CU00994446

BATTLES OF WWII

BATTLES OF WWII

AN ILLUSTRATED ACCOUNT OF THE MAJOR CAMPAIGNS,
FROM EUROPE TO THE PACIFIC ISLANDS

NIGEL CAWTHORNE

ARCTURUS

ARCTURUS

This edition published in 2008 by Arcturus Publishing Limited
26/27 Bickels Yard, 151–153 Bermondsey Street,
London SE1 3HA

Copyright © 2003 Arcturus Publishing Limited

All rights reserved. No part of this publication may be reproduced,
stored in a retrieval system, or transmitted, in any form or by any
means, electronic, mechanical, photocopying, recording or otherwise,
without written permission in accordance with the provisions of the
Copyright Act 1956 (as amended). Any person or persons who do any
unauthorised act in relation to this publication may be liable to
criminal prosecution and civil claims for damages.

Maps by Alex Ingr and Simon Towey, Peter Harper
Book design by typeandimage.com, London

Cover image © TopFoto

ISBN: 978-1-84837-144-6

Printed in Singapore

Contents

National Socialists go
fundraising against cold
and hunger on the streets of
Berlin, 1936. The leadership
cadre of the Nazi Party was
made up of veterans of World
War I. Younger members had been
inspired by dispatches from the front line on
the wireless. They found the Treaty of
Versailles that prevented them building or
importing tanks or aircraft an humiliation.

INTRODUCTION

Aʟᴛʜᴏᴜɢʜ Wᴏʀʟᴅ Wᴀʀ II has been over for more than 60 years and most of those who took part in it are no longer with us, it remains a topic of enduring fascination. How was it that the world could be drawn into such madness, which consumed the lives of some 15 million servicemen and women, and between 20 and 45 million civilians? And how was it that the efficient and well-equipped armies of ruthless warlike states, who seemed initially unstoppable, could be defeated by a coalition of nations who had no desire to go to war?

The hunger that Germans had suffered at the end of World War I returned in 1929, following the Wall Street Crash. Germany was unable to pay its war reparations, and even middle-class families, impoverished by hyperinflation, were forced to live on handouts.

The origins of World War II can be found in World War I. As an ally of Britain, France and America, Italy had been on the winning side in 1918, but it did not do as well out of the peace settlement as it expected. In the period of economic instability that followed the war, the political agitator Benito Mussolini seized power. In 1922, he became the first Fascist dictator, promising his people a return to the glories of imperial Rome. His new empire did not stretch very far though. In 1935–36, he seized Abyssinia (now called Ethiopia) and, in 1939, he occupied Albania.

After World War I, many former members of the German army, including the Austrian corporal Adolf Hitler, were disaffected. They felt that they had been defeated not on the battlefield, but instead by communist agitation at home, a feeling only encouraged by the *Dolchstosslegende* (the stab-in-the-back legend). Many prominent German communists at that time were Jewish. Those who opposed them played on the long tradition of anti-Semitism in Germany. The $33 billion in reparations demanded by the victors in World War I at the Versailles Conference of 1919 bankrupted Germany and brought political infighting to the streets. The result was the rise to power of the Nazi Party and its demagogic leader Adolf Hitler, who became Chancellor in 1933. In 1936, he signed an agreement with Mussolini, forming an anti-communist 'Axis'.

Hitler made no secret of his ambitions. In his political manifesto, *Mein Kampf* (My Struggle), published in two volumes in 1925 and 1927, he makes no attempt to hide his anti-Semitism. He also makes clear that he intends to make Germany a mighty empire on the Continent, with its borders extending to include European Russia, where the Slav peoples would be dominated by the Teutonic master race.

Hitler made his first gains by diplomacy, arguing for the return of territory taken from Germany by the Versailles agreement. He got the Saarland back from France in 1935, reoccupied the Rhineland in 1936 (against the advice of his generals) and took his native Austria into his Third Reich in 1938. (The First Reich – or realm – had been the Holy Roman Empire from 1157–1806; the Second Reich was the German Empire under the Prussian Hohenzollerns from 1871–1918.) After the Anschluss (joining) with Austria, Hitler demanded the Sudetenland, part of Czechoslovakia, and threatened war. A peace conference in Munich in September 1938 dismembered Czechoslovakia, giving Hitler the territory he wanted. In March 1939, however, he seized the rest of Czechoslovakia. What Hitler really wanted was to go to war. He had progressively defied the Versailles agreement that had also disarmed Germany. He rearmed and soon had a powerful army, air force and navy. The Western Allies, particularly Britain and France, had suffered huge losses in World War I, and they had no desire to go to war with Germany again. Their armed forces were ill prepared for a modern war, so they had little choice but to appease the demands of the dictator.

Japan had also been on the winning side in World War I and, again, was disappointed in the territorial gains it was awarded in the peace settlement. The Versailles Conference, however, awarded Japan former German concessions in China. The Japanese had long coveted an empire like the ones Britain, France and the Netherlands had established in the Far East. In 1910, Japan had annexed Korea and, during World War I, had also established a toehold in Manchuria. In 1931, the Japanese further consolidated their hold on Manchuria and, when the Chinese objected, firebombed Shanghai. The Chinese appealed to the League of Nations, which found in China's favour. Japan promptly withdrew from the League. When China was further weakened by the fall of the last Emperor of the Manchu Dynasty, Japan swallowed up Mongolia and parts of China's Hebei province.

Up until this time, the Japanese military had been constrained by a civilian government at home. But, in 1936, the military seized power in Tokyo and signed the anti-Communist 'Axis' pact with Nazi Germany and Fascist Italy. In 1937, the Japanese commanders in Manchuria decided to 'solve the Chinese question once and for all', and launched a full-scale invasion. The United States insisted that Japan be 'quarantined' for this aggression.

On 23 August 1939, the staunchly anti-communist Hitler signed a Non-Aggression Pact with the leader of the Soviet Union –

Communist Russia and its satellites – Joseph Stalin. Everything was set for a war that would engulf the whole world.

Over the six years of war that followed, there were hundreds of battles. Unfortunately, there is not the space to cover them all here. Indeed, whole campaigns are missing, such as the heroic fight by British and Dominion troops against the Japanese in Burma. It has also not been possible to include such decisive action as the Battle of the Atlantic, which maintained the British lifeline from the United States against German submarines and warships, or the RAF and USAAF – the United States Army Air Force, as the US air force was then known – bombing campaign against Germany. But these actions went on day after day for years and are not battles in the conventional sense.

The decisive battles we have picked here do, however, cover the main scenes of action. Taken together, they explain how the war progressed and how the use of improved technology, the harnessing of industrial might, the development of well co-ordinated combined operations and the willingness of individuals to sacrifice their lives for what they thought to be right finally brought victory to the Allies.

Hitler made a brief visit to Paris on the morning of 23 June 1940. With the fall of France, German propaganda heralded him as the 'greatest field commander of all time'. After that, his military directives were almost never questioned by the German High Command.

I

THE
FALL OF
WESTERN
EUROPE

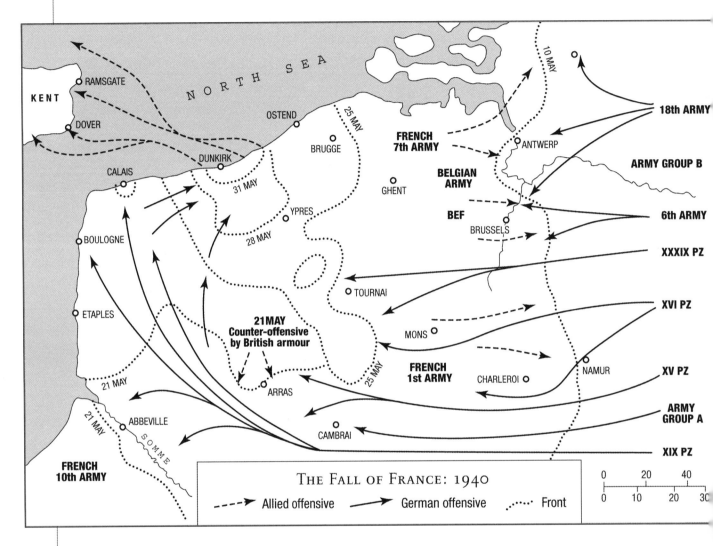

THE FALL OF FRANCE: 1940

- - - → Allied offensive   ——→ German offensive   ······ Front

| 0 | 20 | 40 |
| 0 | 10 | 20 | 30 |

The German offensive in France, June 1940, clearly showing the German Sichelschnitt (sickle stroke) that forced the Allies back to Dunkirk.

O N 1 SEPTEMBER 1939, World War I began. At dawn, a huge German army rolled across the 2,000-km (1,250-mile) Polish border. Immediately, Britain and France ordered a general mobilization. Their ambassadors in Berlin delivered identical messages to the German Foreign Ministry saying that, if Germany did not withdraw its troops from Poland, Britain and France would 'fulfil their obligations to Poland without hesitation'. France had had a military treaty with Poland since 1921, and Britain had pledged its assistance to Poland, if its independence was threatened, on 31 March 1939, marking an end to the policy of appeasement.

Britain had given Germany a deadline for its withdrawal from Poland – 0900 hours on

3 September. Two hours later, British Prime Minister Neville Chamberlain declared war. At midday, the French ambassador in Berlin called the German Foreign Minister Joachim von Ribbentrop, who told him that Germany refused to halt its invasion of Poland. France declared war at 1700 hours.

The fifty-five German armoured and motorized divisions that rolled over the Polish border on 1 September faced just seventeen infantry divisions, three infantry brigades and six cavalry brigades. Poland had mobilized only on 31 August, and thirteen divisions were still moving to their concentration areas, with another nine mustering in their barracks. While the Germans had modern arms and equipment, a large part of the Polish weaponry dated from the 1920s, and fast-moving German Panzers (tanks) were charged by cavalry wielding lances. Against the Polish air force's 842 obsolescent planes, the Luftwaffe – the German air force – could put 4,700 modern aircraft in the air. German planes devastated Polish roads, railways, bridges and power stations, and terror-bombed the cities.

There was little Britain and France could do to help Poland. The French army had been prepared for defence not attack, and there were no British forces on the Continent until the first part of the British Expeditionary Force (BEF) took its place in the line at Lille, in France, on 3 October – one month after Britain had declared war.

Nevertheless, the French did attack Germany on 7 September in Operation Saar. It was a disaster. To avoid violating Belgian neutrality, the French had to attack along the frontier between the Rhine and the Moselle, which had been drawn up after the defeat of Napoleon at Waterloo with the specific aim of discouraging French aggression. The Germans held the high ground and salients into French territory. The Germans had booby-trapped houses and laid cleverly sited fields of anti-tank and anti-personnel mines. The French were completely defensive. They did not possess any mine detectors. Beyond the border was the Siegfried Line, a German defensive wall built during the 1930s. To attack it, the French had to bring their artillery within range of the German batteries, which were well defended inside concrete casemates. French 155mm shells made little impression, and the heavier 220mm and 280mm shells were not fitted with delayed-action fuses which would have allowed them to penetrate the casemates before exploding. Although French fire was rapid and accurate, many of their shells, which were of World War I vintage, failed to explode.

In Poland, however, the Germans were demonstrating the effectiveness of their new tactic of Blitzkrieg – 'lightning war'. Armoured columns would race across the flat Polish landscape, with any defensive action being annihilated by dive-bombers. By 8 September, a German armoured corps was on the outskirts of the Polish capital, Warsaw, having advanced 225 km (140 miles) in seven days. The attack had been so swift that, by 10 September, Polish defence had been reduced to pockets of isolated troops.

Secret Protocol

BY 13 SEPTEMBER, the French decided that the Battle of Poland had been lost, and the French advance into the Saarland, which was

Why? Victims of Nazi air strikes on Poland, September 1939.

The Warsaw garrison held out against the Germans until 28 September, while terror-bombings and artillery barrages reduced parts of the city to rubble. The Germans set the city's flour mills ablaze and destroyed the water supply with no regard for the civilian population. The last serious body of the Polish army held out until 5 October, although some guerrilla fighting went on into the winter. By then, Poland, as an independent state, had ceased to exist. The Germans took a total of 700,000 prisoners; the Soviets took 217,000. The officers were murdered in the Katyn Forest. Many of the rest died as a result of maltreatment. About 80,000 Polish soldiers escaped over the Romanian frontier and continued the fight against Germany from France and Britain. It is not known how many Poles were killed, wounded or missing. The cost to the Germans was 45,000 casualties.

On 27 September 1939, before the Germans had even taken Warsaw, Hitler told his generals that an offensive should be launched immediately against France. Hitler had wanted to defeat France, particularly, to erase the humiliation of Germany's defeat in World War I. The attack should come as soon as possible, as the Western Allies were then ill prepared for war and could only get stronger. Plans were laid to launch an attack between 20 and 25 October.

Hitler was, however, still prepared to make peace. In a speech he gave to the Reichstag – the German Parliament – on 5 October, he proposed a peace agreement on the basis of the partition of Poland, along the lines of that agreed in a new treaty signed with Stalin in Moscow on 28 September. Britain and France declined, so on 9 October Hitler told his army, navy and air force to begin preparations. The

making no significant progress, was told to halt. French casualties were twenty-seven killed, twenty-eight missing and twenty-two wounded. They had also lost nine fighters and eighteen reconnaissance planes, out of an air force that was already significantly under strength.

Then, on 17 September, Soviet forces entered Poland from the east. The country was to be partitioned by Hitler and Stalin under a secret protocol that accompanied their Non-Aggression Pact. On the morning of 18 September, the Polish government and high command crossed the Romanian frontier into exile, and formal resistance was over.

*The swastika
flies over the
Westerplatte
peninsula, on the
Baltic, Poland,
September 1939.*

*German troops
on the march
through Aalborg,
Denmark.*

initial attack, like that in World War I, would be through Belgium, but this time it would also violate Dutch territory in what was known as the 'Maastricht Appendix'. The head of the Luftwaffe Reichsmarschall Herman Göring feared that the Dutch government might retaliate by allowing the British Royal Air Force to use its air bases to bomb Germany, so the plan was altered to take in the invasion of the Netherlands.

Britain and France watched the German build-up on the borders of Holland and Belgium with growing disquiet, but heavy rain that autumn meant that Hitler had to postpone the attack no fewer than thirteen times. Due to the lack of action, that period became known as the 'Phoney War'.

The Race for Norway

BEFORE THE BATTLE of France got under way, Hitler's attention turned to the north. Initially, he had intended to respect Norway's neutrality, but rumours leaked of British designs on Norway. Winston Churchill, then First Lord of the Admiralty, planned to lay mines in Norwegian waters to stop the export of Swedish iron ore from Gällivare to Germany through the Norwegian port of Narvik. The British Cabinet also authorized Churchill to prepare a landing at Narvik.

Hitler feared that, if the British took Norway, they would cut German ports off from the Atlantic and threaten Germany itself through the Baltic. An argument between the French and the British, however, delayed the beginning of mine-laying operations from 5 April until 8 April. On 9 April, with the connivance of the leader of the Norwegian Fascist Party, Vidkun Quisling, Hitler invaded Norway, in the process deploying paratroopers for the first time in warfare. Quisling was rewarded by becoming 'minister president' under a German commissioner. That same day, the German army – the Wehrmacht – overran Denmark, but its neighbour Sweden managed to maintain its neutral status throughout World War II.

The British and French responded by sending in troops of their own to Norway. Despite setbacks elsewhere, on 27 May, the Allies eventually took Narvik after fierce German resistance. But by this time, the Battle of France had begun and, ten days after taking Narvik, the 25,000 Allied troops there were evacuated. For the rest of the war, some 300,000 German troops were stationed in Norway. This guaranteed Germany its supply of Swedish iron ore and gave them naval and air bases for their struggle against the British.

Although the French were ill equipped to attack, it had been thought that they were more than ready to defend themselves. In 1939, France had a standing army of 800,000 men which was thought to be the most powerful in Europe at the time. During the 1930s, the French had also built the Maginot Line, a line of fortifications that ran along France's border with Germany from the Swiss frontier to the Belgian border south of the Ardennes Forest. Its giant pillboxes, underground supply depots, fortified communications facilities and heavy guns pointing eastwards were designed to discourage German aggression. With forty-one divisions manning it, it seemed invincible. There were no fortifications along the border with Belgium, however, although it was defended by thirty-nine divisions.

Two French soldiers push an ammunition cart through a tunnel deep inside the heart of the Maginot Line.

The Dutch army had ten divisions and ten smaller formations, a conscript army of more than 400,000 men. But the Netherlands had managed to stay out of World War I, so these men had no experience of modern warfare. On 10 May, the Germans attacked with just seven divisions. Again they used paratroopers, who captured vital bridges at Rotterdam, Moerdijk, and Dordrecht. They also landed at the airfields around The Hague, but were repulsed. At the same time, the German 9th Panzer Division raced across the country to link up with its airborne troops. On 11 May, the Dutch defenders fell back to Breda, along with the French Seventh Army, which had sped 225 km (140 miles) across Belgium to assist them. By midday on 12 May, German tanks were in the suburbs of Rotterdam. The Dutch retreated into the 'Fortress of Holland', the area north of the Maas and Waal rivers, to protect Amsterdam and Utrecht. But with few planes and few anti-aircraft guns, the Dutch had no defence against German air attacks. Queen Wilhelmina and her government escaped to England on 13 May, where she was later joined by the Norwegian king Haakon VII and his government. The Germans threatened to bomb Rotterdam and Utrecht if Dutch resistance continued and, on 14 May, the Netherlands capitulated – although the city of Rotterdam was bombed anyway due to a mix-up in German communications.

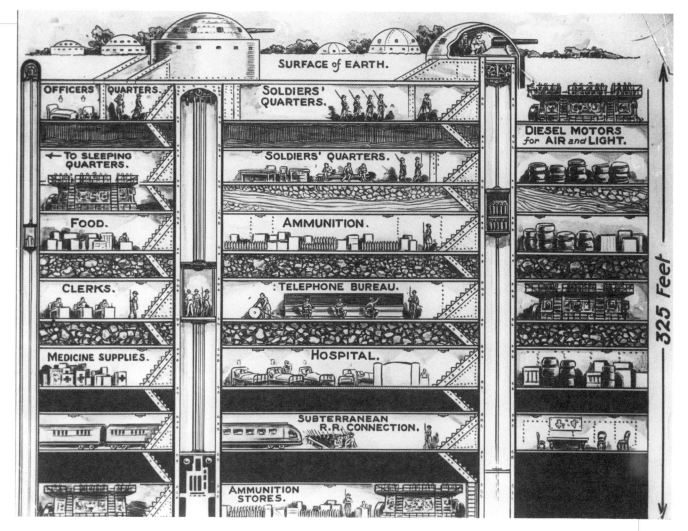

Labels in the illustration:

SURFACE of EARTH.

OFFICERS' QUARTERS.

SOLDIERS' QUARTERS.

← TO SLEEPING QUARTERS.

SOLDIERS' QUARTERS.

DIESEL MOTORS for AIR and LIGHT.

FOOD.

AMMUNITION.

CLERKS.

TELEPHONE BUREAU.

MEDICINE SUPPLIES.

HOSPITAL.

SUBTERRANEAN R.R. CONNECTION.

AMMUNITION STORES.

325 Feet

Cross-section of French gun emplacements, Maginot Line.

But the attack on the Netherlands was a diversion. The main attack would come through Belgium. On 10 May, German paratroops landed in gliders on the top of the fortress of Eben Emael, to the north of Liège, and on bridges over the Albert Canal, which runs from Maastricht to Antwerp, and was the Belgians' forward line of defence. Although the invaders had only four army corps and one armoured corps, along with five hundred airborne troops, at their disposal, air attacks and terror-bombing quickly took their toll on the defenders. On 11 May, the Belgian line collapsed, and German tanks swept through to take Liège from the rear. The Belgian army retreated to a defensive line along the river Dyle, where it was joined by British and French troops. Two tank divisions staged a set-piece battle to check the German advance. The Dyle Line might have held, but by 15 May it had been outflanked and had to be abandoned.

The setbacks in Norway, the Netherlands and Belgium brought with them one benefit, however, which may well have been decisive. On the evening of 10 May, the architect of the policy of appeasement, British Prime Minister

A destroyed bridge bars the way of German tanks, Belgium, 1940.

Neville Chamberlain, resigned from his office and was succeeded by Winston Churchill, who formed a national government.

The British and the French had imagined that the main German attack would come through Liège and Namur, as it had in World War I. The plain there was perfect tank country. Instead, using a plan developed by General Erich von Manstein, the main offensive came on a narrow front through the dense and hilly Ardennes Forest, which the French thought was impassable to tanks.

Again on 10 May, Field Marshal Gerd von Rundstedt threw 1,500,000 men and more than 1,500 tanks – two-thirds of Germany's forces in the west and nearly three-quarters of its tanks – against the weakest part of the front, which was defended by just twelve infantry divisions and four cavalry divisions mounted on horses. The attack was brilliantly organized. A thrust through Luxembourg took just three hours to cover the 50 km (30 miles) to the Belgian border. Another thrust through the forest itself sent the armoured divisions down the narrow lanes. It reached France in less than three days, crossing the border on the evening of 12 May. The infantry followed, using pathways through the woods, travelling so fast that they reached the river Meuse just a day behind the armour. The French had not expected an advance in this area, and the defences there were rudimentary. There were no fortifications in that sector, and the French forces there had few anti-aircraft or anti-tank guns to take on the German dive-bombers or armoured columns; the French cavalry divisions which rode in on horseback to reinforce the sector were forced to retreat to the river Semois on 11 May.

The Road to Dunkirk

ON 13 MAY, after the French defenders on the south bank had been devastated by waves of dive-bombers, German infantry crossed the Meuse on rafts and in rubber dinghies at Sedan – the site of France's defeat in the Franco-Prussian War in 1870. The French had just a handful of aircraft aloft, while the German thrust was supported by a thousand.

The British Expeditionary Force marches back towards the English Channel and the hope of rescue.

The Nazi architect of mechanized warfare, General Heinz Guderian, accompanied the spearhead that drove into France, June 1940.

The next day, German tanks crossed the river and, on 15 May, they broke through what remained of the French defences. It was estimated that the Germans could be in Paris in two days. Instead, the Germans turned westwards towards the Channel. The following day, the German spearhead covered almost 80 km (50 miles) of open country. The advance was so fast that even the German High Command was worried that it was vulnerable; however, when the spearhead advance was joined by a diversionary German force that had come through Liège, French resistance collapsed. Facing almost no opposition, the Germans reached Amiens on 19 May. German tanks entered Abbeville on 20 May and, on 22 May, they turned northwards towards Dunkirk and Calais. The French and British suddenly

found that they had been fighting the wrong war. They imagined that the German advance would sweep across Belgium to the coast and turn southwards, as it had in World War I. Instead, it swept southwards into France, then swept around in an arc to the north. This move was known as the 'Sichelschnitt' (sickle stroke). It broke all communication between Allied forces north and south of this 'Panzer corridor', and the French and British forces that had advanced into Belgium were now threatened with encirclement. As early as 19 May, the British commander Viscount Gort had considered withdrawing the BEF by sea, but the British government wanted action, for the sake of the alliance with France. Gort gave

it to them. On 21 May, he launched an attack southwards from Arras against the Germans' right flank in an attempt to break through to the French forces to the south. This kind of counterattack was just what the German High Command had feared.

By that time, the head of the German column had swept through Boulogne and Calais. Dunkirk was now the only Channel port left in Allied hands through which the BEF could withdraw. The Allies had set up their final defence line along the Canal d'Aire outside Dunkirk. On 24 May, the Germans were crossing the canal, ready to make their final push to take the town, when Hitler ordered them to halt their advance. News of the counterattack at

British troops lie on their backs to shoot up at German aircraft as the British Expeditionary Force is evacuated from the beach at Dunkirk, June 1940.

For the Nazis, the sight of Hitler and his generals arriving in Paris marked the first great achievement of the war.

Arras was confused, and it seemed that the British were a genuine threat.

The German dive-bombers had virtually had the skies to themselves up to this point, but as they approached the coast found themselves under attack from Royal Air Force (RAF) fighters based in England. Nevertheless, Göring promised Hitler that he could finish off the Dunkirk bridgehead with his Luftwaffe alone.

As it was, Gort did not have the armour to break through the Panzer corridor. He was running short of supplies and ammunition and, on 25 May, he ordered the BEF to fall back on Dunkirk. The British government now decided that it had to save what could be saved. On 19 May, it had ordered Admiral Bertram Ramsay to prepare for an evacuation from Dunkirk. Already the call had gone out for small boats. Now the race was on to evacuate the troops before Dunkirk fell to the Germans. Operation Dynamo, as the evacuation was called, began on 26 May. With the British in Belgium withdrawing towards Dunkirk, the Belgian army was left to face the Germans alone. On 27 May, it broke. The following day, King Leopold surrendered unconditionally. Rather than go into exile, he remained a German prisoner for the rest of the war.

As Gort no longer posed a threat, Hitler ordered that the advance on Dunkirk be resumed. But the hiatus had allowed the British to consolidate their defences. When the order came to advance again, the Germans met considerable resistance. Almost immediately Hitler ordered the German armour to stop. Hitler and Rundstedt agreed that it would be best to reserve the Panzers for use against the remaining French army under General Maxime Weygand to the south.

Amateur Sailors

WITH THE RESISTANCE in Belgium over, the Luftwaffe began bombing the harbour at Dunkirk, putting it out of action. The RAF's air cover, however, prevented Göring from

fulfilling his boast that he could destroy what was left of the BEF on the beaches at Dunkirk with his planes. The harbour's bomb-damaged breakwater was still serviceable and allowed many of the troops to be taken off by larger craft. The rest were picked up directly from a 16-km (10-mile) stretch of beach, where they mustered, by small craft largely manned by amateur sailors. In all, 848 British, French and Belgian ships of all shapes and sizes – from destroyers to private motor cruisers – joined the operation. In the eight days during which

Operation Dynamo took place, some 340,000 men, two-thirds of them British, were rescued. Almost all their equipment was abandoned, however, and, of the forty-one destroyers participating in the evacuation, six were sunk and nineteen others damaged.

Another 220,000 Allied troops were rescued from Cherbourg, Saint-Malo, Brest, and Saint-Nazaire in north-western France, bringing the total of Allied troops evacuated to about 560,000. But in three weeks the German army had taken more than a million men prisoner, sustaining some 60,000 casualties itself.

Although the action at Dunkirk was actually a withdrawal, it was hailed as a victory by the British. In the long run, it proved decisive. The bulk of Britain's most experienced troops had been saved. Controversy still rages about why Hitler stayed his hand and allowed the British Army to get away. It may have been one of the several key mistakes he made during World War II, although some believe that Hitler still wanted to make peace with Britain and thought that this might be more easily achieved if the British Army was not forced into a humiliating surrender.

Although the BEF was now safely back in Britain, the Battle of France was not over. The French had lost thirty divisions so far, but General Weygand could still muster forty-nine divisions, along with another seventeen who were still holding the Maginot Line. But the Germans had 140 divisions at their disposal, including ten divisions of tanks. On 5 June, the Wehrmacht started pushing southwards from its positions on the Somme. The French held the Germans for two days, but on 7 June Panzers under Major General Erwin Rommel, the man who was to become known as the

'Desert Fox', broke through south-westwards toward Rouen. Two days after that, they crossed the Seine. That same day, 9 June, the Germans broke through to the south-east, then made a dash for the Swiss border, cutting off the French forces still holding the Maginot Line. To all intents and purposes, the Battle of France was lost.

When Hitler attacked Poland, Italy had not been prepared to go to war and, for some time, the British had hoped that Italy might be persuaded to join the Allied side, as it had in World War I, or at least remain neutral. On 22 May 1940, however, Mussolini had signed a military alliance with Hitler, known as the

In spite of his success in France, Hitler did not enjoy his time in Paris; nor did he visit again. In 1944, however, he ordered the city's destruction.

Opposite: German bombers fly over the Silvertown area of London's docklands during the Blitz, 1940. West Ham greyhound track can be seen near the centre of the picture.

'Pact of Steel'. Plainly, if Mussolini wanted to benefit from this alliance, it would be best if he did not let Hitler win his war against the western democracies single-handedly. On 10 June 1940, Mussolini declared war on France and Great Britain. Some thirty Italian divisions massed on the French frontier, although the attack was delayed until 20 June. Even then, the Italians made little progress against local defence and made no contribution of strategic importance.

As the Germans advanced, the French government under Paul Reynaud left Paris for Cangé, near Tours. There, on 12 June, Reynaud received news from General Weygand that the Battle of France was lost. Reynaud wanted to continue the war from the French possessions in North Africa, but his cabinet was split.

On 14 June 1940, the Germans entered Paris and drove on rapidly south. The French government had to flee southwards from Tours to Bordeaux, to stay ahead of the advance. The French army was now split into a dozen fragments and Weygand pressed for an armistice. Reynaud's position was untenable and he resigned on 16 June. He was replaced by his deputy the elderly Marshal Philippe Pétain, who was France's most-honoured soldier in World War I and hero of the Battle of Verdun. That same day, General Charles de Gaulle, then undersecretary for defence in Reynaud's administration, arrived in London. That night, Pétain's government requested an armistice. While the two sides discussed terms, the German advance continued until it had swallowed two-thirds of the country. On 22 June 1940, the representatives of Germany and France met at Compiègne. This had been

the site of the headquarters of the invading German Army in World War I, and the armistice ending the war in 1918 had been signed in a railway carriage there. The carriage had been preserved as a monument. Hitler came to Compiègne personally to watch the

new armistice being signed in that same carriage. The carriage was then taken back to Germany, where it was destroyed in April 1945 to prevent it falling into Allied hands.

The 1940 armistice divided France into two zones. Northern France, from the Swiss border to the English Channel and a western strip down the Atlantic coast to the Spanish border, was to be held under German military occupation. The rump of the country and its overseas possessions were to be left in the hands of a collaborationist government under Pétain,

German troops marched into Paris on 17 June 1940. For the next 1,500 days, they would march down the Champs Élysées every single day.

The battle lines are drawn for the Battle of Britain. Its outcome would decide the war in the West.

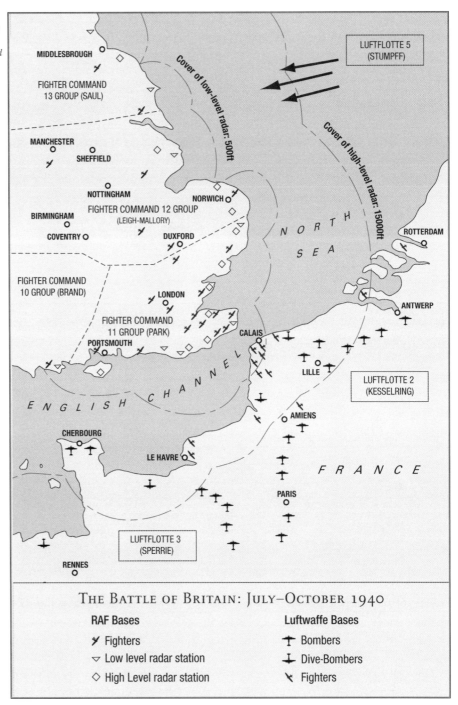

MIDDLESBROUGH

FIGHTER COMMAND
13 GROUP (SAUL)

Cover of low-level radar: 500ft

Cover of high-level radar: 15000ft

LUFTFLOTTE 5
(STUMPFF)

MANCHESTER
SHEFFIELD

NOTTINGHAM
FIGHTER COMMAND 12 GROUP
(LEIGH-MALLORY)

NORWICH

N O R T H
S E A

ROTTERDAM

BIRMINGHAM
COVENTRY
DUXFORD

FIGHTER COMMAND
10 GROUP (BRAND)

LONDON

FIGHTER COMMAND
11 GROUP (PARK)
PORTSMOUTH

ANTWERP

CALAIS

LILLE

LUFTFLOTTE 2
(KESSELRING)

E N G L I S H   C H A N N E L

CHERBOURG

LE HAVRE

AMIENS

F R A N C E

PARIS

LUFTFLOTTE 3
(SPERRIE)

RENNES

THE BATTLE OF BRITAIN: JULY–OCTOBER 1940

RAF Bases

⚔ Fighters
▽ Low level radar station
◇ High Level radar station

Luftwaffe Bases

⊥ Bombers
⊥ Dive-Bombers
⚔ Fighters

based at Vichy. Later, when its overseas possessions were lost, the Vichy government became a mere puppet. On 18 June, however, de Gaulle began broadcasting appeals for France to continue the war from London, where he organized the Free French Forces. On 2 August 1940, he was tried in absentia by a French military court and sentenced to death.

Although the Battle of France had been decisively lost, there was one last action. Britain – with its Empire – now stood alone. Sea power was all-important, and the British government decided that it could not risk the French navy, which was technically under the control of Vichy, falling into German hands. Britain seized all French ships in ports under its control, but the French still possessed a considerable fleet at their naval base at Mers-el-Kébir in Algeria. On 3 July 1940, British ships appeared off the Algerian coast. When the French fleet refused to join the Allies, the British opened fire, putting the fleet out of action. In protest, the Vichy government broke off diplomatic relations with the British. The ships that survived were later destroyed by the Germans.

The Battle of Britain

'WHAT GENERAL WEYGAND called the "Battle of France" is over. I expect the "Battle of Britain" to begin,' Winston Churchill told a hushed House of Commons on 18 June 1940. With France out of the way, Hitler once again sought to make peace, keeping the Continent for himself and leaving Britain its overseas Empire. But as Britain showed no willingness to come to terms, Hitler began to prepare for battle once again.

The enemy, he knew, was in no position to resist him. In Great Britain and Northern Ireland, there were just twenty-nine divisions – including two Canadian divisions – and eight independent brigades, six of which were armoured. They were outnumbered four to one. What is more, the British were poorly equipped. On 8 June, they had just seventy-two tanks. This number was to increase to 200 by August and 438 by September, but – as events in North Africa would later show – they were already obsolescent.

In June, the British Home Forces had just 420 field guns and 163 heavy guns, with 200 and 150 rounds, respectively. The British two-pounder (40mm) guns – of which they had just fifty-four – were of little use against tanks. What was needed was 75mm guns, which had proved their worth as tank-killers in the Battle of France. Fortunately, the United States allowed the British to take over arms contracts that the French had signed. Orders included 900 75mm guns with 1,000 shells each, along with 500,000 rifles. The British had to pay cash for these and transport them to Britain themselves. The British Merchant Navy did this without suffering a single loss to U-boats.

For nearly a month after the fall of France, Hitler dallied, hoping that the British would settle. Then, on 16 July 1940, he signed Führer Directive No. 16, which authorized Operation Sealion – the invasion of England. The month had not been wasted by the British. They had stepped up armament production and prepared their defences. And the delay gave them cause for optimism. It was estimated that the Germans would need at least two months to prepare for the invasion. That meant that it could not come earlier

A flight of Spitfires heads off in search of the enemy during the Battle of Britain.

than 16 September, when rougher autumn weather would be starting in the English Channel. This could prove decisive.

On 19 July, Hitler addressed the Reichstag, saying that he saw no reason for further bloodshed and, again, offering to come to terms with the British. London made no response, so the preparations for Operation Sealion went ahead. The German schedule, however, was much quicker than the British anticipated; D-Day was set at 25 August. The invasion force would consist of forty-one divisions, six armoured and three motorized, along with two divisions of airborne troops. The Sixteenth Army would land between Ramsgate and Hastings, while the Ninth would land

between Brighton and Littlehampton, with a detachment taking the Isle of Wight. This force under Rundstedt would head for a line running from Gravesend through Reigate to Portsmouth. Soon after, the Sixth Army, which was mustered on the Cherbourg Peninsula, would land on the Dorset coast between Weymouth and Lyme Regis. It would strike towards Bristol, with a detachment taking Devon. At that same moment, the Ninth Army would break through the British defences on the North Downs, cross the river Thames at Reading and encircle London from the west.

There was a problem, though. The commander of the Kriegsmarine (German navy) Grand Admiral Erich Raeder pointed

out that, even if he were to requisition every available vessel from the fishing fleets and inland waterways – which would have devastating effects on food supplies and war production – he could not land the first wave of thirteen divisions, even if their numbers were considerably reduced. Besides, the Royal Navy was still a considerable fighting force, and Raeder did not think he would

be able to give the invasion fleet sufficient protection. So the attack on Devon was dropped from the plan and the invasion force reduced to twenty-seven divisions.

The Germans did not have a battle fleet large enough to give the troops landing on the English beaches the necessary artillery support, and the Luftwaffe would not be able to provide total coverage either. So huge batteries were

RAF Hurricane pilots scramble during the Battle of Britain. Of the nearly 3,000 aircrew who fought in the battle, one in three men was killed or wounded.

Radar and ground stations that plotted the incoming attackers and controlled the air defences by radio helped to prevent RAF Fighter Command being destroyed on the ground.

built along the French coast from Sangatte to Boulogne which would pound the invasion beaches. To provide the assault force with support when they got ashore, the Germans developed submarine tanks. These were regular Panzers that had been waterproofed and fitted with a flexible snorkel so that the engine would run, and the occupants could breathe.

They would be dropped offshore by special landing craft, sink to the bottom in 7.5–9m (25–30 ft) of water, then drive up onto the beaches. Experiments off the island of Sylt in the North Sea showed that the submarine Panzers worked perfectly. Even so, the German land forces would need the support of dive-bombers and, as a preliminary, massive Stuka attacks would be needed to destroy the British coastal defences. To do that, the Germans would need air superiority.

On 1 August 1940, Hitler signed Führer Directive No. 17, ordering the Luftwaffe to smash the RAF as quickly as it could. It was to take the RAF on in the air and attack its ground facilities and supply centres. It was to bomb aircraft factories and factories producing anti-aircraft guns. It was also to attack the ports which brought in vital supplies – though leaving intact the Channel ports which would be needed in the invasion. British cities, though, were not to be terror-bombed without the express order of Hitler himself.

The Germans deployed three air fleets against Britain. They flew from Norway and Denmark, Belgium and the Netherlands, and Northern France. Between them they had 2,442 aircraft – 969 heavy bombers, 336 dive-bombers, 869 single-engined fighters and 268 twin-engined fighters.

Although the RAF fighter force – some 620 aircraft – was considerably smaller than the Germans' 1,137, the British had not been sitting on their hands. Fighter production had risen from 157 a month in January 1940 to 496 in July. The RAF did, however, have a shortage of trained pilots. There were only 1,134 in all, but the RAF could draw on the pilots of Coastal Command and the Fleet Air Arm. It also formed one Czech and four Polish squadrons, whose pilots had escaped from Eastern Europe.

The RAF's Hurricanes and Spitfires were much faster and more manoeuvrable than Germany's twin-engined Messerschmitt Bf 110 'destroyer' – which was also known as 'Göring's folly'. On the other hand, the single-seater Messerschmitt Bf 109E was faster than the Mark I Hurricane and about as fast as the Mark I and II Spitfires that were just appearing in frontline squadrons. The Bf 109 could also climb faster than the British fighters, but the British planes were more manoeuvrable. With eight machine guns, they could outshoot their German adversaries, and it is generally reckoned that the Spitfire, although in short supply, was unrivalled as an interceptor at that time.

German heavy bombers were vulnerable to attack from both Hurricanes and Spitfires, particularly in daylight, and did not have the bomb-carrying capacity to deliver a knockout blow. Their effectiveness was also blunted by the lack of an overall strategy. Sometimes they would attack airfields; sometimes factories; sometimes ports. British fighters also found that German dive-bombers could be shot down easily, and German fighters could give them only partial protection, as they were fighting at the limit of their flying range.

The British had other advantages. Since 1938, the British had the most advanced radar defence network in the world, which stretched from Land's End in the south north to the Shetland Islands. Incoming German planes could be detected in time for commanders to get their fighters airborne, so they were not caught and destroyed on the ground. With this radar information, control centres could direct the fighters by radio to intercept the enemy, often taking the Germans by surprise.

As the battle was fought over home soil, the British were able to recover their downed pilots, whereas if a German aircraft was shot down both the plane and crew were lost. For example, on 15 August 1940, seventy German planes were shot down; all their crews were

Hitler's decision to turn the air attack on London caused immense damage, but allowed the RAF to recover and, eventually, prevent a German invasion of Britain.

either killed or taken prisoner. That same day, twenty-eight Hurricanes and Spitfires were also lost, but more than half of their pilots eventually returned to their squadrons.

Although there had been preliminary attacks in June and July, the air war began in earnest on 8 August with the Germans sending up to 1,500 aircraft a day to bomb the British airfields and radar stations. In fighting, on 8, 11, 12, and 13 August, the RAF lost 88 planes, while the Luftwaffe lost 145 aircraft. Between 13 and 17 August, the RAF lost 184, against the Luftwaffe's 255. The battle was becoming so expensive that Göring withdrew Luftflotte V flying from Norway and Denmark, along with his Stuka dive-bombers. In late August, however, the Luftwaffe was close to winning the battle.

Essential British airfields were pitted with bomb craters. The RAF's effectiveness was further curtailed by bomb damage to its radar stations and operations centres which were, unfortunately, sited on airfields. Aircraft were being destroyed on the ground, and it was becoming difficult to co-ordinate formations in the air.

Aircraft losses began to turn in Germany's favour. Between 24 August and 6 September, the Luftwaffe lost 378 planes, against the RAF's 262. Although this appears to give the British an advantage of 45 per cent, the German losses included both bombers and fighters. The British were losing all-important fighters and their experienced pilots. Fighter Command had fewer than a thousand pilots. All of them were in action several times a day and desperately in need of rest. With fifteen to twenty pilots killed or wounded every day, Fighter Command was reaching its last gasp.

Salvation came by glorious accident. Late in the evening of 24 August, a German plane accidentally bombed non-military targets in London. Churchill immediately ordered a retaliatory attack on Berlin. The next night, eighty-one twin-engined bombers took off for

the German capital. Only twenty-nine planes made it. The others became lost on the way. Eight men were killed and twenty-eight wounded. The damage to Berlin was slight, but Hitler had promised the German people that such a thing would never happen. Infuriated, he abandoned the 1 August Directive and ordered the terror-bombing of London. Britain's capital was about to receive the same treatment as Warsaw and Rotterdam.

The sustained German bombing campaign that followed became known as the Blitz –

'lightning'. It began on 7 September, when 330 tonnes of bombs were dropped on London. The terror-bombing campaign was later extended to Liverpool, Coventry and other cities. Although the population suffered terribly from these attacks, the switch of the Luftwaffe's objective gave Fighter Command the breathing space to recover. Between 7 and 30 September, the RAF downed 380 German aircraft for the loss of 178 of its own.

The German air offensive reached a peak on Sunday 15 September with a series of attacks during which British air defences claimed to have downed 185 German planes. The figure was later dropped to fifty-six. But it hardly mattered. The British had defeated the Germans in the air and were shooting down bombers faster than German factories could produce them. By 31 October, the Germans had lost 1,733 planes against Britain's 1,379, and Fighter Command had lost only 414 men. So Churchill was not exaggerating when he told the House of Commons on 20 August 1940, 'Never in the field of human conflict has so much been owed by so many to so few.' It was a view he repeated when he wrote his *History of the Second World War*.

Even so, Hitler continued his preparations for Operation Sealion. The troops of the Ninth and Sixteenth armies gathered at their embarkation points. An invasion fleet comprising 2,500 transports, tugs, lighters, barges and fishing boats was assembled in ports from Le Havre to Rotterdam. The fleet came under attack from the RAF's Bomber Command. Although losses were less than 10 per cent, the craft still had to be replaced. The mine-laying and mine-sweeping programmes that were designed to secure invasion lanes across the English Channel went ahead but, because the Luftwaffe had not gained the upper hand in the air, they were disrupted by attacks by Coastal Command.

Daylight Raids

ON 11 SEPTEMBER, Hitler announced his intention to begin the countdown to Sealion on 14 September – and the landings would begin at dawn on 24 September. But on 14 September, he postponed the decision for another three days – 27 September being the last day the tides were favourable. The strong winds and high seas that could be expected in the English Channel from October onwards would make an invasion impossible.

On 17 September, Hitler ordered that Sealion be postponed and, on 19 September, the invasion fleet was dispersed to protect it from further bombing. Hitler ordered that it should be dispersed in such a way that it could be rapidly reassembled, but this was never to happen. Although daylight raids on British cities continued until the end of the month, German losses continued at such a rate that, at the beginning of October, the Luftwaffe turned to night bombing, which was much less effective militarily. The Blitz continued sporadically until the end of October. By then, it was recognized that the Battle of Britain was over.

Victory for the Luftwaffe in the air would inevitably have led to the invasion and occupation of Britain. Fighter Command had denied the Germans the air superiority they needed. It had created the conditions for Britain's survival, for the continuation of the war and for the eventual defeat of Nazi Germany.

No one knew this at the time, of course. Britain merely felt that it was safe for one more winter. During the following months, the Luftwaffe continued its Blitz with night-time bombing raids on Britain's biggest cities. By February 1941, the bombing offensive had eased, but in March and April it was stepped up again. Some 10,000 sorties were flown, with the bombing concentrated on the East End of London. However, the Luftwaffe never turned its attention back to British airfields. By the time suitable weather for a fresh invasion came the following spring, Hitler had turned his eyes eastwards and was planning his attack on Soviet Russia, which began with Operation Barbarossa in August 1941.

The Invasion of Crete

IN PREPARATION FOR his attack on the Soviet Union, Hitler began drawing other central European countries – Hungary, Romania, Slovakia, Bulgaria, Yugoslavia – into the Axis. Following Germany's huge gains in the west, Italy began to find itself very much the junior partner in the Pact of Steel. Mussolini wanted to make some territorial gains of his own. Without informing Hitler, he sent 155,000 men across the border from Albania, which Italy had invaded in 1939, into Greece. The Italian invasion was a disaster. Mussolini's seven divisions were halted by a handful of Greeks, who pushed the Italians back until, by mid-December, the Greeks occupied one-third of Albania.

The British rallied to the defence of Greece, sending men and planes to air bases on the mainland near Athens. This put them within striking distance of the Romanian

oilfields at Ploiesti which were vital to Germany's attack on Russia. Hitler had no option but to help Mussolini out. In March, there was a coup d'état against the pro-Axis regime in Belgrade, so the Germans decided to invade Yugoslavia with Italian support, and sweep through into Greece. They made a

Paratroopers drop in during the German invasion of Crete. Despite the success of the mission, losses among airborne troops were very high.

The German Panzers arrive in Salonika (Thessaloníki) following the fall of Greece, April 1941.

airfields at Heraklion (Iráklion), Réthymnon and Máleme on Crete.

The Germans needed Crete as well, and not just to starve out Tobruk. From the air bases there, the RAF was still in striking distance of the Romanian oilfields. With the attack on the Soviet Union about to deprive Hitler of Russian oil – albeit temporarily, if all went well – he could not afford to be without a supply from Romania. On 25 April 1940, Hitler's Führer Directive No. 28 ordered the invasion of Crete.

A plan was drawn up to attack the island using an airborne division and three infantry regiments from the 5th and 6th Mountain divisions which would be landed by a hastily requisitioned flotilla, comprising sixty-three motorized sailing ships and seven small steamers. This would be protected by two destroyers and twelve motor torpedo boats from the Italian navy.

Defending the island were 41,500 men, 10,300 of whom were Greek. There were 17,000 British troops and a large ANZAC force, comprising 7,700 New Zealanders and 6,500 Australians who had escaped from mainland Greece. On the way, they had abandoned much of their equipment. They had only sixty-eight anti-aircraft guns, which were far too few to defend an island 261 km (162 miles) from end to end. They were also short of field guns, infantry weapons, ammunition, vehicles, entrenching tools, barbed wire, blankets and mess tins. They were led by General Bernard Freyberg, a hero of Gallipoli who had been wounded twenty-seven times during World War I. But Freyberg was the seventh British commander on the islands in six months, and he had been given just three weeks to prepare the island's defences.

lightning thrust through the Balkans, forcing the British to evacuate their forces from mainland Greece, although 20,000 remained as prisoners of war. By 11 May, the whole of Greece and the Aegean islands, with the exception of Crete, were in German hands.

The British wanted, however, to hold Crete. It was just 800 km (500 miles) from Alexandria and 320 km (200 miles) from Tobruk. The bastion of British resistance in North Africa, Tobruk had to be supplied by sea and would be in great danger if the Germans had the

On 1 May, the RAF had thirty-five operational aircraft on Crete. By 19 May, after incessant bombing by the Luftwaffe, it had only four Hurricanes and three Gladiators left. These were sent to Egypt for safekeeping, but the airstrips were only obstructed rather than put out of action, as it was intended that they be used again as soon as possible.

The Battle of Crete began on 20 May. The Germans had an air fleet of 500 transport planes and 72 gliders, supported by 500 bombers and fighters. At 0715 hours, German gliders carrying elements of the 5th Mountain Division landed to the west and south of Máleme airfield. Soon after more landed on Hill 107, overlooking the airfield, but a third company which aimed to take the nearby Tavronitis Bridge landed among New Zealand troops. Although it took heavy casualties, it managed to take the bridge and hold it.

Then the paratroop drop began. The 3rd Battalion of the 7th Parachute Division was supposed to drop around the airfield but, again, they landed among the New Zealanders and, within three-quarters of an hour, 400 of the 600 paratroopers were dead. The 4th Battalion dropped west of Tavronitis and found itself under attack from a band of civilians, whom they quickly subdued, while the 2nd Battalion landed among Greek troops and armed civilians, who butchered them. Only thirteen of the 2nd Battalion were still alive when they surrendered.

The 3rd Parachute Regiment dropped south of the nearby town of Khaniá (Chania); the 2nd Company of the Luftlande Sturmregiment landed in fifteen gliders to the north-west. They were to take the anti-aircraft batteries there, but soon discovered that the guns were

dummies. The Northumberland Hussars in the area were real enough, though, and the 136 men who landed had soon sustained 108 casualties. But the 1st Company, landing to the south-east, managed to spike the anti-aircraft battery there, before striking out to join up with other troops landing in the area.

The 3rd Parachute Regiment found itself widely dispersed. One company, carrying heavy mortars, dropped into a reservoir. Some men were drowned and all their equipment was lost. The survivors found themselves under fierce attack from the New Zealand and Greek troops in the area. They managed to take the village of Agia, however, and set up their regimental HQ there. The divisional staff then flew in, but the glider carrying the divisional commander split its tow rope and crashed into the island of Aegina.

On the ground, things looked bleak for the Germans. Few of their objectives had been secured, and the landing force was broken up into pockets, which were pinned down by the New Zealanders. A second wave of landings around the airfields at Réthymnon and Heraklion was due that afternoon. But the planes deploying them had to be refuelled by hand on the mainland, which delayed them. Taking off from dirt strips in Greece also kicked up clouds of dust, so the planes carrying the airborne troops had to be dispatched in discrete groups. This meant that the men were landed in small bands, often widely scattered, and preliminary attacks by bombers and fighters had alerted the defenders. One of the battalions landing around Réthymnon found itself among Australian troops. The paratroopers were pinned down in the drop zones and unable to reach their weapons containers. The two other groups landing there dug in, in defensive positions. This meant that there were three discrete pockets of Germans around the airfield.

The troops dropped about Heraklion were even more widely scattered and found themselves under fire from the British troops who were holding the town. So the second wave was even more unsuccessful than the first. None of its objectives was taken. Some 1,800 of the 3,000 men who had been dropped were dead and the survivors were in no shape to mount an offensive action.

While the defenders had overwhelming superiority in men, armour and artillery, Freyberg took a generally pessimistic view of the situation. There were no counterattacks that night that might have disrupted the enemy and finished it off as a fighting force. In the morning, the commander of the 22nd New Zealand Battalion mistakenly thought his forward positions had been overrun and ordered a withdrawal from Hill 107. In the confusion, the New Zealanders really were overrun and the Germans took the vital hill. Shortly after, another 550 paratroopers were dropped and, with these reinforcements, the Germans captured the airfield. The Germans began to fly in ammunition, although incoming planes were subjected to withering machine-gun fire.

Counterattack

REINFORCEMENTS BEGAN landing at 1600. Artillery fire wrecked some of the transports. Others were damaged in collisions on the small airfield, but most of the troops got out safely. By 1800, there were another 1,000 German troops on the ground. The New Zealanders planned a quick counterattack. But by the time they had mustered their troops, the Germans had landed in enough strength to hold on to the airfield.

The Germans also managed to strengthen positions around Heraklion. They had begun house-to-house fighting in the outskirts, when the Greek commander came forward to surrender the town. The British commander knew nothing of this and counterattacked, but was unable to dislodge the Germans.

The Royal Navy caught the first flotilla of German seaborne troops as they came in sight of Máleme and sank it. More than 500 officers and men of the 100th Mountain Regiment drowned, and it was destroyed as a fighting force. But before the Royal Navy could sink the second flotilla in the Mediterranean, it came under air attack. German Stukas sank two cruisers and four destroyers, while the battleship HMS *Warspite* and the aircraft-carrier HMS *Formidable* were so badly damaged they had to be sent to the United States for repairs. Even so, the second flotilla of German troops was taken back to Piraeus, rather than risk further loss of life.

That night, the New Zealanders tried to counterattack again at Máleme to prevent any more reinforcements being landed, but to the east of the airfield they ran into the remnants of the 3rd Battalion of the 7th Parachute Division who had been so badly mauled on the first day. Individual paratroopers scattered across the rough ground put up such a fight that they slowed the New Zealanders' advance considerably. By dawn, the ANZACs were far from their objective and German fighters and dive-bombers forced them to withdraw.

On 22 May, more Germans landed and Major General Ringer flew in to take command. He divided his men into three Kampfgruppen (battle groups) which were to push outwards at dawn the next day. One group moved north towards the sea and found itself up against armed civilians, including women and children. The Cretan Resistance was particularly savage, torturing and mutilating any German who fell into their hands. A second Kampfgruppe moved into the mountains to the east, but was halted by the New Zealanders at the village of Modi. After fierce fighting, the New Zealanders were outflanked, and they were forced to withdraw. This took their artillery out of range of the airstrip and the Germans could now land more reinforcements without coming under fire. Now the Germans brought in their artillery.

On 24 May, there were heavy German air attacks on the towns of Khaniá and Galatas, and new battle groupings were drawn up. The Germans marched 80 km (50 miles) in a flanking movement to cut the main road from Khaniá and Réthymnon, and they joined up with the paratroopers who had remained cut off south-east of Khaniá since their drop on to the island on 20 May.

On 25 May, the Germans made a concerted attack on the key village of Galatas. The New Zealanders were ousted but, in a bitter counter-attack, retook the village. By then, their numbers were so depleted that they knew they could not hold it so, that night, they withdrew. Now Khaniá lay within the Germans' grasp.

Under attack from the skies and with the Royal Navy unable to prevent further landings, Freyberg called for an evacuation on 27 May. Despite the danger, Admiral Andrew Cunningham, commander in chief in the Mediterranean, ordered the Royal Navy to go in and evacuate Freyberg and his men. When one of his aides pointed out that this put his ships in great danger, Cunningham replied, 'It takes the Navy three years to build a ship. It would take 300 years to rebuild a tradition.'

The evacuation of Crete began on the night of 28 May. Altogether some 8,800 British, 4,704 New Zealanders and 3,164 Australians were brought out of the small port of Sfakia on the southern shore of the island and taken to Alexandria. Some 1,464 were wounded. Another 11,835 had been taken prisoner. On board the cruiser HMS *Orion*, Vice Admiral Pridham-Wippell's flagship, a single German bomb killed 260 men and wounded 280. The Royal Navy lost, in all, 2,011 officers and men.

The Germans lost 3,714 killed and missing, along with 2,494 wounded. Eight days' fighting on Crete had cost the Germans more than the entire Balkan campaign. After Crete, Hitler forbade any further large-scale use of paratroops, and plans to invade Cyprus and, later, Malta were abandoned.

The deserts of North Africa provided the perfect terrain for large-scale tank battles. But Panzer warfare would ultimately fail because it was cheaper to build anti-tank guns than tanks.

II

THE WAR IN THE DESERT

The battles of Alamein, October–November 1942.

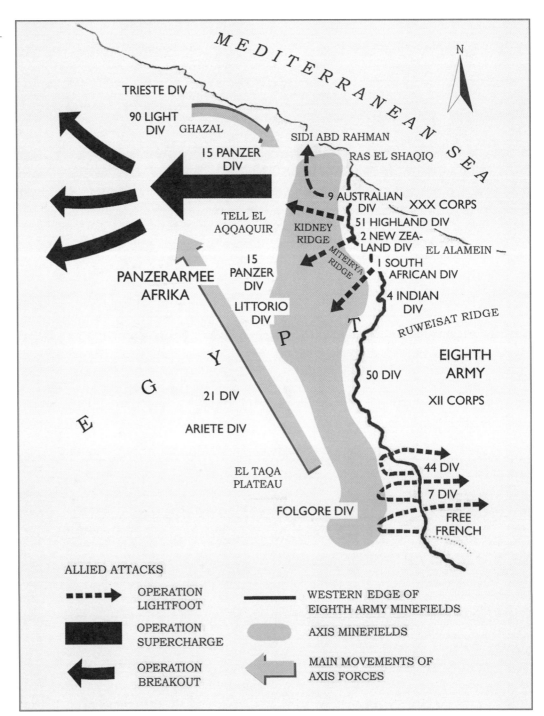

MEDITERRANEAN SEA

N

TRIESTE DIV

90 LIGHT DIV GHAZAL

SIDI ABD RAHMAN

RAS EL SHAQIQ

15 PANZER DIV

9 AUSTRALIAN DIV

XXX CORPS

51 HIGHLAND DIV

TELL EL AQQAQUIR

KIDNEY RIDGE

2 NEW ZEA-LAND DIV

EL ALAMEIN

PANZERARMEE AFRIKA

15 PANZER DIV

MITEIRYA RIDGE

I SOUTH AFRICAN DIV

LITTORIO DIV

4 INDIAN DIV

RUWEISAT RIDGE

E G Y P T

EIGHTH ARMY

21 DIV

50 DIV

ARIETE DIV

XII CORPS

EL TAQA PLATEAU

44 DIV

7 DIV

FOLGORE DIV

FREE FRENCH

ALLIED ATTACKS

- - - ▶ OPERATION LIGHTFOOT

▬▬ WESTERN EDGE OF EIGHTH ARMY MINEFIELDS

■■ OPERATION SUPERCHARGE

▬ AXIS MINEFIELDS

◀ OPERATION BREAKOUT

◀ MAIN MOVEMENTS OF AXIS FORCES

THE FALL OF FRANCE worried Benito Mussolini. He feared that Hitler would make peace with the British, and any pact between Britain and Germany would thwart his territorial ambitions in the Mediterranean. The armistice, particularly, was a disappointment. Mussolini coveted the French possessions in North Africa, but they remained in the hands of the Vichy government.

Italy already had one possession in North Africa – Libya, which it had invaded in 1911. By the outbreak of World War II, some 150,000 Italian colonists lived there. So when the British rejected Hitler's peace overtures, Mussolini turned his attention to Egypt, which had been in British hands since 1882. He ordered Marshal Rodolfo Graziani to launch an offensive eastwards against the British troops in Egypt who were under the command of General Sir Archibald Wavell. On 13 September 1940, the Italian Tenth Army took the small border port of Sollum. They then advanced a further 80 km (50 miles) into Egypt and occupied the British base at Sidi Barrani on 16 September. Six weeks later, the British Western Desert Force under Lieutenant General Richard O'Connor started a 'five-day raid' which pushed the Italians back across the border on 10 December. Reinforced by Australians, the Western Desert Force continued the advance and took the small port of Tobruk in north-east Libya on 21 January 1941. By the time the Italians surrendered on 7 February, the British had driven them back 800 km (500 miles), taking more than 130,000 prisoners, as well as 400 tanks and 1,290 guns. Meeting no further resistance, the Western Desert Force could have gone on to take Tripoli, but its supply lines were already overstretched and Churchill wanted to divert men and resources to Greece.

The Siege of Tobruk

AGAIN HITLER CAME to Mussolini's aid. On 6 February, he sent Rommel and his Afrika Korps to Tripoli. On 24 March, Rommel attacked at El Agheila, capturing O'Connor and pushing the British column back the way it had come. Wavell decided, however, to hold Tobruk while the rest of the British force retreated into Egypt to regroup. As Tobruk had fallen so effortlessly on 21 January, its fortifications were largely intact. Its strongpoints, which were laid out in alternating rows, were protected by concrete about a metre (3 ft) thick, which in turn offered protection against 150mm guns, the heaviest the Afrika Korps had at the time. It had an anti-tank ditch, camouflaged planks and sand, and the perimeter defences described an arc 45 km (28 miles) long round the port and reached 15 km (9 miles) inland. This was to be defended by the 9th Australian Division, reinforced by a brigade of the 7th and the Sikhs of the 18th Cavalry Regiment. Major General Leslie Morshead, commander of the 9th, told his men, 'There will be no Dunkirk here. If we have to get out, we will fight our way out. No surrender and no retreat.'

The artillery support was supplied by the Australian Royal Artillery and Royal Horse Artillery. Although their 25-pounder field guns were not designed as anti-tank weapons, they were very effective against Rommel's Panzers, bearing in mind that the standard anti-tank gun was the two-pounder. Tobruk

Before the beginning of the Pacific War, large numbers of Australian troops were deployed in North Africa, along with New Zealanders and Indians.

was also defended by anti-aircraft batteries with seventy-five guns between them and, in the early days of the siege, four Hurricanes were stationed there, but these were soon either shot down or withdrawn.

On 10 April, Rommel reached Tobruk and sent a motorized detachment to storm the town, but it was repulsed by heavy gunfire which killed its commander. On the night of 13 April, an infantry battalion of the Afrika Korps' 5th Light Division made its way through a minefield and across the anti-tank ditch. A counterattack destroyed the infantry battalion and Jack Edmondson, an Australian defender who went on fighting even though he was fatally wounded in the action, was

posthumously awarded the Victoria Cross. Meanwhile, elements of the Afrika Korps had bypassed Tobruk and reached the Egyptian border. From now on, the 22,000 men at Tobruk would have to be supplied by sea.

This was a dangerous business because the Luftwaffe had complete air superiority. The anti-aircraft gunners managed, however, to keep the harbour open. The heavy batteries were armed with British 3.7-inch guns, which produced shrapnel, while light anti-aircraft batteries used Bofors 40mm and captured Italian 20mm and 40mm Breda guns which fired tracer shells that exploded on impact. Between them, they would throw up a barrage at a predetermined height. But the German pilots grew wise to this and started hanging back to see what height the barrage had been fixed at before starting their bombing runs. So the barrage was then spread more thinly over varying heights to make it more difficult to penetrate. The Luftwaffe's response was to begin dive-bombing the sites of the heavy guns, so the light anti-aircraft batteries with their rapid-fire tracer were moved in closer to protect them.

Pummelled

JUST BEFORE DAWN on 14 April, the Panzers attacked for the first time. They came on the left of the road that led south to El Adem. Thirty-eight tanks broke through the two lines of the zigzagged perimeter defences and headed for the town. About 5 km (3 miles) on they hit the second line of defence – the Blue Line. There they met point-blank fire from British 25-pounders. The Germans' artillery support and machine-gunners had been held up by the Australian infantry who had stayed in position when the tanks broke through. In the face of the 25-pounders, the Panzers had no choice but to retreat. As they did so, British tanks and Australian anti-tank guns pummelled their flanks. The routed Germans left behind seventeen tanks. Twelve aircraft had been shot down, 110 men killed and 254 captured. It was the first time that Hitler's Panzers had tasted defeat.

Rommel realized that Tobruk could only be taken with an all-out attack, but he lacked the resources. Even the 15th Panzer Division, which was on its way, had suffered significant losses when the convoy carrying it was attacked on its way to Libya. By then, operations in the

Balkans and, later, the Soviet Union starved Rommel of the tanks and men he needed to take Tobruk, and the stand-off there went on to become the longest siege in British history.

For the next two weeks, Rommel bided his time and brought up more forces. By the end of the month, he had some 400 German and Italian tanks against the defenders' thirty-one. On the evening of 30 April, he threw his men at Hill 209, known as Ras el Medauur, near the water tower on the south-west corner of the perimeter. Twenty-two Stukas began dive-bombing the Australian positions at 1915 hours, and an artillery barrage opened up at

The ancient and the modern: a British tank crew poses in front of a pyramid, Egypt 1941.

Enemy planes in the desert made an attractive target for the SAS, which specialized in long-range attacks on Axis airfields.

2000. This cut the telephone lines and neutralized the frontline defences.

Under cover of the bombardment, the Germans blew gaps in the wire and cleared paths through the minefield. By 2115 hours, a German machine-gun battalion about 1.5 km (1 mile) inside the perimeter opened fire on the reserve company. The Australians began a counterattack, but with poor communication they could not find the beleaguered perimeter posts in the darkness. By the following morning, it was clear the Germans had punched a hole

Not long after 0800 hours, the Germans advanced again with forty tanks, but were stopped by a minefield. Heavy shelling forced them to retreat, although a dust storm covered their withdrawal. Rommel tried a diversionary tactic with some twenty tanks to draw in the Allied armour, but Morshead was reluctant to commit his tanks, preferring to let mines and artillery shells do their work before risking his precious armoured reserve. Repeated air attacks failed to knock out the Allied artillery, and by 0900 the German attack had petered out.

As they could make no further progress forward, Rommel's Panzers and their infantry support attacked the posts at either side of the mouth of the German bridgehead. One fell at noon, but the heavy shelling prevented the Panzers co-ordinating with their supporting infantry, and their attempts to take the other post failed. Twenty-five light Panzers made it beyond the perimeter posts, however, and ran around the southern edge of the minefield. They were shelled all the way but, by 0915 hours, they had reached Post R12 5 km (3 miles) east of Hill 209. There, they were halted by fourteen cruiser tanks. Rommel sent in another nine tanks. A sporadic tank battle broke out but, although the German tanks outnumbered those of the British, the Panzers nonetheless withdrew after losing three of their number.

The German tanks refuelled and, that afternoon, began a new attack. Again, they were met by accurate British shelling. The Australians in the perimeter posts, armed only with Bren guns and rifles, put up fierce resistance. Two heavy Panzers tried to blast one post into surrender from 70 m (75 yards),

through the outer defences 2.5 km (1½ miles) wide, capturing seven perimeter posts and taking more than 100 prisoners. The Australians had put up such determined resistance, however, that they had taken the momentum out of the German attack.

but the German infantry was repeatedly beaten back. By dusk, half the defenders were wounded. In the twilight, the Germans attacked again with tanks and flame-throwers, and they took the post at 1930. A second post fell the next morning.

Having abandoned any attempt to drive forward directly on the harbour, Rommel continued to push inside the perimeter in the south-east until the bridgehead cleared the southern minefield. But he was stopped by a counterattack against Hill 209 that evening. Impeded by the fading light and the dust kicked up by enemy shelling, the Australians advanced for more than 1.5 km (1 mile) before they met resistance from anti-tank and machine-gun emplacements. By then, they had lost the cover of their artillery barrage. Lacking the machine guns they needed, the men withdrew. They had not retaken Hill 209, but they had forced the enemy on to the defensive and stopped the Germans getting around a vital minefield.

A sandstorm on 2 May halted the German advance, giving the defenders time to lay new minefields, bring up fresh infantry and strengthen their positions. The artillery continued to pummel the German positions and, when the storm cleared the next day, the Germans did not resume their offensive. The garrison had lost just five tanks, while out of the eighty-one German tanks Rommel started the battle with only thirty-five were in action – though, of the forty-six lost, only twelve were completely destroyed. The Panzers had suffered their second defeat, however, and the men's morale was shaken. On the other hand, the Germans had made a breach in the defences and held a large salient.

Jubilant

MORSHEAD PLANNED to do something about that. He would send two battalions to attack the shoulders of the salient, retake the lost posts and cut off the enemy spearhead. At the same time, a third battalion would make deep raids into enemy territory. The problem was that, as the Germans held Hill 209, they could see the Australians as they assembled. This gave them ample warning of the attack. After dark the Australians advanced under an artillery barrage. The Germans fought back with heavy machine-gun fire. Flares lit up the sky, and German mortar and artillery fire brought the Australian advance on the northern flank to a standstill. On the southern flank, they retook one post and attacked another, but could not take it. The other attacks pushed the German outposts back more than 800 m (½ mile). The Germans had lost 1,700 men, compared to the garrisons' casualties of 797 – 59 killed, 355 wounded and 383 missing. The German High Command grew alarmed at the losses and ordered Rommel not to attack again.

Morshead was jubilant. 'The actions before Tobruk in April and May are the first in which armoured formations of the German Army have been defied and defeated,' he said.

Churchill was also impressed. He sent a telegram which read, 'The whole Empire is watching your steadfast and spirited defence of this important outpost of Egypt with gratitude and admiration.'

Wavell's message to Morshead struck a more practical note. It read, 'Your magnificent defence is upsetting enemy's plans for attack on Egypt and giving us time to build up force

for counter offensive. You could *not* repeat *not* be doing better service.'

Nazi radio propagandist William Joyce – a US citizen hanged for treason after the war, and known in Britain as 'Lord Haw Haw' because of his sneering voice – crowed that the garrison was 'caught like rats in a trap'. A German newspaper then dubbed the British defenders the 'Rats of Tobruk', a name they defiantly embraced.

The men of the Afrika Korps were a formidable fighting force – but the Desert Rats defied them.

Until Tobruk, the men of the German Panzer Corps thought they were unassailable.

From the Allied point of view, Tobruk was psychologically important because it showed, for the first time, that the Germans could be stopped. The Panzers were not invincible. The German Blitzkrieg could be defeated by minefields, artillery fire and infantry who stood their ground. Even the terror-bombers could be thwarted by dedicated anti-aircraft gunners. It also gave a vital fillip to British prestige in the Arab world. Strategically, if Tobruk had fallen, Rommel would have rolled on through Egypt, to take the Suez Canal and the oilfields in the Persian Gulf, and cut the British Empire in two. As it was, Britain had time to recover from the disasters of Greece and Crete. In Egypt, British forces were able to regroup, while fresh American aid arrived via Britain.

The defence of Tobruk also kept Turkey – a German ally in World War I – out of the war. That prevented Hitler from using Turkey as a southern springboard for his attack on the Soviet Union and delayed his attack on Russia by at least a month. As winter is considered to be Russia's greatest general, this factor may have been crucial.

The greatest measure of the defenders of Tobruk's success was the fact that it took three battalions of Rommel's best troops and four Italian divisions to hold the salient around Hill 209. Playing on this, Morshead maintained a strategy of aggressive night patrolling to dominate no-man's-land and undermine the enemy's morale. Meanwhile, although short of tanks, the British kept up harassing attacks on Rommel's forces on the Egyptian frontier, to keep him from regrouping his whole force and turning it on Tobruk.

With the Allied evacuation of Greece, fifty tanks were diverted to Egypt. Wavell quickly organized Operation Brevity to relieve Tobruk. On 15 May 1941, the British took the Halfaya Pass on the way to Sollum. They were forced to withdraw on 17 May, however, and the Germans retook the pass.

On the night of 15 May, the Germans launched an attack on three perimeter posts at Tobruk. It was thought that all three were lost, but when one was recaptured it was found that the other two had held out, although desperately short of ammunition. Once they were resupplied, the Australians found they were on a roll and tried to recapture more of their outposts. A smokescreen was laid to prevent observation from Hill 209 and supporting fire came from thirty-nine British guns, while machine-gunners from the Northumberland

Fusiliers swept into the disputed area. But the Germans laid their own smokescreen and barrage. In the dust and smoke, the British tanks lost their way. The Australian infantry carried on alone through intense fire, however, to take two posts. But the Germans were too well established, holding not only the concrete posts, but also intermediate positions that could provide flanking fire. Without the corresponding posts in the zigzag defence, they could not be held. So the Australians withdrew.

By June, the two sides were consolidating their defensive positions. In the salient, the Germans had fallen back to defensive line behind the positions they held on 3 May. By 26 June, the Australians had been able to advance their line about 900 m (1,000 yards), reducing its length from more than 8 km (5 miles) to less than 6.5 km (4 miles). This allowed them to take one battalion out of the line and hold it in reserve. On the other hand, the German line was more closely packed. The Germans had also mined no-man's-land, preventing any further Australian advances.

Wavell made a second attempt to relieve Tobruk, starting on 15 June. This was beaten back by the 15th Panzer Division, and Wavell was replaced as Commander in Chief in the Middle East by General Sir Claude Auchinleck on 1 July.

The Australians had held out in Tobruk for more than three months. The heat, dust, flies, sand and poor food were affecting fighting ability, and the Australian government asked that the men be withdrawn. The bulk of them were evacuated in the late summer and replaced by the British 17th Division under Major General Scobie, supported by the 1st Polish Carpathian Brigade and a Czechoslovak

Battalion. Some Australians, however, along with the original British forces, stayed on.

While Rommel planned a new attack, Auchinleck began organizing Operation Crusader, a third attempt to relieve Tobruk, and formed the Eighth Army under General Sir Alan Cunningham. Cunningham's plan was to send XXX Corps across the Libyan border to the south and deploy it at a place called Gabr Saleh. He expected Rommel and his Panzers to seize the opportunity for a tank battle, which Cunningham believed the better equipped and more numerous British and South African forces would win. Meanwhile, XIII Corps would overrun the frontier positions on the coast and push up the coast road towards Tobruk while Rommel was being crushed in the desert. The danger was that there would be a large gap between the two columns where the British would be vulnerable. So another column was drawn up between them, but it drew its strength from XXX Corps, considerably weakening the force that was supposed to take on Rommel.

Crusader got under way on 18 November in torrential rain. Unfortunately, Rommel had plans of his own. He was readying himself to take Tobruk, so instead of moving to meet XXX Corps at Gabr Saleh he kept his armour around Gambut on the coast road. But worse was to befall Cunningham. The Eighth Army's operational plans, brought to the front by a careless British officer, fell into enemy hands. As Rommel failed to meet XXX Corps at Gabr Saleh, the British pressed on. On 19 November, fifty of their new Crusader tanks were destroyed when they tried to take Bir el Gubi to the south of Tobruk. Another column pushed on towards Tobruk, but was met with a counter-

attack by the Afrika Korps at Sidi Rezegh, which destroyed much of its armour. Rommel could have wiped out the whole of XXX Corps if he had followed up the next day. Instead, he took a gamble. With 100 tanks he made a dash across the desert to the Egyptian border, with the intention of cutting off the entire Eighth Army and attacking it from the rear.

Soldiers of the British 7th Armoured Division, the 'Desert Rats', pose with a field gun before the fall of Tobruk, 1942.

The reverses were to take a terrible toll on Cunningham, who wanted to withdraw. Believing that Rommel's bold move was an act of desperation, Auchinleck urged him on. But the strain was too much for Cunningham, and Auchinleck had to replace him with his own deputy chief of staff Major General Neil Methuen Ritchie, on 26 November. It was Auchinleck, however, who was now really in command.

In a letter home, Rommel described his 'dash to the wire' as a great success. In fact, he had made little impression on the 4th Indian Division who held the rear, nor did he manage to deprive the Eighth Army of its supplies. Worse still, Rommel's radio had broken down

*Opposite:
The British six-pounder was effective when it hit a Panzer in a vulnerable spot. Minefields were laid that directed the enemy armour into gun nests.*

and he had left his Panzer group without orders for four days.

While XXX Corps had been decimated to the south, XIII Corps had had an easier time of it running along the coast road. The New Zealand Division broke through. On 25 November, Scobie received a telegram telling him that the New Zealanders would make another attack on Sidi Rezegh the next day. At the same time, the garrison was to attempt to break out. They did this among fierce fighting. At 1300 hours, they saw tanks on the horizon. Suddenly three red rockets burst in the sky. It was the Eighth Army's recognition signal. Tobruk had been relieved at last. But not for long. In the absence of Rommel, the 21st Panzer Division, which had been on the Egyptian border, was ordered to retreat. Rommel confirmed this order when he reappeared at his headquarters on 27 November. A confused battle followed in which the New Zealand Division was cut in two, with one half thrown back to Tobruk. In the mêlée, the commander of the 21st Panzer Division, General Johann von Ravenstein, was captured.

Meanwhile, Auchinleck reinforced and reorganized XXX Corps, and threw it back into battle. Rommel now had few tanks left, and he was told that he was not going to be resupplied until the latter part of December, so he withdrew his forces attacking Tobruk from the east on 5 December. The following day, a final counterattack failed, and he ordered a general retreat, leaving behind an Italian division with orders to hold out as long as possible. Short of food and ammunition, the Italians surrendered on 17 January.

The Siege of Tobruk lasted 242 days from 10 April to 7 December 1941, fifty-five days longer than the siege of Mafeking in the Boer War. It was the first defeat of German land forces in World War II.

The Drive on Gazala

FOLLOWING THE RELIEF of Tobruk, Rommel was driven back to El Agheila, where the British advance had first halted in February 1941. With the attack on Pearl Harbor in December 1941 and Japan's rapid advance on Britain's colonies in the Far East, the Allies turned their attention there, starving the desert forces of supplies. During his retreat from Tobruk, however, Rommel had been supplied with new tanks. In January 1942, a convoy arrived in Tripoli carrying more reinforcements. Soon the Afrika Korps had 111 tanks with 28 more in reserve, while the Italians had 89.

Rommel quickly counterattacked, destroying nearly half of the British armour. In the swift reversal, the Desert Fox captured huge quantities of supplies as, once again, he made a dash eastwards. By 6 February, he had pushed the British back to Gazala, just 50 km (30 miles) west of Tobruk. There, the British had built a continuous minefield running from the town of Gazala on the Mediterranean coast 50 km southwards to Bir Hacheim in the desert. Another minefield ran from Bir Hacheim to Bir Harmat 25 km (15 miles) to the north-east. A further belt of mines five miles south of the Aslag Ridge joined the two. This area in between the Aslag Ridge and the Gazala Line was known as the 'Cauldron' and would be critical in the outcome of the battle.

The British retreated behind this line, hoping to build up their strength for a new

offensive. Rommel, however, was ready first. The problem with any defensive line in the North African campaign was that it necessarily had an open flank at the desert end. On 26 May 1942, Rommel began an attack that aimed to sweep around the southern end of the Gazala Line and seize Tobruk in just three days.

Rommel's Panzers destroyed the 3rd and 7th Indian Motor brigades south-east of Bir Hacheim, then turned north. The Italians kept up the pressure on the front of the line, while the 15th and 21st Panzers drove up towards the coast behind the Gazala Line to attack the defenders from the rear, and the 19th Light Division headed for Tobruk itself.

But this was not the walkover Rommel had planned. The British 4th Armoured Brigade struck back with its new American Grant tanks, which were equipped with 75mm guns. The 15th Panzer Division lost 100 tanks on the first day of battle, and a counterattack by the 2nd Armoured Brigade forced it on to the defensive near Bir Harmat. The 21st Panzers were halted 16 km (10 miles) north-west of 'Knightsbridge', the British 1st Armoured Division's desert stronghold. And the 19th Light Division was stopped at El Adem, just outside the defensive perimeter at Tobruk.

Rommel's forces were short of fuel and ammunition, and dangerously dispersed, so he pulled them back to the Cauldron, which was protected on three sides by British minefields. There they could be resupplied after the Italian X Corps cut two lanes through the Gazala Line itself. This meant that Rommel's supply lines were no longer vulnerable to disruption by the strong British forces to the south.

The northern supply route, however, was under fire from the British 150th Brigade, supported by the First Army Tank Brigade, at Got el Ualeb. Rommel had to take this stronghold. Infantry, tanks and new six-pounder anti-tank guns were brought up, until the British force was greatly outnumbered. It put up stubborn resistance, but was eventually forced to surrender. The Germans took 101 tanks, 124 guns and more than 3,000 prisoners.

To the north of the Gazala Line, the Italians attacked, but were held off by the South Africans, who were deeply entrenched. On 4 June, General Ritchie then launched Operation Aberdeen to crush the enemy in the Cauldron. It was a failure. It had been planned for 2 June, when Rommel was held with his back to the minefield, before the Italians had broken through and while the 150th Brigade was still a fighting force. Now the situation had changed dramatically.

Ritchie tried to seize the initiative again on 7 June. The South Africans in the northern sector were to attack the Italian positions. However, the Italians were as well dug in as the British, and they, too, had laid minefields. These had to be cleared first. This limited the size of the South African attack, and it was never large enough to overwhelm the defenders.

With supply lines to the west, the Cauldron was now a huge salient in the Gazala Line, and the Free French holding Bir Hacheim to the south were practically cut off. Not only could this salient be defended from the British, but it could also be used to launch an attack. On the night of 1 June, the Italian Trieste Division from the west and the 19th Light Division from the north attacked Bir Hacheim. Despite heavy bombardment by the Luftwaffe, the French put up fierce resistance for eleven days, then surrendered after one of

the bravest defensive actions of the desert war. After Bir Hacheim's fall, Ritchie had to turn his defensive line so it faced south rather than east. He now had a defensive position only 25 km (15 miles) wide, and his back to the sea.

Rommel regrouped his forces at Bir Hacheim. On 12 June, he made a push on El Adem, crushing four armoured brigades on the way. Between them, they lost 185 cruiser and 50 infantry tanks. The next day, he smashed the British armour at Acroma to the rear of the northern sector of the Gazala Line. By 14 June, the British had only fifty cruiser and twenty infantry tanks left. Retreat was inevitable.

This time Auchinleck wanted to abandon Tobruk, but he was ordered by Churchill to hold it. So he told Ritchie to hold an outer defensive line. Auchinleck assumed, however, that Ritchie would have at his disposal the two divisions that were still holding the northern half of Gazala Line. What he did not know was that Ritchie had already ordered the British 15th Division and the 1st South African Division to head back to Egypt. As it was, their direct line of retreat had already been cut by Rommel, and they had to break out westwards through the Gazala Line, then sweep southwards through the desert. As a result, Ritchie simply did not have the manpower to hold the line. Knightsbridge was evacuated. On 18 June, the Afrika Korps cut the road to the east of Tobruk, and the fortress was under siege again. Once again, the Afrika Korps bypassed Tobruk and dashed on eastwards, forcing the RAF to withdraw from Gambut and denying the besieged garrison any air support.

On 15 June, Major General Klopper of 2nd South African Division became commander of the garrison at Tobruk, while Rommel dusted off his plan to attack the south-east section of the defensive perimeter. This was what he had intended to do in November 1941 before he was beaten to the punch by Operation Crusader.

Shortly before 0520 hours on 20 June, the Luftwaffe pummelled the line between posts R58 and R63, which effectively neutralized the Mahratta Light Infantry, which was holding that sector. By 0830, the 15th Panzer Division had crossed the anti-tank ditch. With the 21st Panzer, it drove for 'King's Cross', a key intersection inside the perimeter. A counterattack was delayed by a dispute between the British commanders. At 0930, the 22nd Army Tank Brigade went in, but it was repulsed and, by 1330, King's Cross was in enemy hands. While 21st Panzer headed towards the port, 15th Panzer drove along the Pilastrino Ridge to the west. By dusk, only isolated pockets of resistance were holding out. Major General Klopper had been forced to move his headquarters. He had lost all of his tanks and half of his guns. The situation was desperate.

Early next morning it was decided that any troops that still had transport should be evacuated. Few could get out as, by then, most of the vehicles were in German hands. Klopper wanted to fight on, but realized that the casualties he would sustain would not justify any possible gain. He did his best to destroy the port facilities and the remaining stock of petrol. Then, soon after 0630 hours, he surrendered. Some 32,200 prisoners were taken, including 19,000 British, 10,000 South Africans and 2,500 Indians, along with a large quantity of stores.

Winston Churchill was in Washington when he heard the news. It was a national disaster.

A US Maryland bomber in action over the desert.

Throughout 1941, the defiance of the small garrison at Tobruk of the might of the German army had been a beacon of hope. Now that beacon had been extinguished. Hitler, on the other hand, was delighted and promoted Rommel to the rank of field marshal.

With Rommel's victory on the Gazala Line and the eventual fall of Tobruk, the Axis shelved its plan for an airborne invasion of Malta, and Rommel captured enough stores to push on into Egypt before the British had time to regroup.

El Alamein

THE ALLIES THOUGHT that they could delay Rommel's advance with a line of fortification Ritchie had built running south along the Egyptian border from Sollum to Sidi Omar. But this suffered from the same tactical weakness as the Gazala Line – the desert flank remained open. Rommel swept around it on 24 June, advancing more than 160 km (100 miles) in one day. However, realizing that the line could not be held, the Eighth Army had already fallen back to Mersa Matruh, 200 km (120 miles) east of the frontier. The situation was now desperate. The Luftwaffe was already in range of Alexandria. And if the Eighth Army failed to hold back Rommel, there was nothing to stop him taking both Egypt and the oilfields of the Persian Gulf, and going on to attack the beleaguered Russians' southern flank.

Ritchie intended to make one final stand at Mersa Matruh, but Auchinleck realized that a defensive line there would suffer exactly the same weaknesses as those at Gazala and Sollum. On 25 June, he sacked Ritchie and took personal command of Eighth Army. The next day he issued new orders. There would be no new line at Mersa Matruh. Instead, he intended to keep his all troop formations fluid. Mobile columns would strike at the enemy from all sides. To that end, he reorganized into brigade battle groups made up of artillery – always the Western Desert Force's strength – supported by armour and infantry.

On 27 June, the Axis caught up with the Allies again. There was a series of punishing skirmishes with units of the British forces being bypassed, cut off and having to break out eastwards. Eventually, they fell back on a line at El Alamein, just 100 km (60 miles) from Alexandria. There, Auchinleck blocked any further advance.

What was different about Auchinleck's line at El Alamein and from that at Gazala, 560 km (350 miles) to the west, was that the El Alamein line did not have an open flank to the south. It ended at the Qattara Depression, 18,130 sq km (7,000 square miles) of salt lakes and marshes impassable to tanks and other heavy military vehicles. The German spearhead reached the El Alamein line on 30 June. It was manned by Australians who had been the original 'desert rats' of Tobruk, along with British, South African, New Zealand and Indian troops who had fallen back across the desert. And at El Alamein, critically, they would be supported by the RAF.

Having come so far, so fast, the Afrika Korps was now exhausted. And it was at the end of a very long supply line. Its first assaults failed to break through, so it halted to build up its forces, and began to lay minefields. Throughout July 1942, assault was met with counterstroke, with neither side giving way.

General Bernard Montgomery (later to be promoted to field marshal) knew that he had to be instantly recognizable to his men, so he always wore two badges on his beret – those of the Royal Tank Regiment and a British General Officer.

On 13 July, Rommel launched his newly re-equipped Afrika Korps into what became known as the First Battle of El Alamein. Again the Panzers were halted and, that night, Auchinleck counterattacked. Indians and New Zealanders overwhelmed two Italian divisions, and held a counterstrike by the Panzers.

The battle became a war of attrition, leaving some 10,000 dead. Rommel quickly used up all the supplies that he had taken at Tobruk. He had been reinforced with 260 tanks but, after the fall of Tobruk, US President Frankin D. Roosevelt had sent 100 self-propelled guns and 300 Sherman tanks. The Shermans were armed with 75mm guns that at last gave the British a tank to rival the Mark III and Mark IV Panzers.

Although Auchinleck had stopped Rommel's advance, he had not thrown him back and, on 4 August, Churchill arrived in Cairo to see what could be done. Auchinleck told him that he intended to delay any offensive until September to give the new reinforcements that he had just received time to acclimatize. Churchill sacked him and appointed Sir Harold Alexander Commander in Chief in the Middle East. Command of the Eighth Army was given to General Bernard Montgomery, who took over on 13 August. Montgomery quickly reorganized the Eighth Army again so that it fought in divisions, with units giving each other mutual support.

The Eighth Army was expecting Rommel to go on the offensive at some time around the full moon on 26 August. It was anticipated that he would attack, as usual, to the south of the line, aiming to break through, surround the Eighth Army within a matter of hours and rush on to take Cairo. The spot he would choose for his attack was defended only by a minefield. But Montgomery had spotted the weakness in his defences too. Behind it he prepared positions so that any attacking force would have to run the gauntlet between six-pounder anti-tank guns and dug-in tanks.

Rommel's long supply lines meant that he had problems obtaining fuel. This delayed the attack until 31 August, giving the Allies more time to prepare. He had been hoping that his attack would take the British by surprise. But two hours before the attacking force – 200 Panzers, 243 Italian medium tanks and 38 light tanks – set off, it came under attack from

the RAF. Troops advancing in front of the tanks to lift the British mines came under heavy fire from well dug-in troops. More air strikes were called in. The commander of the Africa Korps was badly wounded; the commander of the 21st Panzer Division was killed.

Rommel narrowed the front. His column made its way through two minefields, but was stopped by a third. The Panzers also found that they could make only slow progress on the soft sand. Casualties were heavy, and the stalled column came under heavy artillery fire. But then a sandstorm blew up, grounding the RAF and hampering the artillery.

On 1 September, the storm lifted and the Panzers continued their advance. British

General Erwin Rommel was actually respected by the British, who called him the 'Desert Fox'.

armour drove them back. They tried another offensive in the afternoon, but were beaten back again. Montgomery tightened a ring of steel around the Afrika Korps. It tried to break out and failed, sustaining heavy casualties. Meanwhile, it was being bombed day and night. By the afternoon of 3 September, Rommel's men were in retreat. Montgomery now aimed to go on the offensive, but he did not feel that his reinforcements were sufficiently welded together to give chase. As it was, he let the Germans hold on to a strongpoint between the two minefields at the end of the El Alamein line.

New Preparations

ON 7 SEPTEMBER, Montgomery broke off the battle and began making new preparations. He had worked out a plan of deception to keep the enemy's strength at the south end of the line. He deployed a dummy pipeline, dummy supply dumps and dummy vehicles in that sector. Radio traffic was stepped up in the southern part of the line to suggest that an attack would be launched from there early in November.

The real attack, though, would be launched further north. The guns and tanks massed there were moved in at night and camouflaged carefully. Slit trenches were dug out into the desert for the infantry to attack from. These, too, were camouflaged to prevent German aerial reconnaissance knowing the British intentions. As the six-week period of preparation grew to a close, the RAF stepped up its attacks on enemy airfields, effectively grounding the Luftwaffe by 23 October – the night of the attack.

Montgomery abandoned the conventional wisdom of desert warfare. He would not attack to the south and try to turn the flank. Nor would he take on the enemy's armour, then deal with the infantry later. He would begin by sending a diversionary force against the armour in the south to make Rommel think that the main thrust would come there. Meanwhile, there would be a massive bombardment, first of the artillery positions in the north, then the infantry positions there. Next, Montgomery's infantry would infiltrate down the slit trenches to take on German troops still dazed from the bombardment. While there would inevitably be vicious hand-to-hand fighting, Montgomery reckoned his men would get the best of it. The armour would then pour through the hole made by the infantry, systematically finish off the German infantry, and get into position at the rear to take on any remaining armour on ground of his choosing. Even if he could not destroy the Panzers completely, without infantry they could not hold ground and would have to retreat.

There was a full moon on the night of 23 October. This was vital, as thousands of mines would have to be lifted to make a hole in the enemy's defences. The minefields were 4,570–8,230 m (5,000–9,000 yards) in depth, and strengthened with booby-trap bombs and barbed wire. At 2140 hours, the Second Battle of El Alamein began, when more than 1,000 guns along the whole line opened fire simultaneously on the German artillery. Twenty minutes later, they switched their aim to the enemy's forward positions. As a huge curtain of dust and smoke rose over the enemy, the British infantry moved in with fixed bayonets to the skirl of the pipes.

The Germans resisted valiantly, but by 0530 the next morning two corridors had been opened, and the armour began moving down them. Then things began to go wrong. The infantry still had not made it all the way through the minefields when it was met with fierce resistance. This left the armour dangerously exposed. By dusk the following day, one column of armour had made it through. But the 10th Armoured Division was still in the middle of the minefields and taking shelter behind the Miteiriya Ridge. Its commander General Herbert Lumsden had always been critical of Montgomery's plan. He thought that it was suicide to send tanks through narrow corridors in minefields where there was heavy anti-tank artillery, well dug in. If one tank was hit, those behind it could not move and would be sitting ducks.

Lumsden was summoned to Montgomery's HQ and explained his position. Montgomery then called Brigadier Alec Gatehouse who was commanding the spearhead, and ordered him to send the 10th Armoured Division over the ridge. Gatehouse refused to waste his division in such a reckless fashion. After a robust exchange of views, Montgomery ordered him to send one regiment over the ridge,

British cavalry soldiers charge in North Africa. Actions of this type were rare on any front during World War II – most 'cavalry' units were, in fact, equipped with tanks.

instead of the entire division. Of the forty-nine tanks of the Staffordshire Yeomanry that went over, only fifteen limped back. Gatehouse had been right.

Nevertheless, the advance continued and, by the morning of 25 October, two armoured columns had reached the enemy's positions. But the situation on the battlefield had grown confused. The Germans made a number of bloody counterattacks. One, on the vital salient known as Kidney Ridge, was led by Rommel himself. All were repulsed. Gradually, things turned in Britain's favour. On 27 October, 1st Armoured Division alone knocked out fifty German tanks, and repeated sorties by the RAF broke up the Panzer formations.

With the two armies locked in fierce fighting, it became apparent to Rommel that everything depended on which side would be exhausted first. However, Montgomery had been skilfully pulling units out of the line to build up a force that could deliver a knockout punch. Those that remained were told to adopt a defensive posture, but to use aggressive patrolling and artillery fire to give the impression that the advance was continuing.

On the night of 28 August, the 9th Australian Division drove a wedge down the coastal road. This was what Rommel was hoping for. If the British attempted to move around him to the north, he could cut their forces in two. Hence he moved his Panzers to the north. Montgomery, however, did not follow up with a major attack down the coast. Instead, he sent the 2nd New Zealand Division against a weak point in the German line which was defended by the Italians.

The battle was reaching its climax. Rommel told his commanders that they must fight to the death, although shortage of fuel meant that he was already considering withdrawing. Then, on the night of 30 October, he thought he had got lucky. The Australians came up out of their trenches and moved forward against fierce resistance. This would inevitably exhaust the tenacious Australians. But a force of Panzergrenadiers found themselves surrounded in a fortified position known as 'Thompson's Post'. The Panzers attacked repeatedly in an attempt to relieve them. After three days of fighting, they managed to get through to the survivors.

Meanwhile, in Operation Supercharge, the full weight of Montgomery's remaining forces was thrown against a 3,660-m (4,000-yard) stretch of the front. At 0100 on 2 November, two British infantry brigades moved through the New Zealanders' lines and attacked. They were followed by 123 tanks of the 9th Armoured Brigade. The objective was to destroy the anti-tank screen, especially the lethal 88mm guns. Montgomery told its commander Brigadier John Currie, 'I am prepared to accept one hundred per cent casualties'. Currie led the attack personally.

The tanks, which were followed by infantry with bayonets fixed, ran over mines. As the sun came up, they were hit by dug-in German anti-tank guns. All but nineteen of the 9th Armoured Brigade's tanks were knocked out, and 230 of Currie's 400 men were killed; however, the attack succeeded in its objective. Through the new corridor it had created plunged the 1st Armoured Division. When Rommel realized that he had been tricked, he sent formations of Panzers south. The following day anti-tank guns were moved into position, but by that time the British had

expanded their salient to the south and were pushing relentlessly westwards. A tank battle ensued, but the German and Italian tanks were held in check by the RAF and artillery fire. After two hours, the German counter-attack petered out. That afternoon, Rommel tried again, throwing an Italian armoured division into the fray. But more and more British reinforcements were pouring through the gap and fanning out behind it.

The Afrika Korps was down to just thirty-five tanks when Rommel decided to withdraw. But he received an order from Hitler, telling him to hold the position to the last man.

'There will be no retreat, not so much as a millimetre,' read the Führer's message. 'Victory or death.'

Rommel knew that to hold his current position would be suicidal. But then, it would also be suicidal to disobey Hitler. When General von Thoma, head of the Afrika Korps, asked for permission to retreat, Rommel refused to give it, but he turned a blind eye when Thoma pulled back anyway. Thoma was captured soon after and did not have to face Hitler's wrath. After twelve days of fighting, the Axis forces were now in full retreat. Fuel was low and there were only enough vehicles for the Germans to get away. The hapless Italians were abandoned, and surrendered by the thousand.

Brigadier Gatehouse wanted the 10th Armoured Division to give pursuit. He was sure that he could outrun them in forty-eight hours and destroy them. But Montgomery was more cautious. Rommel had already shown that he could suddenly mount a counter-attack that could turn a rout into a new offensive. The retreating column was bombed and strafed by the RAF, and the 8th Armoured Brigade managed to head off a German column taking a large number of prisoners, tanks and lorries. Other units also gave pursuit, but a downpour on 7 November turned the road into a quagmire, and the Afrika Korps got away. It left 10,000 men behind it. Another 20,000 Italians had been captured. A further 20,000 had been killed or wounded. On the battlefield, there were 450 knocked-out tanks, along with 75 abandoned by the Italians due to lack of fuel. More than 1,000 enemy guns had been destroyed or abandoned.

During the Battle of Alamein, the British Eighth Army sustained 13,500 casualties. Some 500 British tanks had been knocked out – though 350 of those could be repaired – and 100 guns were lost. In Britain, the church bells had been silent for years as they were to act as an invasion alarm. Churchill ordered that they be rung out in celebration. Speaking of the victory at El Alamein at the Mansion House in the City of London on 10 November 1942, he said memorably, 'Now is not the end. It is not even the beginning of the end. But it is, perhaps, the end of the beginning.'

For Britain, the Battle of Alamein was a turning point. For three years, the British had been battered in Europe, in the Atlantic and in the Far East.

'After Alamein,' wrote Churchill, with some justification, 'we never had a defeat.'

Operation Torch

THE UNITED STATES had joined the war after the Japanese attacked Pearl Harbor on 7 December 1941 (*see* Chapter IV: Pearl Harbor to Midway). On 11 December, Hitler

had declared war on the United States, and the United States declared war on Germany and Italy. The sides were now drawn up. The strategy agreed between Britain and the United States was that they should take on Hitler before dealing with the Japanese. The United States would maintain only defensive operations in the Pacific, while the bulk of its effort would go into defeating the Axis powers. As soon as the United States joined the war, the US military had wanted to launch an amphibious assault on the coast of France. But after two years of fighting, the British were more cautious and persuaded the United States to join in the fight in an area of the world where they had already had some success – North Africa.

On 8 November 1942, with Rommel in full retreat from El Alamein, a 117,000-strong Anglo-American task force under General Dwight D. Eisenhower was to land in French North Africa. Some 45,000 men under Major-General George S. Patton would sail directly from the United States and seize Casablanca and the Atlantic coast of Morocco. Another 39,000 US troops under Major General Lloyd R. Fredendall would sail from Scotland and take the Mediterranean port of Oran in Algeria, while a 33,000-man Anglo-American force under Major General Charles Ryder would take the port of Algiers itself. This was to be code-named Operation Torch.

The situation in French North Africa was far from clear, and no one knew what the reaction to the invasion would be. Officially, the French forces in North Africa were loyal to the collaborationist government in Vichy, although many in the military had sympathies with General de Gaulle and the Free French. There was still a

American troops wade ashore in North Africa. This was where the raw recruits of the US Army would first prove themselves. By the time they were landing in Italy and France, they had become an unstoppable force.

lot of bitterness, however, about the Royal Navy's attack on the French Fleet in the port of Mers-el-Kebir in July 1940, which killed more than 1,200 French sailors.

Three weeks before the invasion a small team of officers under Major General Mark Clark was landed secretly near Algiers. There they had talks with sympathetic French officers. These were inconclusive, but Clark's team made contact with General Henri Giraud, an officer sympathetic to the Allied cause and not tarnished by any association with Vichy. They offered Giraud Anglo-American support if he would take command of the French forces in North Africa. They also contacted Admiral Jean Darlan who, by chance, was in Algiers visiting his sick son. Darlan was Pétain's deputy and Commander in Chief of all French forces under the control of Vichy. Darlan was equivocal; as the landings went ahead, no one could be sure what resistance they would meet.

Operation Torch had been planned hastily. The men were poorly trained for their task, and the American forces were new to war. The amphibious landings went ahead on 8 November in high seas and losses in landing craft were heavy. If they had met determined French resistance, the operation could easily have turned into a disaster. As it was, after the fall of Algiers, Darlan was persuaded to order all French forces to cease fire. But this came too late to prevent heavy fighting at Oran, where the French fought bitterly for two days before surrendering to Major General Terry Allen's US 1st Infantry Division. The Axis powers took Darlan's ceasefire as a violation of the armistice Pétain had signed, and invaded unoccupied France. The remains of the French Fleet in Toulon then scuttled its ships. Giraud

then became Commander in Chief of the French forces in North Africa. Darlan was shot by a young anti-Vichy fanatic on 24 December.

While General Patton's troops remained in Morocco training, the rest of the Allied forces turned east towards the western border of Tunisia; Rommel's Afrika Korps was retreating towards its eastern border. With Libya lost, Hitler was determined to hold on to the key ports of Tunis and Bizerte. The Luftwaffe attacked Eisenhower's forces on land, while U-boats sank Allied supply ships at sea.

The British First Army, under Lieutenant General Kenneth Anderson, was to lead the assault on Tunis, which was 800 km (500

miles) east of Algiers. Transporting fuel, food and ammunition all that way down the primitive road network of northern Algeria proved to be a logistical nightmare. When Anderson arrived at the Tunisian border, he found it strongly defended, and his first assault was repulsed. The major threat came from the Luftwaffe in Tunisia, which had been strengthened to 445 aircraft earlier that month. The nearest Allied all-weather air base was at Bône, 190 km (120 miles) from the front lines. The Luftwaffe's nearest air base was just 8 km (5 miles) from the battlefield.

By the end of November 1942, the Axis forces in Tunisia had grown in size to around 25,000 men. These forces included fresh reserve units from Germany, Italy and France, along with reinforcements that had been destined for the Afrika Korps. Organized by General Walther Nehring, a former commander of the Afrika Korps who was convalescing after being wounded, the troops were supported by seventy Panzers – twenty of which were armed with the new 88mm guns. This was already a formidable force. But Field Marshal Albert Kesselring, Commander in Chief in the Mediterranean, was convinced that it was vital to block General Anderson's advance on Tunis, and sent a further three divisions to bolster the numbers.

Hastily planned, the landings of Operation Torch could have ended in unmitigated disaster if they had been met by determined French resistance. However, US commander General Eisenhower told Vichy troops: 'We have come amongst you to repulse the cruel invaders who would remove for ever your rights to live your own lives in peace and security.'

Night-firing: a British 25-pounder field gun in action during the Battle of Gazala, June 1942.

German counterattack supported by tanks on Christmas Day brought the Allies to a halt. Casualties were high on both sides, but any attempt to take Tunis would now have to be postponed. From the end of December to March, the rains come to North Africa, turning the parched landscape into a sea of mud.

The Allied forces would have to sit out the cold Tunisian winter at the end of long, tenuous supply lines. If aircraft strayed off their makeshift runways, or trucks left the road, they would sink irretrievably into the mud. There was friction between the Allies with plenty of bar-room brawls between British and American troops. Eisenhower decided to put a stop to this. When one of his senior officers called his counterpart a 'British bastard', Eisenhower bellowed, 'There are no British, American or French bastards in this headquarters. There are certainly bastards aplenty and I am looking at one.'

Ill-suited Bunch

In December, Anderson made a second attempt to take Tunis, but the Allied forces were inexperienced. Neither the British First Army nor the US II Corps had been tried in battle. Added to this was the difficulty of fighting as a coalition, which the Allies had by no means yet perfected. The Allied air force could not give them the close air support the Luftwaffe gave to its men. Anderson's men were still fighting as reinforced brigades as the British had in Libya and Egypt under Auchinleck; however, a joint British–French–US force reached Longstop Hill overlooking the Gulf of Tunis in December. The battle there lasted four days, until a powerful

PART OF THE FRICTION came from the fact that the British Army, which had a fighting tradition centuries old, rubbed up against a peacetime US Army suddenly thrust into global war. The British found the inexperienced Americans brash and boastful, while the Americans found the British professionalism and sang-froid patronizing. Anderson, particularly, came in for criticism, not least from Montgomery, who said that he was no better than 'a good plain cook'. Even Field Marshal Alan Brooke, Chief of the Imperial General Staff, lamented the quality of his army and corps commanders, mourning the loss of so many good men in World War I.

It has to be said that the Americans were not a lot better. General Mark Clark was mistrusted by fellow Americans as being an intriguer who issued contradictory orders. And Eisenhower discovered that Fredendall not only held Anderson and the French in disdain, but also viewed Major General Orlando W. Ward, commander of the 1st Armored Division, with outright contempt.

Against this ill-suited bunch, Hitler pitched the experienced Colonel General Hans-Jürgen von Arnim. He was moved from the Eastern Front to take command of the Fifth Panzer Army and the defence of Tunisia. Arnim had more than 100,000 veteran German troops under his command and, by January 1943, he had all the mountain passes around Tunis under Axis control. Meanwhile, Eisenhower's planners developed Operation Satin. This was a plan for American and French forces, at the 400-km (250-mile) stretch of southern front they now occupied, to punch their way through a mountain range called the Eastern Dorsal to the coast, south of Tunis, thereby cutting Arnim's forces off from Rommel's retreating army. When this was raised at the conference between Churchill and Roosevelt in Casablanca, Morocco, in January 1943, the British condemned the plan on the grounds that the inexperienced Allied troops would stand no chance against the veteran Panzer divisions that opposed them. Operation Satin was shelved.

When Montgomery reached Tripoli in late January 1943, he decided that his troops must rest and essential repair work must be done on his armour before he tackled Rommel again. As a result, Rommel halted when he reached the Tunisian border and established the formidable Mareth Line there. He knew that he could not defeat Montgomery's veteran Eighth Army. If he could hold them with minimal troops at the Mareth Line, however, he could launch an attack on the inexperienced and ill-supplied troops to his rear. With his Panzers he would destroy the untested and understrength US II Corps, then push along another mountain range called the Western Dorsal to the coast near Bône, knocking out the Allied airfield.

Rommel did not, however, have the Panzers to pull this off. He did not get on with Arnim, a Prussian aristocrat who did not trust Rommel's flair, and Arnim would not go along with this daring plan. Arnim would, however, support a more limited attack to strengthen his position on the Eastern Dorsal. On 14 February, German dive-bombers attacked the American forces guarding the town of Sidi Bou Zid in the Faid Pass. Then the tanks and infantry of the 10th Panzer quickly overran them, inflicting huge losses. The 21st Panzers attacked from the south through the Maizila Pass. By noon, the defenders of Sidi Bou Zid had been routed. The Americans quickly counter-attacked with a force of light tanks and infantry on half-tracks. This has been compared to the charge of the Light Brigade. The Americans lost more than 2,000 men, of which 1,400 were taken prisoner, including Patton's son-in-law Lieutenant Colonel John Waters. Only 300 got out. Some ninety-four tanks were lost, along with sixty half-tracks and twenty-six self-propelled guns. But Arnim would not give Rommel the support he needed to follow up on this success.

It was only on 19 February that Rommel received the authority to proceed. Even then

Arnim withheld part of the 10th Panzer and some newly arrived Tiger tanks. Rommel's forces were under strength when they began their attack on the Kasserine Pass in a rainstorm. This was held by Task Force Stark, which occupied the high ground on either side of the pass. It was not taken until the following day. The British then fought a brilliant delaying action as Task Force Stark withdrew along the road to Thala, where the advance was halted. Although Rommel had won another tactical victory at the Kasserine Pass, it was a strategic failure. Allied reinforcements were on their way. He had lengthened his supply lines, and his flanks were now open to attack. And it would only be a matter of time before Montgomery turned up at the Mareth Line. Rommel called off the offensive on 22 February.

In early March, Rommel advanced again – this time towards Medenine and Montgomery's advancing forces. By this time Montgomery knew Rommel well. At the first hint of the attack, he turned the 2nd New Zealand Division, two other infantry brigades and two armoured brigades, and positioned them along a line 39,300 m (43,000 yards) long at right angles to Rommel's line of attack. Rommel found himself attacking across open terrain against 810 medium, field and anti-tank guns, including many of the new 17-pounder anti-tank guns in use for the first time. Salvos of concentrated fire knocked out fifty-two tanks and inflicted 640 casualties before the Germans retreated. The British lost one Sherman tank and 130 men. Again, Montgomery expressly forbade his men to pursue the fleeing enemy, who disappeared behind the Matmata mountains. Two days later,

Rommel – now out of favour with Hitler – left Africa and his command was ceded to Arnim.

Another British victory did nothing to help American morale. So far the Americans had sustained 6,000 casualties with nothing to show for it. Their equipment was no match for the Germans'. The British contended that the Americans' gung-ho attitude was no more than bravado, while in their intercepted communications the Germans were openly contemptuous. General Alexander, who was brought in as overall commander of ground forces, despaired that, from private to general, the Americans 'simply did not know their jobs as soldiers' and 'lacked the will to fight' – although he told Eisenhower, diplomatically, that once they had overcome their inexperience they would match any soldiers in the world. Chief of the Imperial General Staff Field Marshal Alan Brooke feared that the American forces would be 'quite useless' in the European theatre of war. Only Rommel had any time for them. He saw that their tactical defence of the Kasserine Pass was superb. He also knew that the United States' industrial might would mean it would soon be out-producing Germany with equipment equal to anything the Wehrmacht had. For the moment, though, the American forces' main problem was leadership.

Inexperienced

EISENHOWER WAS STILL a very inexperienced general, and he had not tackled the personality problems in his own chain of command. The stridently anti-British attitudes of General Fredendall were causing problems, but Eisenhower felt that he could not replace

him as he was a favourite of General George C. Marshall, then the US Army Chief of Staff in Washington. Instead, he called in veteran cavalry officer Major General Ernest Harmon from the 2nd Armored Division in Morocco and sent him to Fredendall's II Corps HQ. These were 105 km (65 miles) behind the lines and housed in an enormous underground bunker it had taken 200 combat engineers three weeks to build. When Harmon arrived there at 0200 on 23 February, a nervous Fredendall asked him if he thought the corps headquarters should be moved. Harmon thought that this was a strange question to ask in the middle of the night when he had had no time to assess the situation and he said, simply, 'Hell, no.'

Fredendall then took to his bed for a day, and Harmon effectively took over command. The first thing he did was visit the British in Thala, who were still holding off the 10th Panzers. He immediately countermanded Anderson's order to withdraw the US artillery and sent his men into battle. 'I figured if I won the battle I would be forgiven,' Harmon said. 'If I lost, the hell with it, anyway.'

Harmon then sent a report to Eisenhower saying that Fredendall was unfit to command. He told Patton that Fredendall was a moral and physical coward. Eisenhower dismissed Fredendall. The US Army's leaders, however, were afraid of the adverse effect dismissing the officer in charge of the first US ground troops in combat against the Axis might have on American public opinion. So it was made out that he was being transferred home because of his invaluable expertise in training. He arrived back in the United States to a hero's welcome and was later promoted.

Eisenhower offered Fredendall's command to Harmon, but Harmon refused it on the grounds that he could not take over from a commander whose relief he had recommended. Instead, Harmon suggested that Patton be brought in to command II Corps. He was joined by Major General Omar N. Bradley, first as an observer, then – when Patton refused to have 'one of Ike's goddam spies' in his command – as his deputy. Although the two men could hardly have been more dissimilar – Patton was volatile and outspoken, while Bradley hated theatrics and any kind of profanity – they instinctively got on. Patton began reorganizing II Corps along the lines of Montgomery's Eighth Army, while Alexander streamlined the overall command structure.

As the Germans withdrew through the Kasserine Pass and down the Eastern Dorsal, they were harassed by the planes of the Northwest African Tactical Air Force, now commanded by Air Marshal Arthur Coningham, who had previously led the Desert Air Force which had done such an effective job supporting Montgomery.

With the Germans now on the retreat in the west, Alexander planned for his ground forces to tie up with the Eighth Army, which was massing to drive through the Gabes' Gap – a narrow corridor between salt lakes of Chott el Fedjadj and the sea – and punch its way through the Mareth Line. The Eighteenth Army Group, as the combined command was known, would then bottle the Axis forces up in northern Tunisia, while the Allied air forces and navies would deny them any possibility of escape or reinforcement.

In preparation, Alexander asserted his authority and made it clear that the British

attitude of professionalism should take over from American amateurism. British officers set up training programmes, so the inexperienced troops could be toughened up before they were thrown into battle. Even so, in battle, British formations would be used ahead of American ones. This destroyed Eisenhower's strategy of building a truly equal alliance. However unpopular his policy was, Alexander enjoyed the respect of the American commanders in Tunisia. However unpalatable the truth might be, they knew that their troops were going to have to improve their performance before they won the respect of the British. Fortunately, in Patton, Bradley, Harmon and others, they had the officers who could inspire their men to deliver just that result.

Ten days after he took command, Patton was ordered to stage a diversionary attack to draw troops away from the Mareth Line. Alexander wanted him to take back the ground the Americans had lost the previous month and take the airfield at Gafsa, which would be used as a supply base when Montgomery broke through. Patton had other plans. He intended to push on past Gafsa and reach the coast at Gabes, cutting the Axis forces in two. Patton had brought a whole new attitude with him to II Corps.

'Gentlemen, tomorrow we attack,' he told his commanders. 'If we are not victorious, let no one come back alive.'

Despite heavy rains, on the night of 16 March, Patton's 1st Infantry Division took Gafsa. Arnim reacted as Alexander had predicted and sent the 10th Panzers to defend the pass at El Guettar, and Maknassy Pass which led from the Eastern Dorsal to the sea. The 10th Panzer arrived at the Maknassy Pass

US troops walk the streets of Oran, Algeria. The French garrison based there held out for two days before surrendering to Major General Terry Allen of the US 1st Infantry Division. This was the only significant resistance to the landings in French North Africa.

on 22 March, just as the 1st Armored Division also made it there. General Ward, commanding, realized that they had already exceeded Alexander's orders. He was also fearful of the Luftwaffe, which was flying from bases nearby, so he stopped to regroup. Patton was furious and replaced Ward with Harmon.

The following day, an armoured battle group of the 10th Panzers, supported by artillery, infantry and Stukas, advanced across an open plain along the road that led from Gabes to Gafsa to the east of El Guettar. They were ambushed by tank destroyers, massed artillery and 1st Infantry Division, which lay in wait in the hills flanking the road. By the time they withdrew in disarray, the Germans had lost thirty-two tanks and large numbers of infantrymen.

By the standard of the war, the Battle of El Guettar a was small engagement, but to the Americans it was a decisive battle. They had shown the Germans – and the British, too – that they could fight. Naturally, Patton then wanted bigger fish to fry.

'Let me meet Rommel in a tank,' he said, 'and I'll shoot it out with the son-of-a-bitch.'

Unfortunately, Rommel was back in Germany by then.

While Patton was making his thrust down the Eastern Dorsal, Montgomery launched his offensive against the Mareth Line on 19 March. He used the same tactics as Rommel, sending Freyberg's New Zealand Corps around the south end of the line. They would go through the Tebega Gap in the Matmata Hills and attack the line from the rear, while XXX Corps attacked the line from the front across Wadi Zigaou. But the winter weather favoured the defenders. The wadi, which was usually dry, was full of water. The tanks that made it across were subjected to a fierce counterattack by the 15th Panzers, which took a fearful toll on them and their supporting troops.

After twenty-four hours, Montgomery called off the frontal assault. He now had to depend on Freyberg, and sent the British 1st Armoured Division, under Lieutenant General Brian Horrocks, to reinforce him. The 4th Indian Division, under Major General Francis Tuker, was also to swing to the south on a shorter route to attack a section of the Mareth Line weakened by the withdrawal of the 164th Light Division, which had been sent to reinforce the 21st Panzer at the Tebega Gap. Freyberg had been halted by this formidable force but, with Horrocks reinforcing him and an all-out attack by the Desert Air Force, he broke through after nine days' fighting. The Axis forces fell back through Gabes, but turned to fight again at Wadi Akarit 16 km (10 miles) further on. After another furious battle which cost the British 1,300 casualties, the remains of the German and Italian forces fell back to Endifaville, just 80 km (50 miles) short of Tunis.

The Battle for Tunis

AN ATTEMPT WAS made to cut off the fleeing forces by a provisional British corps commanded by Lieutenant General John Crocker. The men were ordered to break out of the Eastern Dorsal at Fondouk, cutting the line of retreat at Sousse. The American 34th Division under Major General Charles Ryder was to take the pass at Fondouk in a frontal attack. Ryder planned to encircle the enemy,

but was overruled by Crocker. The assault failed, costing the 34th heavy casualties. Crocker blamed Ryder and ordered the 34th to be withdrawn for retraining.

Bradley feared that this would damage American morale. He had been at West Point with Ryder and knew that he was a good tactician. With Patton, who had now been designated American invasion commander for Sicily, he opposed the withdrawal of 34th Division and Alexander overruled Crocker. Nevertheless, the Americans were becoming fed up with the contempt in which they were still held by the British. Patton struck back, blaming poor close air support for the short-comings of II Corps. Air Marshal Coningham responded by saying that II Corps was not battleworthy. In an attempt to heal the rift, Eisenhower ordered Coningham to apologize personally to Patton.

By this time, the Axis forces were confined to a small enclave at the tip of the Tunisian peninsula; however, it was clear to the Allies that they would not give up without a fight. Alexander drew up Operation Strike, his plan to finish them off. But once again he gave the Americans only a minor role. Marshall wrote to Eisenhower from Washington, complaining. He pointed out that the American press were saying that the 34th Division had already ruined the British chances of trapping the remains of the Afrika Korps. Bradley also put pressure on Eisenhower, who persuaded Alexander to change his plan and let II Corps take Bizerte.

Key to the success of the attack was a German strongpoint called Hill 609. Bradley assigned Ryder's 34th Division to the task. 'Get me that hill and no one will ever again doubt the toughness of your division,' he told Ryder.

The result was one of the most ferocious actions in the entire campaign. For five days, the 34th battled to take the surrounding high points. They finally took Hill 609 with a combined assault using tanks and infantry. They then successfully fought off a series of bloody counterattacks. After that, Harmon restored the 1st Armored Division's tarnished glory with a thrust through the German defences on the road to Mateur. This broke the back of Bizerte's defences and cut off the Axis forces' only escape route. Arnim was determined to fight on, but Hitler turned a deaf ear to his requests for more ammunition and supplies. By then, the remains of the Axis forces were encircled on the plain of Tunis and, on 12 May, Arnim surrendered along with 250,000 crack troops – at a time when tens of thousands more were being wasted on the Eastern Front.

Overall Allied loses between 12 November 1942 and 13 May 1943 were 70,341. The French had lost 16,180; the British 35,940. The Americans had lost 18,221, including 2,715 killed. Tunisia, however, had been the American proving ground. Bradley said, 'In Africa we learned to crawl, to walk, to run.'

The British did not recognize how far the US forces had improved in so short a time, and the bitterness and rivalry between the two Allied armies continued. But between them the Allies were now masters of North Africa.

To their north lay what Churchill called the 'soft underbelly of Europe'. From North Africa they could attack either in Greece, the Balkans, Italy or the South of France. They chose to take Sicily, then fight their way up the Italian peninsula.

The Germans were ill prepared for the scale of Russia, and the conditions they would find there.

III

THE
RUSSIAN
FRONT

Operation Barbarossa: the German invasion of the Soviet Union, June 1941. The speed of the German attack meant that millions of Russian soldiers were encircled and taken prisoner – many perished in captivity. But Stalin was able to call upon millions more soldiers to go into battle.

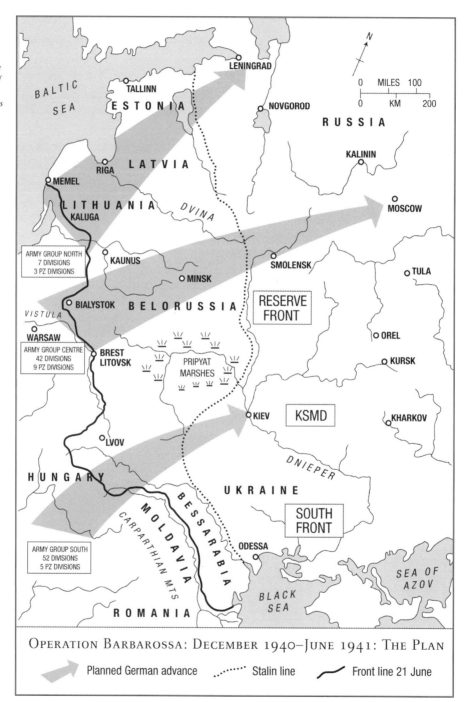

OPERATION BARBAROSSA: DECEMBER 1940–JUNE 1941: THE PLAN

Planned German advance ······· Stalin line ⎯ Front line 21 June

HITLER WAS AN avowed anti-communist. When he came to power in 1933, Joseph Stalin, leader of Communist Russia and its satellites, collectively known as the Union of Soviet Socialist Republics, was concerned about Hitler's rush to rearm Germany, fearing a German military expansion in the east. After the Munich Agreement of 1938 ceded Czech territory to Germany in an attempt to buy peace, Britain and France sought to establish an alliance with the Soviet Union to encircle the German Reich. But Stalin believed that such an alliance would have guaranteed a Nazi attack on the Soviet Union and sought to make a pact with Germany instead.

On 3 May 1939, Stalin fired the Soviet Commissar of Foreign Affairs Maksim Litvinov, an advocate of an alliance with the western powers and a Jew, and replaced him with Vyacheslav Molotov, who began negotiations with the Nazi foreign minister Joachim von Ribbentrop. On 23 August 1939, in Stalin's presence, Molotov and Ribbentrop signed what is known variously as the Nazi-Soviet Non-Aggression Pact, the German-Soviet Treaty of Non-Aggression, the Hitler-Stalin Pact or the Molotov-Ribbentrop Pact. The pact came as a surprise not only to Britain and France, but also to the Soviet people, who had been subjected to years of anti-Nazi propaganda. Now Nazi Germany was a trusted friend.

The Molotov-Ribbentrop Pact contained a number of secret protocols which divided Eastern Europe into German and Soviet spheres of influence. Poland would be divided between the two, while Finland, Estonia, Latvia, Lithuania and Bessarabia (now divided between Ukraine and Moldova) would be ceded to the Soviet Union. On 1 September 1939, Germany invaded Poland, starting World War II. Soviet troops invaded from the east on 17 September, meeting the advancing Germans near Brest-Litovsk two days later. The German Blitzkrieg had progressed so quickly that the Germans had already moved into areas that were to be in the Soviet sphere. The dividing line between the German and Soviet zones was altered a little in Germany's favour, and the partition came into effect on 29 September. According to Molotov, Nazi–Soviet co-operation was now 'cemented in blood'.

While Hitler had honoured the secret protocols, for now, he had no intention of honouring the Non-Aggression Pact itself. In his political treatise *Mein Kampf*, written in prison in the 1920s, Hitler said that the destruction of Communism was one of his primary goals. He also wanted Russian territory as far as the river Volga as Lebensraum (living space) for the German people. The Slavs who lived there, regarded as subhuman under the Nazi ideology, would provide slave labour for Hitler's 'Thousand Year Reich'. After the failure of Operation Sealion and defeat in the Battle of Britain, Hitler believed that a swift invasion of Russia would be such an awesome demonstration of German military might that it would keep the United States out of the war and force Britain to sue for peace.

Operation Barbarossa

IN FEBRUARY 1941, British intelligence learned that Germany planned to invade the Soviet Union that spring. The United States picked up similar information. Both informed Moscow. Stalin refused to believe it, however, and he assured the Soviet people that Germany intended to live up to the Non-Aggression Pact.

Then, seemingly out of the blue, the German ambassador in Moscow went to see Molotov and, at 0530 on 22 June 1941, he delivered a declaration of war. The reason – or excuse – was 'gross and repeated violations' of the Molotov–Ribbentrop Pact. A huge German army was already pouring across a 3,000-km (1,900-mile) front from the Baltic to the Black Sea. Even though the Soviets had been tipped off, the Germans achieved total surprise. Stalin had believed it when he had been told that the Axis forces massing on his borders were there for military manoeuvres.

In Operation Barbarossa, named for the 12th-century German founder of the First Reich, Hitler threw some 180 divisions into Russia – more than 3,000,000 German troops, supported by thirty Romanian and Finnish divisions. There were nineteen Panzer divisions with 3,000 tanks; 2,500 aircraft were involved along with 7,000 artillery pieces. The German forces were divided into three army groups. The first, Army Group North, was commanded by Field Marshal Wilhelm von Leeb; the second, Army Group Centre, by Field Marshal Fedor von Bock; while the third, Army Group South, was commanded by Field Marshal Gerd von Rundstedt. The plan was to destroy all Soviet resistance in lightning advances on Leningrad (St Petersburg), Moscow and Kiev.

'We have only to kick in the door,' said Hitler to Rundstedt, 'and the whole rotten structure will come crashing down.'

It was said that Stalin had a 'nervous collapse' when he was told of the invasion. He did not speak for eleven days. The Soviet Union, however, was hardly defenceless in the face of this attack. Stalin had twice or maybe even three times the number of tanks and aircraft the Germans had and, while many of the aircraft were obsolete, the Russians' heavy tanks, the KV series, were superior to any the Germans threw against them, and the Russian T-34 medium tank was arguably the best of the entire war.

In one of his more lucid moments, Hitler said, 'At the beginning of a campaign one pushes a door into a dark, unseen room. One never knows what is hiding inside.'

In the Barbarossa campaign, what was hiding inside was the vast manpower upon which Stalin could call. German intelligence estimated correctly that Stalin had about 150 divisions in the western Soviet Union, and reckoned that he might be able to muster fifty more. In fact, by the middle of August, Stalin had brought up 200 fresh divisions, dwarfing the German onslaught. They were badly led, however, as many of their best generals had been killed during the 1930s when Stalin had purged the Soviet Red Army of supposed anti-Communist elements.

The Germans were also better trained and, after the campaign in the west, more experienced. They also had the element of surprise on their side and, as they made their advance into Russia, they attacked in places where they would have decisive superiority. The Russians were poorly deployed to meet the attack, and their defensive positions were quickly overrun. In the Baltic states and areas of the Ukraine and Belorussia which had been under Soviet

Communist rule since 1917, the Germans were greeted as liberators. Even the Jews of Kiev welcomed the Germans, as they had been well treated by the Germans who had invaded the Ukraine in World War I. But within days 100,000 Ukrainian Jews had been massacred at Babi Yar, a large ravine to the north of the city. SS death squads also sought out Soviet commissars for execution, and Slavs were summarily killed.

Rapid Progress

ARMY GROUP NORTH began its advance from East Prussia. It was to sweep through the Baltic states, then advance towards Leningrad. Hitler believed that, with the capture of Leningrad, Army Group Centre would be able to move on Moscow. Although Army Group North was the weakest of the three army groups and faced the most powerful opposition, it made the most rapid progress. Despite the swampy, forested terrain and unpaved roads, by 26 June, Army Group North had already taken Lithuania and was well into Latvia.

One of the major obstacles the Germans faced on their way to Leningrad was the river Dvina. But, on 26 June, the 8th Panzer Division and the 56th Panzer Corps seized the road and rail bridges over the Dvina at Dvinsk (now Daugavpils) and went on to seize the city before the Red Army was able to reduce it to rubble. After five hours of street fighting, the Germans had crushed all resistance. Three days later, Army Group North had captured Riga, the capital of Latvia, then halted to regroup.

On 3 July, Stalin had rallied sufficiently to make a radio address to the Russian people. He called on their nationalism and reminded

them of the fate of Napoleon and Kaiser Wilhelm, who had invaded their country in World War I. Both had been toppled from power by their military adventures. He told Soviet citizens in the territories already occupied by the Germans to form partisan groups. He also announced a 'scorched earth' policy, like the one that had been used against Napoleon's invasion of Russia in 1812. The Germans, Stalin said, must be not be allowed to take 'a single engine, or a single railway truck, and not a pound of bread nor a pint of oil'. The Soviet economy was turned over to war production. Entire factories were moved eastwards, out of the reach of the Germans,

In 1941, when the Germans reached Kiev, they took the city's Jews out to Babi Yar, a large ravine on the northern edge of the city. There, at least 100,000 were murdered by the Einsatzgruppen of the SS, who were ordered to shoot Jews, Gypsies and Soviet commissars. Babi Yar was to become a symbol of the first phase of the Holocaust.

German troops pause for a meal break in the Russian town of Vitebsk on their way to Moscow, August 1941. On arrival in the town, they found that it had been torched by the retreating Soviets.

and began turning out tanks and aircraft at an astonishing rate.

Far from scaring the British into surrender, Operation Barbarossa gave them new heart. At last, they had a powerful ally – one corner of the grand alliance Churchill intended to build to defeat Hitler. Both Britain and the United States began supplying the Soviet Union, via the Arctic Ocean to the northern Russian port of Arkhangelsk (Archangel) and through Persia (Iran), which Britain and the Soviet Union jointly occupied.

On 2 July, Army Group North had resumed its offensive. The Red Army had hopes of stopping the German advance at Pskov on the border of Estonia, the most northerly of the Baltic states, but by 8 July the German armour had broken through. Sixteenth Army took Opochka and moved on towards Lake Ilmen, south of Leningrad, while in the west Eighteenth Army took Tallinn, the capital of Estonia, on the Gulf of Finland.

Army Group North then advanced towards the river Luga, where the Red Army hoped, once again, to stop it. But the Germans simply split their corps either side of the Soviet concentration and crossed the river in full strength on 15 July. Army Group North was

now poised to make a thrust towards Leningrad. The Red Army had had no time to fortify the approaches to the city. The German High Command, however, told Army Group North to stop to regroup and shore up its supply lines.

When Army Group North got under way again the following month, Eighteenth Army took Narva on the Gulf of Finland and Sixteenth Army seized Novgorod on the north side of Lake Ilmen on 16 August; 4th Panzer Group reached Krasnogvardeisk (Gatchina), 34 km (21 miles) from Leningrad, on 20 July.

Russia had seized parts of Finland under secret protocols of the Molotov-Ribbentrop Pact. But after Barbarossa began, the Finns seized the opportunity to side with Germany. On 10 July, they began their offensive to take back the lands they had lost. By 16 August, they had advanced approximately 100 km (60 miles) along the western shore of Lake Ladoga. This cut Leningrad off from the north, but the Finns stopped at the Russo-Finnish border and could not be persuaded to advance any further.

As the Germans closed on Leningrad from the south, the Red Army suddenly mounted a counterattack. This gave the population of the city enough time to dig anti-tank trenches and build a defensive perimeter. By 9 September, the Germans had pushed the Red Army back until they were within artillery range of Leningrad. They also began bombing the city. German tanks broke through the last fortified line, but they could make little headway in the narrow streets, where tanks are particularly vulnerable. It was then decided that the Panzers would be more use in the south, so they were withdrawn. The German infantry and artillery remained, however, to besiege the city.

One million of the city's inhabitants had already been evacuated. The remaining two million were now completely cut off, with the Finns to the city's north and the Germans to the south. A siege began that lasted 900 days. During that time, Leningrad's only lifeline was across Lake Ladoga, by barge in the summer and by truck and sled across the ice in the winter. When the siege was finally lifted on 19 January 1944, some 200,000 civilians had been killed by the German bombardment and at least 630,000 had perished as a result of starvation and disease.

In the first weeks of Operation Barbarossa, Army Group South quickly overtook most of the Ukraine, giving Hitler the benefit of its summer harvest. When Stalin ordered a counterattack in the south-west, Hitler reacted by sending both Romanian and more German forces into the southern front, and a massive struggle ensued between the German and Russian armoured divisions. By the end of the first week, the Soviets' twenty-four divisions were looking decidedly threadbare. Army Group South hit at any weak spots it found in the Soviet lines and, by 11 July, the German army was 16 km (10 miles) from Kiev. Stalin did not want to lose his hold on the river Dnieper. On 31 August, however, the German army crossed the river and pounded the Russian flanks. Although the Russians were taking heavy losses, Stalin refused his generals' request to pull out of Kiev, and replaced his commander. Then as the losses mounted, Stalin made a snap decision to pull out. It was too late. On 20 September, the Soviet Fifth Army and its Russian armoured column were encircled and captured. Some 520,000 prisoners were taken.

The German army marches on towards Leningrad. Unable to overcome its defences, the German forces starved the city's population in a siege that lasted nearly 900 days.

Army Group Centre, under Field Marshal Fedor von Bock, was the strongest of the three army groups. It consisted of Fourth and Ninth armies, as well as 2nd and 3rd Panzer groups, later redesignated as Panzer armies, and it was supported by 2nd Air Fleet under Field Marshal Albert Kesselring. Its Panzer and motorized formations burst out from the area north of Warsaw on 22 June, tore huge holes in the Soviet defences and smashed the Soviet forces in Belorussia. Its primary task was to guard Army Group North's right flank as it swept through the Baltic states towards the city of Leningrad. Hitler had decreed that only after Leningrad had been captured should Army Group Centre advance on Moscow.

Its Panzer spearheads reached Minsk, the capital of Belorussia, on 29 June, encircling four Soviet armies and taking 287,000 prisoners. On 16 July, the German pincers reached Smolensk, 420 km (260 miles) from Moscow, surrounding another large Russian force and taking a further 300,000 prisoners. By July's end, the Germans controlled an area of Soviet territory more than twice the size of France.

By early August, Army Group Centre had covered two-thirds of the distance to Moscow. Feeling that the Red Army could not successfully resist a German advance upon the Soviet capital, Bock urged the High Command to let him push on to Moscow. But Hitler insisted that taking both Kiev and Leningrad was the priority. His aim was to prevent the bulk of the Red Army escaping eastwards into the depths of Russia, and he diverted Army Group Centre's forces northwards and southwards to assist. The result was the encirclement of the huge Russian force at Kiev, yielding another 665,000 prisoners.

With Kiev now taken and Army Group North menacing Leningrad, Hitler gave Bock permission to resume his march on Moscow in Operation Typhoon. But Army Group Centre was not able to regroup and renew the offensive until 2 October, which gave the Russians

the chance to prepare defensive positions and bring up reinforcements. Once it had regrouped, Army Group Centre quickly made deep thrusts into the Russian lines. Using its superior mobility, it encircled large pockets of Red Army troops at Vyazma and Bryansk. The Vyazma pocket yielded 663,000 prisoners; Bryansk another 100,000. By then, the Russians had only 824 tanks left on the Western Front, no air support and all their massed armies had been lost. All that was left were a few divisions of defeated men and some improvised workers'

91

German troops interrogate a Russian peasant. The soldiers in the background wear the metal half-moon badges of the Feldgendarmerie, or Military Police, nicknamed 'headhunters' by ordinary German troops.

battalions. The road to Moscow was now open. Foreign diplomats were evacuated from the city, and the embalmed body of Lenin, founder of the Soviet Union, had been removed from his tomb in Red Square for safekeeping.

Stalin was about to flee the city, then changed his mind. He imposed martial law and recalled Marshal Georgii Zhukov, his ablest general, from Leningrad to command

the defence of Moscow. The Germans were also experiencing severe problems and hardships. The troops were exhausted. The Soviets' scorched-earth policy had destroyed any housing that could be used as a billet, and their equipment was wearing out. Every advance stretched the German supply lines and, at night, the Russians would attack the German guards and destroy their supplies.

The diversion of some of Army Group Centre's strength to Kiev and the time it had taken to regroup had delayed its advance. It was now October, and the weather was changing. Whenever it rained, the roads turned into a sea of mud, and the advance slowed to 10 km (6 miles) a day. The German Panzers to the north of Moscow, under the command of General Hermann Hoth, were not able to make a rapid attack in formation through the dense forest there. General Guderian's force, however, could attack from the south across the open country there. But Zhukov had stationed his last independent tank force, the 4th Armoured Brigade, to the south. The men were well trained and equipped with T-34

German Panzer IIIs, fitted with armoured skirting to protect their vulnerable tracks, pass through a deserted village in the Soviet Union during the latter stages of the invasion.

tanks, which had armour that could not be penetrated by the German artillery. Fourth Armoured stopped the German advance almost within sight of Moscow.

Hoth continued to push forward, though. The Russians responded with Katyusha rockets, whose multiple launchers were nicknamed 'Stalin organs' by the Germans, and the Soviet Air Force was airborne again. But Hoth pushed on and, by 12 November, he was in a position to attack the city. By then, though, Zhukov had 1,700 tanks and 1,500 aircraft to defend Moscow, along with fresh troops brought in from Siberia.

The Germans launched their final thrust on Moscow on 15 November. They moved rapidly at first, as the roads were now frozen, and the 7th Panzer Division reached the Moscow-Volga canal, just 32 km (20 miles) from Moscow. On 4 December 1941, the Soviets began a counterattack. Army Group Centre was forced back in spite of Hitler's insistence that it hold its positions regardless of the cost. But the situation was hopeless. The weather had closed in. Blizzards and snowdrifts hampered the movement of supplies, and the scorched-earth policy meant that the Germans could not support themselves from the land. The German Army was not prepared for the brutal Russian winter. Hitler had been so confident of a quick victory that he had not provided his men with winter clothing. Soon almost everyone was suffering from frostbite. Nor was German equipment built to withstand the freezing temperatures. Oil froze in the tanks' engines; packing grease in the artillery froze; automatic firing mechanisms seized up.

Hitler blamed his generals. He promptly fired them and took over as Commander in Chief himself. There was nothing, however, he could do about the weather. That winter was the coldest for 140 years. It was so cold, in fact, that boiling soup ladled out from pots in German field kitchens froze within minutes. Axe-shafts splintered when meat was being hacked up, and butter had to be cut with a saw. By the end of the year, 100,000 cases of frostbite had been reported, and more than 14,000 were so serious that a limb had to be amputated. Then, on 7 January 1942, Stalin ordered another offensive. Using the last of his reserves, Zhukov pushed the Germans

back and, by the end of January, the front had stabilized some 65 km (40 miles) west of Moscow. Operation Typhoon had been thwarted, and the city had been saved.

Army Group Centre did, however, continue to hold a position at Rzhev, 160 km (100 miles) west of Moscow, until March 1943, when Hitler finally allowed it to withdraw. Hitler did not try to take Moscow again. Instead, he sought to defeat Russia in the south, concentrating his strength on the battle for Stalingrad, a battle which would prove to be a turning point in Hitler's war.

Stalingrad

DURING THE WINTER of 1941, despite the privations of his men on the Eastern Front, Hitler was not downhearted. Most of the Soviet Union's European territory was now in his hands and, by February 1942, the Soviets' winter counterattack had petered out. Hitler now began to make plans to crush the Red Army once and for all. The renewed campaign would attack Stalingrad (now Volgograd), a city that stretched some 50 km (30 miles) along the Volga, 1,000 km (600 miles) south-east of

During the Battle of Stalingrad, the city was reduced to rubble. When the Germans finally surrendered, a Soviet colonel pointed to the ruins and shouted: 'That's how Berlin is going to look!'

The Battle of Stalingrad, 1942. Both the Red October factory and the tractor factory were held by the Soviets throughout the entire battle.

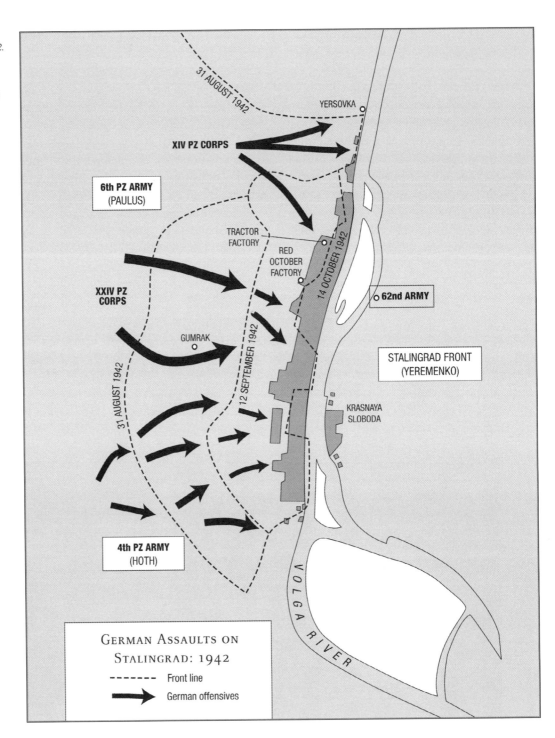

31 AUGUST 1942

YERSOVKA

XIV PZ CORPS

6th PZ ARMY
(PAULUS)

TRACTOR FACTORY

RED OCTOBER FACTORY

14 OCTOBER 1942

XXIV PZ CORPS

62nd ARMY

GUMRAK

STALINGRAD FRONT
(YEREMENKO)

12 SEPTEMBER 1942

31 AUGUST 1942

KRASNAYA SLOBODA

4th PZ ARMY
(HOTH)

VOLGA RIVER

GERMAN ASSAULTS ON
STALINGRAD: 1942

- - - - - - Front line

➤ German offensives

Moscow. It was a huge new industrial city and was paraded as one of the great achievements of the Soviet system. It also bore the name of the Soviet Union's leader, who had organized its defences against the White Russians in the civil war that followed the founding of the Soviet state. Stalin realized that the city must be held at all costs. If it fell, so would he.

For Hitler, too, Stalingrad was important. It was a symbol of Communism and had to be crushed. It was also an important centre for mass production of armaments. Once it had been taken, his victorious army would head up the Volga to encircle Moscow, while another second army would move south-east to take the oilfields of the Caucasus and threaten Turkey and Persia.

Army Group Centre was then split into two groups, under the overall control of Field Marshal Bock. Army Group B, under General Freiherr von Weichs, was much the stronger of the two. It comprised Fourth Panzer Army under Hoth, Second Army, and the powerful Sixth Army, under General Friedrich Paulus, supported by other crack infantry and Panzer divisions. By comparison, Army Group A was practically a reserve force. It had the crack First Panzer Army under Field Marshal Ewald von Kleist, which was going to take the oilfields of the Caucasus, and Seventeenth Infantry Army. But the numbers were made up with Italian, Romanian and Hungarian troops. Altogether there were now twenty-five Panzer divisions, compared with nineteen only the year before. Still, the war was very different now. The Wehrmacht no longer seemed to be invincible, and Hitler was no longer considered infallible. German soldiers now feared being posted to the Eastern Front.

The brutal treatment of the civilians there – including mass shooting, burnings, summary execution of prisoners and the deliberate starvation of men, women and children – was sure to invite retribution.

In the spring of 1942, Stalin made a counter-attack in the Kerch Peninsula in the Crimea. This was crushed, and the Germans took 100,000 prisoners. Two fresh Siberian divisions sent to relieve Leningrad were encircled. Then 600 Russian tanks, two-thirds of the Soviets' force, punched through the Romanian Sixth Army to take Kharkov. But then the trap closed. Kleist crushed the southern flank of the Soviet advance on 18 May, while Paulus swept down from the north the following day. The Soviets lost nearly a quarter of a million men, along with all their tanks. Now the stage was set for Hitler's summer offensive.

On 28 June, on a wide front stretching from Kursk to Rostov, the Panzers went roaring across the open steppes. The dust pall they kicked up could be seen for 65 km (40 miles), and it was soon joined by smoke from burning villages. There were no significant forces to oppose them, as the reserves were still being held back for the defence of Moscow. The Red Army put up a fight at the industrial town of Voronezh. When Bock attempted to crush the Soviet forces, rather than bypass them and continue the offensive, Hitler sacked him. Army Group A, led by Kleist's Panzers, then crossed the river Don and headed southwards towards the oilfields, while Army Group B headed for Stalingrad.

While Army Group A progressed quickly and was almost in sight of the oil derricks of the Caucasian field by 9 August, Fourth and Sixth armies, with 330,000 of Germany's finest

soldiers, advanced more slowly over the 320 km (200 miles) to Stalingrad and became strung out. As they massed to mount an assault, Stalin made the decision to commit the Moscow reserve to the defence of Stalingrad and the desperate race to get them there began.

Between 25 and 29 August, Paulus's Sixth Army made a ferocious attempt to storm the city before reinforcements could arrive. Meeting stiff opposition, Paulus asked Hoth's Fourth Panzer Army for help. It attacked from the south, forcing the Soviet Sixty-Fourth Army, which was defending the southern part of the city, to extend its flank to meet the threat. The Soviet front was now 130 km (80 miles) long, but only 80 km (50 miles) wide. Paulus threw his entire Sixth Army, now supported by the Fourth Army Corps, against it. On 22 August, German troops penetrated the northern suburbs and on the next day reached the Volga, within mortar range of a vital railway bridge. The Soviet Sixty-Second Army in the northern sector was now outflanked. The Luftwaffe was then called in to deliver an all-out night bombardment. The idea was to demoralize the defenders and cause panic among the citizens.

Much of the civilian population fled to the other side of the Volga, and the authorities began evacuating the largest factories. When Stalin heard of this, he stopped the evacuations. As a result, the factories themselves became centres of resistance. Workers in the tractor factory continued producing new tanks and armoured cars until the Germans were on their doorstep. They would then sling ammunition belts over their overalls, pick up grenades, rifles and anti-tank weapons, and take up their positions in the firing-points or

A German soldier makes his way around a water-logged shell crater, Stalingrad, 1942. Six months of fighting had reduced the city to an almost alien landscape.

In winter, the map of Russia changes radically. To preserve the surface of regular roads used in spring, summer and autumn, new snow roads across fields are constructed from compacted snow and ice.

bunkers with their comrades from the Red Army, while the remaining women, children and the elderly hid in cellars, sewers and caves in the cliffs above the Volga.

Despite fierce fighting following the terror-bombing, the German advance in the north of the city was halted. In the south, Hoth's Panzers pushed the Sixty-Fourth Army back, but failed to penetrate the line. And once they entered the heart of the ruined city, their advance, too, ground to a halt.

For Hitler, Stalingrad was going to be where the war was won or lost. He summoned his commanders to his new forward headquarters at Vinnitsa more than 800 km (500 miles) away

in the Ukraine. The drive up the Volga was vital to the success of his Russian campaign, he told them. New Hungarian and Romanian armies were brought in to protect the left flank along the Don, and three new infantry divisions were sent to reinforce Sixth Army. Stalin, too, believed that the war would be won or lost at Stalingrad. He moved in a new team of commanders headed by Zhukov.

The Germans were the masters of the Blitzkrieg. They were not used to slow, grinding, man-to-man fighting through the rubble of a ruined city. The Russians, by contrast, quickly learned to adapt their tactics to the new situation, and every move the Germans made cost them dearly. After weeks of ceaseless fighting against crack German troops, the Red Army still held a 14-km (9-mile) strip along the banks of the Volga. A series of gentle curves in the Volga and a number of small islands prevented German ground troops bombarding all the river crossings with artillery and mortar fire. Nor did the Luftwaffe bomb either them or the Soviet artillery on the other bank. Instead, they continued to throw everything they had against the Soviet enclave on the west bank.

On 12 September, Hitler authorized a new offensive. The following day, Paulus sent in three Panzer divisions backed by eight divisions of infantry. Against them, the Soviets had forty tanks, all but nineteen immobile. The Sixty-Second Army had been reduced to just three infantry divisions, the remnants of four others and two battle-damaged tank brigades. And there were no reserves, as every man had already been thrown into the battle. The Soviet headquarters, however, were on the spot. General Vasili Chuikov had made the dangerous crossing of the Volga and had set up his command post in a dugout, by the river near Puskin Street bridge. With their backs to the river, his men were inspired by these words from Chuikov: 'There is no land across the Volga'. For those who did not get the message, there were firing squads to deal with the deserters. Hundreds were shot.

Vital Link

THE GERMANS FLUNG themselves at the middle of the Russian line and, on the afternoon of 14 September, they broke through and seized Mamaye Hill. From the high ground there, they could concentrate artillery fire on the vital ferry link from Krasnaya Sloboda. The 76th Infantry Division overwhelmed the defenders at a ruined hospital in the middle of the Soviet line. Victory now seemed certain, and many Germans got drunk on looted vodka. The only resistance now seemed to be snipers.

Chuikov then threw his nineteen tanks in, and the battle resumed. That night, the fighting came within 180 m (200 yards) of Chuikov's headquarters, and staff officers joined in. But the Germans still pushed forward, and the vital central landing stage came under machine-gun fire from close range. On the night of 14 September, Russian Guardsmen had to scramble ashore under fire. There was no possibility of them counterattacking as a coherent division, and they were soon dispersed among the ruins in isolated pockets with no intercommunication.

The street fighting had also broken up the German formations. They now fought through the devastated streets in small battle groups comprising three or four Panzers and a company of German infantrymen, which had to laboriously clear each pocket individually. Russian riflemen and machine-gunners hid in ruined buildings, craters and behind mountains of rubble. They waited until the Panzers had gone by, then attacked the infantry. The Panzers then found themselves attacked by roving T-34s, or they ran into anti-tank guns or dug-in tanks. In the narrow streets, the Panzers were very vulnerable both to grenades dropped from directly above and to anti-tank guns, which the Russians had a plentiful supply of, while their armour-piercing shells made a comparatively small hole in a building, most of which had been destroyed, anyway.

The battle hinged on house-to-house combat fought with bullet, grenade, bayonet and flame-thrower.

The Germans found that it took a whole day and numerous casualties to take 180 m (200 yards). Even then, the Russians reappeared at night, knocking holes in attic walls so that they could reoccupy buildings over the heads of the Germans. Despite that, victory seemed near. A German salient ran down the Tsarita tributary to the Volga itself. They had almost complete control of much of the city. And the landing stages and most of the river crossings were within range of their guns. The Russians' only lifeline lay to the north, where the ferries were out of range.

But it did not seem to matter how much of the city the Germans occupied. The Russians would not give up. The remains of the 92nd Infantry Brigade formed isolated pockets of resistance across the south of the city. The grain elevators there, although bombed and blasted, still stood defiant. At all levels from top to bottom, they were occupied by pockets of Guardsmen and Russian Marines who repelled wave after wave of attackers. Their stout resistance brought the German assault inexorably to a halt.

For the Germans, two months of fighting for a narrow strip of the ruined city of Stalingrad was a propaganda disaster. The German people were told that the Russians were throwing wave after wave of men into the battle and were exhausting their reserves. In fact, the opposite was true. During September and October, the Germans threw no fewer than nineteen newly formed armoured brigades and twenty-seven infantry divisions into the battle. In that same period, only five Soviet divisions crossed the Volga. Zhukov sent only the bare minimum needed to hold off the Germans, so that he could build up strength for a counterattack.

Around this time a crucial change was made in the Red Army. As the Red Army was formed in the wake of the 1917 Revolution, its officers, many of whom came from the former Imperial Army, had been stripped of their badges of rank and their every move was watched over by political commissars attached to each unit. Now, old-fashioned gold-braided epaulettes were distributed. Old regimental traditions were revived. Political interference ceased, and soldiers were told that they were fighting for Mother Russia, not for the Communist party.

While Russian spirits received a boost, German morale sagged. Russian artillery fire grew steadily heavier. Meanwhile, the nights began to draw in. The skies became grey and the weather chilly, and the Germans began to fear that they would be spending another winter in Russia. Quickly Paulus planned a fourth all-out offensive. This time he was determined to score a great victory, as he had heard that Hitler was considering promoting him to Chief of the High Command, and Hitler had also publicly promised that Stalingrad would fall 'very shortly'.

Forty thousand Russians now held a strip of the city barely 16 km (10 miles) long. At its widest, it reached 2 km (1¼ miles) inland from the west bank of the Volga; at its narrowest, it was about 450 m (500 yards). The Russians defending it, however, were hardened troops who knew every cellar, sewer, crater and ruin of this wasteland. They watched German advances through periscopes and cut them

down with machine-gun fire. Snipers stalked the cratered streets, or lay camouflaged and silent for hours on end awaiting their prey. Against them were pitched veteran German troops, who were demoralized by the losses they had taken, or raw recruits, who could be in no way prepared for the horrors they were about to face.

On 4 October, the Germans were about to launch their offensive when the Russians counterattacked in the area around the tractor factory. This threw the Germans off balance. Although little ground was lost, it cost them many casualties. The Luftwaffe sent in 800 dive-bombers, and the German artillery pounded the city mercilessly. Occasionally, a pet dog, escaping from a bombed building, would race through the inferno, leap into the river and swim to freedom on the other side. After a five-hour bombardment, which

One of the most effective Soviet weapons was the Katyusha truck-mounted multiple rocket launcher. Known as the 'Stalin Organ', it could deliver a withering barrage.

Opposite: A German field gun in action during the fighting for Stalingrad, winter 1942.

shattered glass deep below ground and killed sixty-one men in Chuikov's headquarters, the German attack eventually went ahead.

Killing Grounds

ON 14 OCTOBER, two new armoured divisions and five infantry divisions pushed forward on a front just 5 km (3 miles) wide. They found themselves lured into special killing grounds the Russians had prepared, where houses and sometimes whole blocks or squares had been heavily mined. Combat became so close that the Germans would occupy one half of a shattered building, while the Russians occupied the other. When the Russians prepared a building as a stronghold, they would destroy the stairs so that the Germans would have to fight for each floor independently. And when it came down to hand-to-hand fighting, it was usually the Russians who came off best. If they lost a building, the survivors would be sent back with the first counterattack to retake it. That day, 14 October, according to Chuikov, was 'the bloodiest and most ferocious day of the whole battle'.

By sheer weight of numbers, the Germans pushed forward towards the tractor factory. The Soviets reinforced it with 2,300 men. After an entire day, the Germans had taken just one block. But although the Germans took enormous casualties, the tractor factory eventually ended up in German hands and the Soviet forces were pushed back so close to the Volga that boats bringing supplies across the river came under heavy machine-gun fire.

Next door to the tractor factory, the ruined Red October factory looked as if it might fall, too. But at the last moment a Siberian division

was put in. Its men were told to fight to the death. They dug in among shattered concrete, twisted girders, heaps of coal and wrecked railway wagons. Behind them were the icy waters of the Volga – there was nowhere to retreat to.

Unable to shift the Siberians, the Germans bombarded them with mortars, artillery and dive-bombers. But the Siberians had dug a series of interconnecting trenches, dugouts and strongpoints in the frozen ground around the factory. When the barrage was lifted and the German armour and infantry went in, they found themselves under blistering attack. After forty-eight hours of continuous fighting, hardly a man was left of the leading Siberian regiment. Nonetheless, the German offensive had been halted.

For the next two weeks, the onslaught on the Red October factory continued. The Germans made 117 separate attacks – including twenty-three on a single day. But, backed by artillery from across the river directed by observation posts hidden in the ruins, the Siberian division held out.

'Imagine Stalingrad,' wrote a German veteran, 'eighty days and nights of hand-to-hand fighting. The streets are no longer measured in metres, but in corpses. Stalingrad is no longer a town. By day it is an enormous cloud of burning, blinding smoke. It is a vast furnace lit by the reflection of the flames.'

Paulus's offensive was at a standstill. The defenders of the city were unyielding, and he had no more men to throw against them. For the moment there was a stalemate, but winter was on its way. The Sixth Army then received reinforcements in the form of a number of battalions of Pioneers, frontline engineering and sapper troops. These would be used in the

vanguard of a new offensive along a front just 365 m (400 yards) wide. Instead of fighting from house to house, they would move through the sewers, cellars and tunnels under the city.

The offensive began on 11 November with a bombardment that turned what remained of the city into rubble. The first rush of fresh troops took the Germans through the last 275 m (300 yards) under the city, to the bank of the Volga. But when they reached it, the Germans were cut off by the Russians, who emerged from their hiding places behind them. The German advance troops were trapped. But surrender was not an option. They were far past the point where prisoners were taken. The attack collapsed into sporadic pockets of desperate hand-to-hand combat in hidden caverns under the rubble. On both sides men fought with unmitigated savagery. The troops were filthy, smelly, unshaven and red-eyed. They were high on vodka and benzedrene. No sane, sober man could fight in such conditions. After four days, only Russians were left. Then a terrible silence fell over Stalingrad – the silence of death.

But at first light on 19 November, the air was full of sound again. Two hundred Russians guns opened fire to the north of the city. The next day, hundreds more opened up to the south. While the Germans had been exhausting their forces fighting inside the city, Zhukov had been busy building up a new army. He had massed 900 brand-new T-34 tanks, 115 regiments of the dreaded Katyusha multi-rocket launchers, 230 artillery regiments and 500,000 infantrymen.

Two spearheads attacked the northern and southern tips of the German forces. The German flanks were turned 80 km (50 miles)

north and 80 km south of Stalingrad, and the Red Army rushed forward to encircle the German forces inside the city. This took the Germans completely by surprise. Paulus had imagined that the Russian reserves were drained, and the German High Command was bracing itself for a new Russian winter offensive against Army Group Centre at Rzhev. The flanks of Paulus's Army were held by Romanian troops who were ill equipped and had little stomach for fighting. As far as they were concerned, this was Germany's war.

The Germans never knew what had hit them. They found it impossible to judge the scale or direction of the offensive. Paulus sent Panzers to the north, but they could not stem the tide there. About 30 km (20 miles) to the rear of the main German forces besieging Stalingrad was the town of Kalach and its bridge across the Don, a vital link in Paulus's supply line. Demolition charges had already been placed so that the bridge could be blown if the Russians threatened to take it. But, on 23 November, the Russians took the Germans by surprise by turning up in a captured Panzer. They machine-gunned the guards and removed the demolition charges.

Meanwhile, the Russians' southern pincer had smashed through the German lines and turned northwards, and the two spearheads met at Kalach that evening. They had encircled 250,000 Germans and made the most decisive breakthrough on the Eastern Front. They had defeated an Italian army, a Hungarian army and a Romanian army, and had taken 65,000 prisoners. Three days later, the Russians had thirty-four divisions across the Don and were breaking out to the north. Some armoured columns stayed behind to trouble Paulus's rear, while Russian infantry moved around the Germans and dug in. More than a thousand anti-tank guns were deployed to prevent a German break-out, and the Germans menacing Stalingrad were bombarded by heavy artillery from the other side of the Volga.

Not Convinced

HITLER TOLD PAULUS to hold his ground until 'Fortress Stalingrad' was relieved. Göring told Hitler that his Luftwaffe could fly in 500 tonnes of stores a day. Paulus was not wholly convinced and, knowing that the winter was imminent, he prepared a force of 130 tanks and 57,000 men for a break-out. Hitler countermanded this. He had not given up on Stalingrad and ordered General Erich von Manstein, author of the attack through the Ardennes, to collect up the remaining Axis forces in the region and relieve Paulus.

Reinforcements were rushed to Manstein from Army Group Centre at Rzhev and Army Group A in the Caucasus. The attack began on 11 December and was led by Hoth and his Fourth Panzer Army. Following them was a convoy of trucks carrying 3,000 tonnes of supplies. They would make their attack from the south-west and punch their way into the city where Paulus was still holding his position. The ground was frozen, which made the going better for the Panzers, and the heavy snow made them difficult to spot. The Russians in Stalingrad were also having a hard time and ice floes coming down the Volga menaced their ferries.

But the Russians also knew how to turn the snow to their advantage. The winter sky denied the German's air reconnaissance. As Hoth made progress towards Stalingrad, he did not notice Russians hidden behind the snow in the gullies that crisscrossed the landscape. At dusk and dawn, T-34s would emerge and attack the infantry's trucks and the supply convoy following the Panzers. The German armour would then have to halt, turn around and deal with them. This slowed the German advance. On 17 December, however, Hoth reached the river Aksay, 56 km (35 miles) from Stalingrad, where Zhukov had sent 130 tanks and two infantry divisions to meet him.

The powerful 48th Panzer Corps was planning an attack to relieve Stalingrad from the north-east. But 450 Russian T-34s suddenly came rumbling across the ice of the river Don, smashing the Italian, Romanian and Hungarian armies in that sector and pushing on towards Voronezh. The 48th was so busy containing this thrust that a counterthrust towards Stalingrad was out of the question.

To the south, Hoth was in trouble, with his north-eastern flank crumbling along its entire 320-km (200-mile) length. Manstein now realized that the only hope for the quarter of a million Germans in Fortress Stalingrad was for Paulus and Hoth to attack at the same place on either side of the Russian line simultaneously. Paulus refused to try to break out, saying that Hitler had ordered him to stay where he was. There was to be no retreat from Stalingrad. Besides, his ill-fed troops were not physically strong enough to make the attack and they had only the fuel to go about 30 km (20 miles), only just enough to reach the Russian lines. Göring was still promising that he would supply them, and Hitler wanted Paulus's army in position for a new offensive in the spring.

On 19 December, Hoth crossed the Aksay and, two days later, Manstein talked to Hitler, telling him that it was vital for the Sixth Army to attempt to break out to meet him. But Hitler backed Paulus. Manstein had no choice but to recall Hoth. He had lost 300 tanks and 16,000 men in the failed attempt to relieve Paulus. With Hoth pulling back, Army Group A also had to withdraw, as it risked being cut off in the Caucasus.

The Sixth Army was now left to its fate. It was fanciful to believe that it could hold its position all winter. The infantry was running short of ammunition. The maximum allocation was thirty bullets a day. The Russians now had the 250,000 beleaguered Germans surrounded by 500,000 men and 2,000 guns. Meanwhile, the retreating German forces were being chased out of southern Russia by a new Soviet offensive.

In an effort to free up more manpower, the Soviets offered Paulus the chance to surrender on 8 January on the best possible terms. There would be food for the hungry, medical care for the wounded, guaranteed repatriation for everyone at the end of the war and the officers would even be allowed to keep their weapons. But Hitler had taken personal charge of Fortress Stalingrad from his bunker in Poland and refused these terms. Instead, he promoted Paulus to the rank of field marshal and told him to fight on.

It had been estimated that the remains of Sixth Army could be sustained on 550 tonnes of supplies a day – fifty less than Göring, at his most optimistic, had promised. The Luftwaffe had 225 Junkers Ju 52s available for the task. The nearest airfields were then an hour-and-a-half's flying time away, and it was assumed that

Lines of German troops march into captivity after the Soviet recapture of Stalingrad, February 1943. Almost 90,000 German soldiers were taken prisoner after the battle; few were to see their homeland again.

each plane could make one flight a day. In fact, there were rarely more than eighty Junkers serviceable on any one day. Two squadrons of converted Heinkel 111 bombers were brought in, but they could carry only about 1.5 tonnes of supplies each. Then, as the Russians advanced, the Sixth Army had to be supplied from airfields even further away. As the weather closed in, supply by air grew erratic. The Soviets massed anti-aircraft guns along the flight paths, and the Sixth Army could then only be resupplied at night. In all,

536 German transport planes were shot down, and the average supply drop fell to 55 tonnes a night. The bread ration was cut to one slice a day, and 1 kg (2¼ lb) of potatoes had to feed fifteen men. The horses of the Romanian cavalry were eaten. Dogs, cats, crows, rats – anything the soldiers could find in the ruins was consumed. The only drinking water came from melted snow.

As the tightening Russian noose forced them to retreat, the Germans found that they were too weak to dig new defences. They slept with their heads on pillows of snow. Frostbite was endemic. Any wound, regardless of its severity, almost inevitably meant death. Even if the wounded man's comrades were strong enough to carry him to the first-aid post, there were few medical supplies left and little the doctors could do. Suicide was so common among the German troops that Paulus had to issue a special order declaring it dishonourable. Even so, when the rumour circulated that the Russians were taking no prisoners, everyone kept one last bullet for themselves.

On 10 January, the Russians began their final attack. The perimeter shrank by the hour. By 24 January, the Germans were forced back behind the line the Russians had held on 13 September. The command structure collapsed. Medical posts and makeshift hospitals were full of wounded men begging their comrades to kill them. The airstrips – their only lines of supply – were taken, and the remnants of the Sixth Army were forced back into the ruined factories, the cellars and the sewers of the city. But still Hitler would not surrender.

Finally, on 30 January, Paulus's command post was overrun and he was captured. Two days later, resistance was at an end. In all, 91,000 frozen and hungry men, including twenty-four generals, were captured. As they were marched away, a Soviet colonel pointed at the rubble that was Stalingrad and shouted angrily at a group of German prisoners, 'That's how Berlin is going to look.' Two entire German armies were wiped out, including their reserves. Some 300,000 trained men had been lost. They were irreplaceable. The battle had been a bloodbath. In the last stages alone, 147,200 Germans and 46,700 Russians had been killed.

Stalingrad was the decisive battle on the Eastern Front. It humiliated what was once thought to be an invincible German army. On 5 February 1943, the Red Army newspaper *Red Star* wrote:

> *What was destroyed at Stalingrad was the flower of the German Wehrmacht. Hitler was particularly proud of the Sixth Army and its great striking power. Under Von Reichmann it was the first to invade Belgium. It entered Paris. It took part in the invasion of Yugoslavia and Greece. Before the war it had taken part in the occupation of Czechoslovakia. In 1942 it broke through from Kharkov to Stalingrad.*

Now it was no more. This was a terrible blow to German morale. With the destruction of the Sixth Army at Stalingrad, the German offensive in Russia was over. The Soviets' staggering repulsion of Germany subtly turned the tide of the war, easing the pressure on the Allied landings of D-Day during the invasion of Normandy in 1944, while the Red Army would eventually push the Wehrmacht all the way back to Berlin and beyond.

In captivity, the tide turned for Paulus, too. Once one of Hitler's favourites, he agitated against the Führer among German prisoners of war. If they did not make peace, he warned, the whole of Germany would be turned into one 'gigantic Stalingrad'. He joined the Soviet-backed 'Free Germany Movement', broadcasting appeals to the Wehrmacht to give up the fight. After the war, he testified at the International Military Tribunal at Nuremberg. After his release in 1953, Paulus settled in East Germany and died in Dresden in 1957.

During the Pacific War, aircraft carriers came into their own. But while their aircraft could deliver a swift attack on any foe, the carriers themselves were highly vulnerable to air attack.

IV

PEARL
HARBOR
TO
MIDWAY

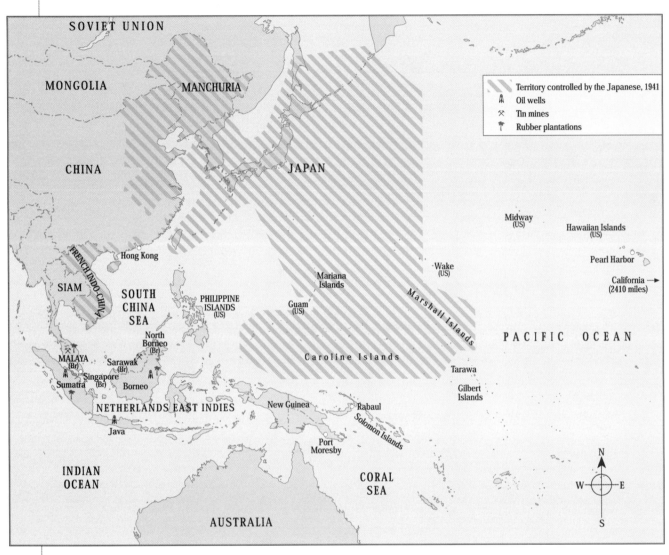

The Pacific region showing British, American and Japanese possessions before World War II broke out in the East, December 1941.

A T 0753 HOURS ON Sunday, 7 December 1941, 181 Japanese warplanes attacked the US Pacific Fleet as it lay at anchor in Pearl Harbor, the great US naval base on Oahu in the Hawaiian Islands. Forty minutes later, a second wave of 170 planes staged a second attack. While there had been no formal declaration, the fact that the United States was now at war was inescapable.

Brewing Conflict

ALTHOUGH THE ATTACK at Pearl Harbor was a surprise, a war between the United States and Japan had not been entirely unexpected.

In the early 20th century, Japan had risen to be a great naval power, beating the great Russian Imperial Fleet in the Russo-Japanese War of 1904–05. In the 1930s, militarists gained the upper hand in the government. Already the Japanese held Korea and Manchuria, and, in 1937, they attacked China. To add to their growing possessions on the mainland, they aimed to take over the British, French and Dutch colonies in the Far East, along with the Philippines, which was under US control, and establish what Japan called a 'Greater East Asia Co-Prosperity Sphere' – in other words, a Japanese empire.

Washington backed Chiang Kai-shek, the Chinese nationalist leader who was resisting

An aerial shot of Pearl Harbor shows that, while it was well protected from attack from the sea, it was wide open to attack from the air.

Japanese planes prepare to take off for their attack on Pearl Harbor. While the air strike took the US Pacific Fleet completely by surprise, it did not catch its aircraft carriers in port, nor did it destroy the dockyards or the fleet's fuel stocks – this meant that the Americans could strike back.

the Japanese onslaught, and imposed sanctions on Japan. The Japanese joined the Axis and signed the Tripartite Pact with the Germans and Italy on 27 September 1940. Just as the United States wanted no part of the war in Europe, it was equally reluctant to go to war in the Far East. But diplomatic talks between America and Japan went nowhere.

When Hitler attacked the Soviet Union in June 1941, he had invited Japan to join the war and seize Russia's eastern seaboard. But Japan decided to benefit from the German attack, rather than aid it. Operation Barbarossa effectively neutralized the Soviet Unon as an enemy in the Far East, and it presented the Japanese with the opportunity to attack to the south and seize the European colonies there – provided any threat from the United States could be neutralized as well.

On 20 November 1941, America received an ultimatum from the Japanese government, saying that the United States must withdraw its support from the Chinese government, lift its trade embargo and supply Japan with the one vital commodity it lacked – oil.

The United States could not comply. Any concession to the Japanese would mean that China would fall, along with British possessions in the Far East. Without its Empire, Britain would fall, leaving the whole of Europe, Africa, and Asia to the Axis. America would then be surrounded on all sides by hostile dictatorships.

On 26 November, Washington sent a reply to the Japanese ultimatum that simply outlined the principles of self-determination once more. The United States knew that this would not be acceptable to the Japanese, but it did not know that the Japanese fleet had already sailed. For Japan, there was no time to lose. The Germans seemed on the brink of victory in Europe. In that case, they would soon arrive in the Far East to seize their enemies' colonies as spoils of war. If Japan was to have its empire, it had to strike straight away – at Pearl Harbor.

The man who had drawn up the plan for the attack on Pearl Harbor was the Commander in Chief of the Japanese Imperial Navy, Admiral Isoroku Yamamoto. He was opposed to a war with the United States. He believed that Japan could not win such a war. It could not invade and hold such a vast country. And as naval attaché to Washington, he had seen the United States' industrial might at first hand. Asked about Japan's chances of victory,

Yamamoto replied, 'If I am told to fight regardless of the consequences, I shall run wild for the first six months or a year, but I have absolutely no confidence about the second and third years.'

The Japanese government gambled that six months was enough. In that time, its forces could sweep through Southeast Asia and seize the Indonesian oilfields and enough raw materials to supply its industry for a prolonged war.

The Japanese navy had realized that aircraft carriers, not battleships, would be the crucial weapon in a war in the Pacific. It had built a carrier fleet and equipped it with dive-

An aerial view of Ford Island during the Japanese attack on Pearl Harbor. A plume of water rises from an explosion, as planes swoop over the island.

A Japanese fighter-bomber returns to its mother ship. Pearl Harbor burns in the background.

(66 ft) before beginning its run. In Pearl Harbor, it was thought, torpedoes would bury themselves harmlessly in the mud. But the Japanese simply added wooden fins to their torpedoes, which gave them extra buoyancy. It also helped them to run straight and, during practice in Kagoshima Bay in southern Kyushu, the strike rate rose to 70 per cent.

While increasingly hostile diplomatic traffic was exchanged between Washington and Tokyo, Yamamoto secretly massed an armada under Vice Admiral Chuichi Nagumo in the Kurile Islands to the north-east of Japan. There were six huge aircraft carriers – the *Akagi*, *Kaga*, *Hiryu*, *Soryu*, *Shokaku* and *Zuikaku* – carrying 423 warplanes between them. They set sail on 26 November in two columns of three, flanked by the heavy cruisers *Chikuma* and *Tone*, while the battleships *Hiei* and *Kirishima* brought up the rear. The light cruiser *Abukuma* and nine destroyers were also deployed to protect the convoy. The strike force sailed slowly eastwards at 13 knots so that the oilers – the vital refuelling ships – could keep up. Meanwhile, radio traffic was generated so that it would appear that they were still in their home ports.

The fleet took a northerly route, staying out of the shipping lanes, and maintained radio silence. It arrived in position north-east of the Hawaiian Islands on 6 December. That day, the government in Tokyo began sending a long message to the Japanese embassy in Washington, D.C. This brought any further negotiations to a conclusion, although it fell short of a declaration of war. It was to be delivered to the Secretary of State Cordell Hull the following morning, before the attack. Delay in decoding such a long letter, however, meant

bombers, torpedo bombers and fighters that were the best in the world. Yamamato's plan was to knock out the US Pacific Fleet at Pearl Harbor in an attack so swift that it would have no time to react. He knew that the element of surprise would be on his side. The received wisdom was that making a surprise attack nearly 6,400 km (4,000 miles) from its home port without being detected was impossible. The Americans also thought that their fleet was safe at Pearl Harbor. Although the British had destroyed the Italian fleet with torpedo planes at Taranto in November 1940, it was thought that Pearl was too shallow to launch torpedo attacks. The anchorage was only 12 m (40 ft) deep and an airborne torpedo sank to 20 m

that it was not delivered until after the first wave of Japanese planes had gone in and the second was on its way.

Submarine Sighting

ON THE NIGHT of 6 December, two Japanese submarines sailed close to the coast of Oahu to deploy five two-man midget submarines, which were also to attack the Pacific Fleet. At 0342 hours, the minesweeper USS *Condor* spotted the periscope of a midget submarine just outside Pearl Harbor's anti-submarine nets. She summoned the destroyer USS *Ward*,

which began searching the area. The contact was reported, but submarine sightings were not uncommon.

By this time it was known that the Japanese fleet had sailed. But no one knew where it was. Some historians have claimed that President Roosevelt knew where and when the attack was coming. Although Roosevelt had won the 1940 US presidential election on the promise of keeping the United States out of the war, his growing support of Britain – and, later, the Soviet Union – indicates that he felt the United States would be dragged into the war sooner or later. After the attack on Pearl Harbor, there

Both the USS West Virginia *(pictured here) and the USS* Tennessee *were hit by Japanese air strikes during the attack on Pearl Harbor.*

was no doubt in the minds of the American people that they should go to war. Crucially, the Pacific Fleet's aircraft carriers were not in port. When it sailed, the Japanese fleet thought that all six US aircraft carriers were in Pearl Harbor. Five had been, but the *Hornet* and the *Yorktown*, had been transferred to the Atlantic, while the *Saratoga* had been pulled back to protect the United States' West Coast. And, on 28 November, the *Enterprise* and the *Lexington* set sail westwards to deliver planes to Wake Island and Midway.

An accusing finger has also been pointed at Churchill, whose strategy from the beginning had been to get the United States into the war. Not only had the British broken the German Enigma codes, but they were also reading the Japanese equivalent, called 'Purple'. The Americans had also broken Purple; however, not being on a war footing, they did not have the necessary manpower to decode the amount of material they were intercepting. Churchill read all intercepted messages, but Roosevelt was considered a security risk and was not shown raw intelligence data. So Churchill would have had a better idea of what was going on in the Japanese mind. He repeatedly told Roosevelt that the first attack would be on Singapore. To maintain this fiction, he reinforced the garrison there with Australians, even though a recent assessment of its defences showed that it could not be held. This deceit cost the British 130,000 fighting men, captured when Singapore fell to the Japanese in February 1942.

At 0550 on the morning of 7 December, the Japanese carriers turned into the wind. Japanese pilots assembled on deck and tied around their heads ceremonial *hachimaki*

scarves carrying the Japanese characters meaning 'certain victory'. The ships' crews were allowed time off from their duties to witness this historic moment. Conditions were far from perfect. The wind was gusting and the sea was high, but only one of the 183 planes in the first wave was lost on take-off. Another developed engine trouble and had to turn back. But by 0620, forty-nine bombers, fifty-one dive-bombers, forty torpedo planes and forty-one Zero fighters were heading to Oahu, while the second wave was being marshalled on the flight deck.

At 0630, just off Oahu, the USS *Antares*, a supply ship, spotted another submarine. The *Ward* closed in, put a shell through its conning tower, then finished it off with depth charges. In the battle of Pearl Harbor, it was first blood to the United States.

At 0700, Commander Fuchida, the attack force flight leader, picked up music from a Hawaiian radio station and locked onto it. Five minutes later, two American radar operators in the newly established US military radar station on the north of Oahu spotted a blip. This indicated that a group of more than fifty planes was bearing down on them. They reported what they had seen, but were told that a flight of American B-17s was expected from the mainland that morning.

The Japanese planes stayed above a thick layer of cloud, out of sight. Below, Oahu was quiet and sleepy. The Japanese had deliberately chosen a Sunday morning to attack. Few navy men were on deck. Most were still in their bunks sleeping off their shore leave the night before. The ships were moored close together, making them an easy target. No smoke was coming from their stacks, and none was ready

Opposite: There was little the defenders could do at Pearl Harbor – to prevent sabotage, the ammunition that they needed had been locked away in storage boxes. This meant that few of the Japanese planes were shot down.

to sail. Of the 300 planes based at the airfields on the island, only three were airborne, with those on the ground parked in close formation. With a large Japanese population on the islands, there was a fear of sabotage; the planes were easier to guard when they were close together. They also made a better target.

At 0753, Fuchida sent the famous radio message 'Tora, Tora, Tora' – 'Tiger, Tiger, Tiger' – which meant that the Americans had been taken completely by surprise. And the Japanese planes went in for the kill.

Under Attack

WHEN THE FIRST BOMB dropped, those of the Americans who heard it assumed that it had been dropped by accident by one of their own planes. It was only when a dive-bomber blew up a hangar at the Ford Island Command Center that Commander Logan Ramsey realized that the island was under attack. Frantically, he sent the radio message, 'Air raid, Pearl Harbor. This is no drill.'

By 0755 hours, the Pacific Fleet and the surrounding airfields were under full-scale attack. For the next two hours, bombs rained down and torpedoes sliced through the unprotected hulls of the US Navy's prize battleships. Amid the explosions gunners managed to return fire, but they were hampered by firing from capsizing decks and a shortage of ammunition. To prevent sabotage, it had been kept in the locked storage boxes. Meanwhile, the Japanese planes bombed and strafed American airfields against virtually no opposition.

The havoc the Japanese wrought was immense. The battleship USS *Arizona* blew up and was completely destroyed. The *Oklahoma*

capsized. The *California*, *Nevada* and *West Virginia* sank at their moorings. Three other battleships, three cruisers, three destroyers, and several other vessels also suffered damage. Some 169 aircraft were completely destroyed and 150 damaged, mainly on the ground. In all, some 2,403 Americans were killed, including sixty-eight civilians. Another 1,176 were wounded.

The Japanese lost between twenty-nine and sixty planes – some sacrificed in kamikaze suicide attacks. Another ten or fifteen made it back to their carriers, but were so badly damaged they were pushed overboard to make room for incoming planes. Around another forty were damaged but repairable. All five midget submarines had been lost, along with one, perhaps two, fleet submarines and fewer than a hundred men. It seemed an overwhelming victory; however, a fatal mistake had been made. Despite the pleadings of Fuchida, Admiral Nagumo had refused to send in a third wave of planes already fuelled, loaded with bombs and waiting on the flight decks. With the defences at Pearl now crippled, a third or fourth wave could have finished off the battleships, destroyed some of the lighter shipping and put the airfields out of action. An attack on the US Navy fuel depot would have sent the United States' complete naval strategy for the Pacific up in smoke.

To pick up incoming planes, however, the Japanese fleet had sailed to within 300 km (190 miles) of the island and was now vulnerable. Nagumo did not know where the US carrier fleet was, but by now it would be looking for them. He had fulfilled his mission. According to the damage reports he had been receiving, the US Pacific Fleet would be out of

action for at least six months, which was all that was required. Why risk turning a victory into a defeat? So Nagumo's flagship, the *Akagi*, hoisted the signal flag ordering a withdrawal to the north-west. Below decks, the disappointed pilots said, 'Now we can live to be a hundred.'

The following day, President Roosevelt addressed a joint session of the US Congress:

Yesterday, December 7, 1941 – a day which will live in infamy – the United States of America was suddenly and deliberately attacked by the naval and air forces of the Empire of Japan. The United States was at peace with that nation and, at the solicitation of Japan, was still in conversation with its government and its emperor looking toward the maintenance of peace in the Pacific. Indeed, one hour after Japanese air squadrons had commenced bombing in Oahu, the Japanese ambassador to the United States and his colleague delivered to the Secretary of State a formal reply to a recent American message. While it stated that it seemed useless to continue the existing diplomatic negotiations, it contained no threat or hint of armed attack.

In fact, the Japanese had never been overly concerned about the niceties of a declaration of war. On 7 February 1904, Admiral Togo Heihachiro's fleet had won a great victory when it attacked the Russian fleet in the harbour of Port Arthur in Manchuria without declaring war. That had been the first attack of Asian people on Europeans, and the first significant use of torpedoes, in modern warfare. After the attack on Pearl Harbor, the Japanese government maintained that an Imperial proclamation declaring war had been released at 0900 Tokyo time, but it was later admitted that it had not been signed by the Emperor until 1145.

Pearl Harbor was not the only target that came under attack by the Japanese on 'the day of infamy'. President Roosevelt went on to list for Congress what else had happened on that day:

Yesterday the Japanese government also launched an attack against Malaya. Last night Japanese forces attacked Hong Kong. Last night Japanese forces attacked Guam. Last night Japanese forces attacked the Philippine Islands. Last night the Japanese attacked Wake Island. This morning the Japanese attacked Midway Island. I ask that Congress declare that, since the unprovoked and dastardly attack by Japan on Sunday, December 7th, a state of war has existed between the United States and the Japanese Empire.

The Senate passed the resolution 82 to 0; the House of Representatives by 388 to 1 – the only vote against coming from Representative Jeanette Rankin of Montana, who had also voted against US entry into World War I. And at 1610 that afternoon, 8 December, President Roosevelt signed the declaration of war. That same day, Britain also declared war on Japan.

But although the attack on Pearl Harbor had been a crushing defeat for the United States, within it were the seeds of victory. It had awoken the sleeping giant. For Americans, isolationism was over. The country was now at war, and the American people rallied to the cause. Although the West Coast was now vulnerable to attack, the situation in the Pacific was far from hopeless. The carrier fleet was unscathed. And, while the rest of the fleet had been sunk, the vital oil storage facility and the naval dockyard at Pearl Harbor remained intact. Indeed, all of the ships sunk by the Japanese that day – with the exception of the *Arizona* and the *Oklahoma* – were repaired and returned to service.

In Tokyo, initial misgivings had turned to jubilation. At first, people did not know what to make of an attack on the United States, a country they had long sought to emulate. The attacks on Hong Kong and Singapore, however, were particularly gratifying, as Britain was seen as Japan's real enemy in the Far East. The following day, the Japanese occupied Bangkok and landed on Tarawa and Makin in the Gilbert Islands. Then, on 10 December, Britain's two most powerful warships east of Suez – the ultra-modern 35,000-tonne battleship *Prince of Wales* and the 32,000-tonne battle cruiser *Repulse* – steaming to the defence of Singapore, had been sunk in the Gulf of Siam. That same day, the Japanese landed on Camiguin Island and at Gonzaga and Aparri on the main Philippine island of Luzon. A US destroyer, two submarines and a minesweeper had been damaged.

What was the purpose of these unprovoked attacks? 'To assure the stability of eastern Asia and to contribute to world peace,' an Imperial Japanese spokesman said.

On 11 December 1941, Hitler made another blunder – perhaps the biggest blunder of the war. He declared war on the United States. He was not obliged to do that under the Tripartite Pact, just as Japan had failed to declare war on the Soviet Union. Although the

American people were eager to get their own back on the Japanese, Roosevelt was by no means assured of getting a declaration of war on the Axis powers through Congress. As it was, the United States returned the compliment and declared war on Germany and Italy. Now the sides were drawn.

Roosevelt already had an agreement with Churchill that, apart from defensive actions in the Pacific, they would pursue the war in Europe first. But the American public was baying for blood. The commander of the Pacific Fleet Admiral Husband E. Kimmel and the garrison commander General Walter C. Short were relieved of duty, although subsequent reports found them guilty of errors of judgement, rather than dereliction of duty. Admiral Chester W. Nimitz replaced Kimmel and began rebuilding his fleet.

The three carriers that had been out to sea when the Japanese had attacked – the USS *Lexington*, *Saratoga* and *Enterprise* – along with five others – the *Langley*, *Ranger*, *Wasp*, *Hornet* and *Yorktown* – would be the backbone of the US fleet that fought the Pacific war. There would be some twenty battles with the Imperial Japanese Navy. Five of them would be fought between aircraft carriers, and four would be fought within a six-month period in 1942 that would decide the outcome of the war in the Pacific.

The Battle of the Coral Sea

IN THE MONTHS following Pearl Harbor, nothing could stop the Japanese advance. They overran the Philippines, the East Indies, Guam and Wake Island. By mid-April, they held most of the South Pacific. Their next objective was to

take Tulagi to the north of Guadalcanal in the British Solomon Islands and Port Moresby on New Guinea. They would then cut the supply route between the United States and Australia, in preparation for the invasion of Australia itself. An invasion force assembled at Truk in the Carolines. On 30 April, it sailed for Rabaul in northern New Britain, where Vice Admiral Shigeyoshi Inouye was mustering a separate naval force as part of his intricate plan. The Japanese now occupied much of the area, and Inouye's ships would be supported by 140 land-based aircraft.

Australia was a British dominion whose soldiers were fighting fiercely in North Africa. It was also a long-time friend of the United States, and Nimitz rallied to its defence. He sent Task Force 17, under the command of Rear Admiral Frank J. Fletcher, to the Coral Sea. His flagship was the *Yorktown*, which had been transferred back from the Atlantic after the attack on Pearl Harbor. It was accompanied by the *Lexington*, a converted cruiser, under Rear Admiral Aubrey W. Fitch. These two carriers were escorted by seven cruisers and a screen of destroyers. They carried three types of plane. They had thirty-six Douglas TBD-1 Devastators, which were the first all-metal monoplanes to be carried by the US Navy. Designed in 1934, they were slow and had a poor rate of climb and a limited range, and carried a torpedo which tended towards

The USS West Virginia *was hit by two bombs and seven torpedoes. She capsized and sank at her moorings. The ship was repaired and took part in the Allied landings in the Philippines and the Battle of Leyte Gulf.*

Admiral Chester W. Nimitz became Commander in Chief of the Pacific Fleet after Pearl Harbor. He commanded both the land and maritime forces that island-hopped across the Pacific.

the war, Fletcher had more dive-bombers. The US carriers also had radar and the *Yorktown's* planes carried IFF – Identification, Friend or Foe – equipment. The Japanese possessed neither of these innovations.

Takagi's strike force set off from the Carolines and swung to the east to stay out of the range of US reconnaissance planes for as long as possible. On 3 May, a small force landed on Tulagi and, by 1100, the island was in Japanese hands. It was here that Fletcher decided to strike back. At 0630 on 4 May, twenty-eight Dauntless dive-bombers and twelve Devastators took off from the *Yorktown*. At 0815 hours, they were over the island. The first two strikes sunk a destroyer, three minesweepers and a patrol boat. A third sank four landing barges and five Kawanishi H6K Mavis flying boats. Returning to the *Yorktown* at 1632, they had lost one Devastator, downed over the target, and two Wildcats which had strayed off course on their return to the carrier and crash-landed on Guadalcanal. Their pilots were recovered later.

Meanwhile, Takagi's strike force had headed west towards the Coral Sea; however, due to bad weather, US reconnaissance planes were unable to find it. A Japanese flying boat spotted the US fleet, but it was shot down by Wildcats.

The New Guinea invasion force set off from Rabaul with six Japanese army transports, five navy transports and a destroyer escort, under the command of Rear Admiral Kajioka in his flagship *Yubari*. It rendezvoused with a support group under Rear Admiral Marushige off the island of Bougainville and headed south towards the Jomard Passage, which would take it into the Coral Sea.

the unreliable. The bomber force comprised seventy-two Douglas SBD-2 Dauntless dive-bombers, which were already considered obsolete. Fighter support was provided by thirty-six Grumman F4F-3 Wildcats.

Fletcher's ships would meet Rear Admiral Takagi's main strike force, which comprised two of the aircraft carriers that had attacked Pearl Harbor, the *Shokaku* and the *Zuikaku*, two cruisers and a screen of destroyers. They carried forty-two Mitsubishi A6M5 Zero fighters, forty-two Aichi D3A Val dive-bombers and forty-one Nakajima B5N torpedo planes. Although the Japanese planes were superior to anything the Americans had at this point in

The fleets then began to sight each other. The *Yorktown* and the *Lexington* were spotted by a Japanese flying boat, although the report did not reach Takagi until 18 hours later. Meanwhile, the *Shoho*, which was supporting the invasion force, was spotted by USAAF B-17Es on 6 May. However, they did not spot Takagi's strike force due to the bad weather. That evening the two fleets were within 110 km (70 miles) of each other, though they did not know it. Later, they both changed course, and the gap widened again.

Encoding Error

THERE WAS ANOTHER Allied force in the area. Under the command of Rear Admiral Crace of the Royal Navy, it comprised two Australian cruisers, one US cruiser and a destroyer escort. On 7 May, Fletcher told Crace to close the southern end of the Jomard Passage, while Fletcher himself closed in from the south-east. At 0815, US reconnaissance planes reported seeing 'two carriers and four heavy cruisers' approaching the Louisiade Archipelago, north of the Jomard Passage. Fletcher thought that this was the main force and, between 0926 and 1030, ninety-three planes were sent off to attack it, leaving only forty-seven with the fleet. When the spotter plane returned, it became clear that there had been an error in encoding. It had only seen two heavy cruisers and two destroyers. But, soon after 1100, Lieutenant Commander Hamilton, leading *Lexington*'s squadrons, spotted the *Shoho* and its escort of four cruisers and a destroyer off Misima Island in the Louisiades. Despite its powerful escort, five of the *Shoho*'s aircraft

were blown over the side by first wave of US planes. Successive waves hit the carrier with six torpedoes and thirteen bombs, leaving it listing and on fire. It sank at 1135 with 600 of its 800 hands. Six US planes had been lost.

The invasion force now had no air cover and halted north of the Louisiades until the Jomard Passage was cleared. That afternoon, Crace's fleet was attacked by waves of land-based torpedo bombers, but they failed to sink any of the Allied ships. Meanwhile, reconnaissance planes from Takagi's strike force had mistakenly reported that they had located Fletcher's carriers. They launched more than sixty sorties and sank the USS *Sims*, a destroyer, and the oil tanker USS *Neosho*. At 1630, fifteen torpedo planes and twelve dive-bombers were launched with instructions to seek out Fletcher's force and destroy it. But the weather closed in and, without radar, the Japanese planes had little chance of finding the US fleet. The US fleet, however, picked up the bomber force on radar, and the *Lexington* sent up its Wildcats. They shot down nine bombers, losing two fighters in the process.

The Japanese torpedo squadron did not find the fleet either and gave up the search. They dumped their torpedoes in the sea and headed back to their carriers. But they had been closer to the American fleet than they had realized. At 1900, three of the Japanese planes spotted an Aldis lamp sending out Morse code from the *Yorktown*, but got clean away. At 1720, another Japanese plane was not so lucky and was shot down. A further 11 planes failed to find their carriers and crashed into the sea in the darkness. Of the original twenty-seven, only six planes returned safely to their carriers.

The Japanese aircraft carrier Shoho was hit by seven torpedoes and thirteen bombs on 7 May 1942, during the Battle of the Coral Sea. The first Japanese aircraft carrier to be sunk, she went down in forty minutes with the loss of 631 men. Captain Izawa and 202 crewmen were rescued by the destroyer Sazanami.

Japanese Advantage

UNABLE TO CLEAR Crace's force from the Jomard Passage, the invasion force withdrew, leaving Fletcher and Takagi to fight it out in the Battle of the Coral Sea – the first sea battle in history in which the opposing ships neither saw nor engaged each other. That night, the two fleets deliberately sailed away from one another, neither willing to risk a night engagement. Next morning, while the skies over Takagi's fleet remained overcast, Fletcher's fleet was bathed in sunshine. At around 0600, both sent out reconnaissance planes. Even though the weather gave the Japanese the advantage, at 0815 hours one of the *Lexington*'s Dauntlesses dived through the clouds and saw ships. As it went in for a closer look, the plane was rocked by a shell exploding near its left wingtip and it quickly climbed back into the clouds. The Japanese fleet was 282 km (175 miles) north-east of the American position. Its position was radioed back. At 0850, twenty-four dive-bombers and two fighters took off from the rolling deck of the *Yorktown*. They were followed by nine torpedo planes escorted by four fighters. Ten minutes later, the *Lexington* started sending a flight consisting of twenty-two dive-bombers, eleven torpedo planes and nine fighters. By 0925, all the planes were away.

The Japanese had also spotted the US fleet and, while the American planes headed for the Japanese fleet, fifty-one bombers and eighteen fighters were going the other way. At 1030 hours, the American dive-bombers saw the *Zuikaku* and the *Shokaku* 13 km (8 miles) ahead and pulled up to hide in the clouds until the slower torpedo planes caught up.

Then, as the *Shokaku* appeared from under the cloud cover, they attacked. Seeing them coming, the Japanese sent up fighters, which downed three of the Dauntlesses. This disrupted the American attack, and only two of their bombs hit the ship. One damaged

the flight deck enough to prevent any more fighters taking off, while the other started a fire in a machine shop. But the *Shokaku* still responded to the helm and weaved violently. As a result, all of the torpedoes either missed or failed to go off.

The *Lexington's* dive-bombers failed to find the carriers. They ran low on fuel and had to return to the 'Lady Lex'. But the torpedo planes and their fighter escort continued the search and spotted the enemy 25 km (15 miles) out. They were immediately attacked by Japanese

Crew members jump for their lives after the USS Lexington *is hit by two torpedoes and two bombs on 8 May 1942, during the Battle of the Coral Sea. When fires reached the bomb room and the torpedo store, the ship was abandoned.*

Zeros, which drove off the Wildcats. The low-flying Devastators managed to release their torpedoes; again, none of them hit. By this time, the *Shokaku* was on fire and out of action. One hundred and eight of its crew had been killed, but it had not been hit below the waterline. It limped back to Truk, while most of its planes transferred to the *Zuikaku*, which emerged briefly from the murk, only to disappear again.

The US fleet had no such protection. Above it, the skies were clear and it had little fighter cover. The Wildcats were low on fuel and were badly positioned for a fight, even though the bandits had been spotted on radar 110 km (68 miles) out. Only three Wildcats spotted the Japanese planes as they started their attack at 1055; they were at 3,050 m (10,000 ft) and did not have the fuel to climb up to meet the Vals, which began to dive from 5,490 m (18,000 ft). Twelve other Dauntlesses, having been trained to expect a low-level attack, patrolled at 610 m (2,000 ft) 5 km (3 miles) outside the destroyer screen. The Japanese torpedo planes and their fighter escort flew over them at 1,830 m (6,000 ft), only to drop to release height inside the ring of destroyers. Still, the Dauntlesses reacted quickly, managing to down two Kates before they could release their torpedoes. They also shot down two Zeros, a Val and two more Kates for the loss of four Dauntlesses.

The *Yorktown* managed to dodge the eight torpedoes launched at her port quarter and everything the dive-bombers threw at her. Five minutes later, however, when a second wave of Japanese planes arrived, an 800-pound bomb went through her flight deck and exploded three decks down, killing sixty-six US sailors. Black smoke streamed from the gaping hole in her deck. She was on fire, but still afloat.

Listing Badly

THE JAPANESE PILOTS then turned their attention to the *Lexington*. They attacked both bows, dropping their torpedoes at between 15 and 60 m (50 and 200 ft), 915 m (1,000 yards) out. Two hit, and all three boiler rooms were flooded. Two dive-bombers also scored hits, and the *Lexington* was listing badly when they turned for home. Although both US carriers

The crew prepares to abandon the USS Yorktown. She was hit by three bombs and four torpedoes on 4 June 1942, during the Battle of Midway. Still afloat two days later, she was being towed to port when she was sunk by a Japanese submarine.

had been hit, the returning planes were still able to land on them.

But the jubilant Japanese pilots returning to the *Shokaku* found that they had to ditch in the sea. This left the Japanese fleet with only nine planes, while the Americans still had twelve fighters and thirty-seven attack aircraft. At that point in the battle, the Japanese had lost eighty planes and some 900 men; the Americans sixty-six planes and 543 men. But worse was to come. Fuel was escaping, and vapour built up inside the damaged *Lexington*. At 1247, a spark from a generator ignited it, and the ship was rocked by a massive explosion. A second internal explosion tore through her again at 1445. The fires on board got out of control and, at 1710, the crew abandoned ship. At 1956, a destroyer put her out of her misery with five torpedoes, and the *Lexington* went to her watery grave.

The Battle of Midway

THE OUTCOME OF the Battle of the Coral Sea had been indecisive; however, the Japanese were forced to cancel their seaborne invasion of Port Moresby. But it did not ruin their appetite for a fight. Yamamoto went back on the offensive. He planned to take Midway Island, 2,100 km (1,300 miles) north-west of Oahu. From there, he would be able to mount further attacks on Pearl Harbor, denying the United States a navy base west of San Francisco. This was a response to the 'Doolittle' raid, where Lieutenant Colonel Jimmy Doolittle led a force of sixteen B-25s from the USS *Hornet* on a bombing raid on Tokyo on 18 April 1942. As it was, the *Hornet* could not get close enough to Japan for Doolittle's planes to land

back on the carrier, and they had to fly on to airstrips in China. But Yamamoto wanted to push the Japanese naval perimeter back so that no US aircraft carrier could get in range of the imperial capital again.

As the United States now employed enough code breakers to read all the Purple intercepts they collected, Admiral Nimitz knew what to expect. Yamamoto's plan was to stage a diversionary attack on the Aleutians, the chain of islands belonging to the United States that run out into the Pacific from the coast of Alaska. They would invade and occupy two of the inhabited islands – Attu and Kiska – and intern the people there. Such a humiliation would force the United States to react. To make sure that America sent sufficient of its strength northwards, Yamamoto would also have to commit capital ships, including the aircraft carrier *Junyo* and the light carrier *Rjujo*, which would have been useful at Midway.

Admiral Nagumo, the victor of Pearl Harbor, would lead the attack on Midway with four of the carriers that had been there that day – the *Akagi*, *Kaga*, *Hiryu* and the *Soryu* – while the light carrier *Zuiho* would be part of a central covering force that could help out either in the Aleutians or at Midway. They would face the *Enterprise* and the *Hornet*, along with the rapidly refitted *Yorktown*, which was ready to put to sea again after only three days in the all-important navy yard at Pearl. Its fighter complement had been increased from eighteen to twenty-seven, as it was carrying the new F4F-4 Wildcats, which had folding wings allowing the carrier to accommodate the extra planes, and six machine guns instead of four. Her pilots were the survivors from the *Yorktown* and *Lexington*, who now had combat experience.

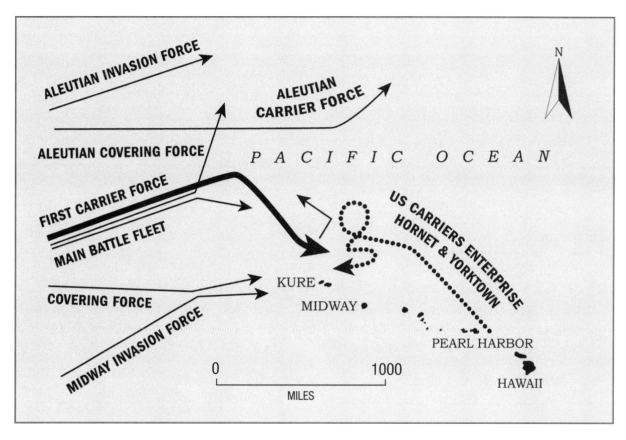

ALEUTIAN INVASION FORCE

ALEUTIAN CARRIER FORCE

ALEUTIAN COVERING FORCE

FIRST CARRIER FORCE

MAIN BATTLE FLEET

COVERING FORCE

MIDWAY INVASION FORCE

P A C I F I C   O C E A N

N

US CARRIERS ENTERPRISE HORNET & YORKTOWN

KURE

MIDWAY

PEARL HARBOR

HAWAII

0   1000

MILES

Strike Force

ON 30 MAY, Admiral Fletcher sailed north-westwards to meet up with the two cruisers and five destroyers surviving from Task Force 17. They then joined up with Task Force 16, under Admiral Raymond Spruance on board the *Enterprise*. On Midway itself, the USAAF stationed four squadrons of Flying Fortresses and some B-26 Marauders, while the Marine Corps had nineteen Dauntless dive-bombers, seven F4F-3 Wildcats, seventeen Vought SB2U-3 Vindicators (or 'Wind Indicators', as the Marines called them), twenty-one obsolete Brewster F2A-3 Buffaloes and six new Grumman TBF-1 Avenger three-man torpedo bombers.

Yamamoto himself led the main Japanese force from the battleship *Yamoto* and sent Nagumo's carrier strike force towards Midway from the north-west, while the minesweepers, transports and supply ships of the invasion force approached further to the south. A US Catalina reconnaissance flying boat spotted the invasion fleet 1,130 km (700 miles) west of Midway on 3 June. At 1230, nine Flying Fortresses took off. Four hours later, they found the invasion force 920 km (570 miles) to the west. Short of fuel, they dropped their bombs amid heavy anti-aircraft fire, but hit

The Battle of Midway, 3–7 June 1942.

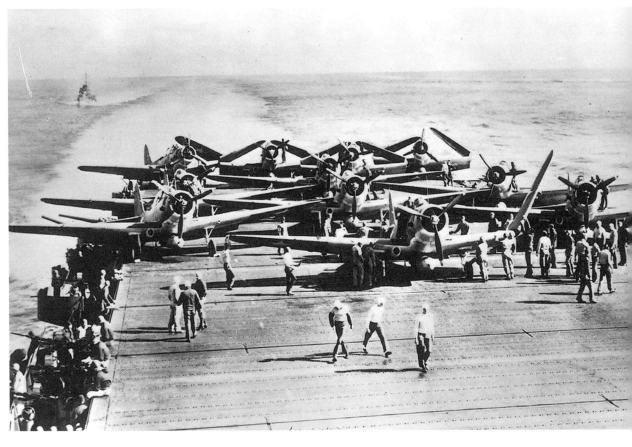

US Devastator torpedo-bombers aboard the aircraft carrier USS Enterprise *off Midway, June 1942. The US carrier force would play a major role in defeating the Japanese.*

nothing. At dawn the following morning, however, four Catalinas from Midway torpedoed a tanker.

At 0415 hours, fifteen Flying Fortresses were on their way to bomb the invasion fleet again, when they received word that another fleet – complete with carriers – was approaching Midway and was then only 233 km (145 miles) away. Fifteen minutes later, ten Dauntless scouts were airborne, searching for the carriers to the north of the island. At the same time, thirty-six Val dive-bombers, thirty-six Kate torpedo-bombers carrying 800-kg bombs and thirty-six Zeros took off from Nagumo's

carriers. They headed for Midway, intending to soften up its defences for the invasion which was scheduled two days later. Once the strike force was airborne, more Kates were hoisted up to the flight deck, armed with torpedoes to attack shipping. At the same time, spotter planes were despatched to hunt for the US fleet. Here, the United States got lucky. One of the two floatplanes launched from the cruiser *Tone* was delayed for half an hour, when the catapult malfunctioned. It was headed for the search sector where the fleet was.

At 0534, a Navy flying boat reported to Midway that there was a Japanese carrier fleet

400 km (250 miles) away to the east. The *Yorktown* also picked up the message, and Fletcher told Spruance to take the *Enterprise* and *Hornet* to attack the Japanese carriers. Radar operators on Midway spotted 108 Japanese planes heading for the island at 0553. They warned the flying boats and Flying Fortresses to stay away, while the seven Wildcats and twenty-one Buffaloes of the island's defence force went to take on the attackers. They managed to shoot down four Japanese bombers and damage several others, before they were overwhelmed by the nimble Zeros. In the ensuing dogfights, three Wildcats and thirteen Buffaloes were shot down. Seven more were damaged beyond repair. Of the twenty-eight US planes, only five survived intact – and one of those had not even been involved in the engagement as it had engine trouble and had to turn back. They had managed to down just two Zeros. A further three Japanese planes were downed by ack-ack fire over Midway.

Furious Fire

WHILE THIS DISASTROUS dogfight had been going on, six Grumman Avengers and four Marauders headed off to attack the Japanese fleet. As they attacked at low level, seventeen Zeros pounced on them from 915 m (3,000 ft). The unprotected bombers were easy prey and turned back. Two of the B-26s made it back to Midway, where they crash-landed. The Avengers managed to loose their torpedoes, but furious fire from the Zeros and the fleet shot down five of them. Only one Avenger, badly damaged and with a wounded radio operator and a dead gunner on board, made it back to Midway.

However, this attack convinced Admiral Nagumo and the strike force commander Lieutenant Joichi Tomonaga that a second wave of bombers needed to be sent against Midway, so the Kates were lowered from the flight deck to be rearmed with bombs. This was a time-consuming process. At 0728, the *Tone*'s second floatplane had finally located the 'ten enemy surface ships' around 390 km (240 miles) from Midway. Nagumo waited, weighing up the information. Then, at 0813, he ordered the Kates' torpedoes to be replaced. Then a report came, saying that the ships were only cruisers and destroyers – not carriers – and posed no imminent threat as they were well out of range, so arming the Kates with bombs could resume.

It was then that Midway's bomber force, fifteen USAAF Flying Fortresses and sixteen Marine Corps Dauntless dive-bombers, arrived. The Flying Fortresses dropped their bombs from 6,100 m (20,000 ft). But when the pluming sea subsided, the Japanese carriers were still intact. As the Flying Fortresses turned for home, Nagumo could see that the pilots of his eighteen airborne Zeros were wary of these heavily armed bombers. They needed reinforcing. He ordered the thirty-six Zeros intending to escort the Kates to take off in time to intercept the Dauntlesses as they came in. The Zeros fell on the American dive-bombers, whose inexperienced pilots were bringing them in too low. As these Dauntlesses were land-based, their pilots had not been trained to attack shipping and posed no threat to the Japanese fleet. Only a handful got close enough to release their bombs. Just eight of the sixteen made it back to Midway, and they were riddled with shrapnel and bullet holes.

Nagumo then received the bad news. The *Tone*'s floatplane now reported that the ten US ships they were shadowing were a vanguard for the carrier force which was following in the rear. They were streaming south-east and were now just 320 km (200 miles) away – well within range. And carrier aircrew were trained to attack enemy ships. Nagumo's second-wave attack aircraft were still below decks being rearmed. His fighters were getting low on fuel and ammunition, and his first-wave force was expected back any minute.

realized that he had the upper hand. If he bided his time, he could attack the Japanese carriers when they were at their most vulnerable – when their decks were full of returning aircraft. His timing was immaculate and, within a few minutes of the last Japanese plane arriving back from Midway putting down, Nagumo's destroyer screen reported US planes approaching.

The timing may have been immaculate, but the tactics were not. Broken cloud along the route had scattered the American formations. Nagumo's change of course meant that the Japanese carriers were not where they were thought to be. Some planes grew short of fuel as they searched for the fleet and had to return. Others lost their fighter escort, and ten Wildcats ditched in the sea. But, piecemeal, the US squadrons found their target.

A Japanese heavy cruiser of the Mogame class on fire after being hit by planes from Task Force 16 under Admiral William 'Bull' Halsey at the Battle of Midway.

Blown out of the Skies

THE FIRST INTO the attack were fifteen obsolete Devastators. They came skimming in at 90 m (300 ft) but, unescorted, they were no match for the fifty Zeros that attacked them. Fourteen were blown out of the skies before they got near enough to release their torpedoes. But the last one, piloted by Ensign George H. Gay, who was wounded in the leg and arm, and carried a dead gunner, pressed on. He managed to loose his torpedo, before he skimmed over the deck of the carrier and crashed in the sea. The torpedo missed its mark, but Gay managed to get out of his plane before it sank, and he kept himself afloat with his rubber seat cushion which had floated clear. When night fell and he was no longer in danger of being strafed by Zeros,

Rather than muster what planes he had that were ready to go, Nagumo decide to retire to the north until his fighters were refuelled and his first wave recovered. He would then send a properly armed force into the attack. Admiral Spruance coolly assessed the situation and

he inflated his dinghy. The next day he was picked up by a US Navy Catalina.

The Japanese sailors were still cheering when fourteen more Devastators from the *Enterprise* arrived and began attacking the *Kaga* from the starboard. At the same time, twelve more Devastators from the *Yorktown* turned up and attacked the *Soryu*. They were accompanied by seventeen Dauntlesses and six Wildcats. These drew some of the Zeros away from the Devastators. Even so, eleven of the *Enterprise*'s torpedo planes were downed.

With the support of the six Wildcats, the *Yorktown*'s Devastators were within 5 km (3 miles) of their target before they were attacked. Almost immediately, one Wildcat was downed and two others so badly damaged that they had to break off. The remaining three could do little to help the torpedo planes, other than try to draw some of the Zeros off. And they, too, were soon forced to break off and return to the *Yorktown*.

As well as being attacked by the Zeros, the cumbersome Devastators drew withering fire from the Japanese ships. Some of them managed to release their torpedoes before they were blasted from the skies. Again, not one of the torpedoes hit its target, but two passed within 15 m (50 ft) of the *Kaga*.

These three suicidal attacks had served to keep the Zeros at low altitudes, however, and some were landing to refuel when the Dauntlesses came in. They saw below them an unforgettable sight – four Japanese carriers completely unprotected. Three dive-bombers from the *Yorktown* peeled off and attacked. One bomb hit the *Akagi* amidships, ripping through the hangar deck and exploding among the stored torpedoes, carelessly stowed bombs and refuelling tanks, setting off secondary explosions. A second set the planes on the flight deck ablaze. The stern was shattered and the rudder useless and, as the huge ship lurched drunkenly around, Nagumo's officers begged a stunned admiral to abandon the blazing hulk.

Then a squadron of Dauntlesses from the *Enterprise* turned up and directed its attentions to the unprotected *Kaga*. The carrier took four direct hits. Three bombs hit the planes that were being prepared for take-off, setting them ablaze. The fourth hit a petrol tank on deck. Burning gasoline engulfed the bridge, killing the captain and the staff officers, and putting the ship out of action.

The *Yorktown*'s dive-bombers regrouped and attacked the *Soryu*. In minutes, she was a raging inferno. All three carriers stayed afloat while they burned. But they had to be abandoned and were later sunk by Japanese or American torpedoes. The *Hiryu* had escaped, however, and its air group, now augmented by twenty-three Zeros seeking refuge from their blazing carriers, still posed a threat. Also, Yamamoto had not yet abandoned his plan to invade Midway. Thinking there was only one US carrier in the area, he steamed on towards the island. The rest of the task force was to join up with his battleships and bombard the island's defences before the Japanese invasion force, standing by 800 km (500 miles) away, went ashore.

Still in Danger

IN THE ATTACK on the *Akagi*, *Kaga* and *Soryu*, seven Dauntlesses had been lost, while eight Zeros had been shot down. However, eleven more Dauntlesses had been ditched when they ran out of fuel on the way back to their ships.

Fletcher knew that his fleet was still in danger. He ordered the remaining Dauntlesses aloft to search for the *Hiryu*, while twelve Wildcats flew a defensive patrol around the *Yorktown*. What Fletcher did not know was that a reconnaissance plane from the *Soryu* had already spotted the *Yorktown*, and eighteen Vals and six Zeros from the *Hiryu* were on their way. At midday, they were picked by the *Yorktown*'s radar about 75 km (46 miles) out. The Wildcats intercepted them 25 km (15 miles) out and shot down four Zeros and seven Vals. The surviving bombers broke away and attacked the *Yorktown*. Six more were shot down – two by anti-aircraft fire from the American cruisers. Before breaking up, however, one of them managed to lob a bomb through the *Yorktown*'s flight deck, causing a fire in the hangar below. A second bomb knocked out the engine room, while a third caused a fire that threatened the forward ammunition stores and petrol tanks. Despite severe loss of life, the crew managed to get the fires under control.

While the *Yorktown*'s Wildcats refuelled and rearmed on the *Enterprise*, engineers on board the *Yorktown* managed to get her under way again, and Captain Elliot Buckmaster ran up a huge new Stars and Stripes. As it fluttered defiantly above the wrecked ship, a second wave of Japanese planes came screaming low over the horizon. This time there were ten Kate torpedo planes, escorted by six Zeros. The Wildcats managed to down three Zeros, at a cost of four F4Fs. Five Kates were also downed in the curtain of fire put up by the cruisers. But four torpedoes were launched within a range of 460 m (500 yards). Two hit the *Yorktown* below the waterline. They knocked out all power, lights and communications, and

the great ship listed to port. Fearing a further wave, Buckmaster gave the order to abandon ship at 1500.

Revenge was not long in coming. A US scout plane had already spotted the *Hiryu*. Fourteen Dauntlesses from the *Enterprise*, along with ten transferred from the *Yorktown*, set off to attack the remaining Japanese carrier. They were followed by sixteen more dive-bombers from the *Hornet*. As they neared the *Hiryu*, they were intercepted by thirteen Zeros, which shot down three Dauntlesses as they dived. Nevertheless, four bombs pierced the *Hiryu*'s flight deck, causing uncontrollable fires. When the planes from the *Hornet* arrived, they turned their attention to a battleship and a cruiser in the carrier's escort. Some Flying Fortresses en route from Hawaii to Midway also joined in, to little effect. Some of the Zeros attacked the B17s, but the fighters were soon out of fuel and ditched in the sea. That night, more bombers set out from Midway to try to discover what had happened to the *Hiryu*, but could not find it and flew back to their base guided by the fires still burning on Midway.

The loss of the *Hiryu* still did not put paid to Yamamoto's plan to invade Midway. However, he knew his invasion force would be vulnerable to the land-bombers. To have any chance of carrying off the invasion, they would have to attack that night. But then came the news that two of the cruisers he had designated to bombard the island could not make it before nightfall. Then he learned that there were other US carriers in the area and he bowed to the inevitable. At 0255 on 5 June, he issued an order, saying, 'The occupation of Midway is cancelled.'

The USS Yorktown *goes down fighting during the Battle of Midway, June 1942. Although the* Yorktown *was lost, the battle was a resounding victory for the United States.*

His admirals were mortified. Some would rather lose the entire fleet than lose face.

'How can we apologize to His Majesty for this defeat?' asked one.

'Leave that to me,' said Yamamoto. 'I am the only one who must apologize to His Majesty.'

The *Hiryu* was finally abandoned and sunk by Japanese torpedoes. But the defenders of Midway did not know this and went on searching. Yamamoto had already turned for home and was out of range, but a dozen dive-bombers put the *Mikuma* and the *Mogami*, two heavy cruisers, out of action. The *Mikuma* was badly damaged, not by a bomb, but by the Dauntless of Captain Richard E. Fleming hitting the rear gun turret. Gasoline from the aircraft seeped into the engine room and ignited, killing the entire engine-room crew.

The last victim of the Battle of Midway was the *Yorktown*. Now unable to sail under her own steam, she was being towed back to

A Grumman TBF Avenger torpedo-bomber takes off from the USS Yorktown *during the Battle of Midway. She will have no mother ship to return to.*

Pearl Harbor by a minesweeper when, soon after dawn on 6 June, a Japanese submarine torpedoed her again and sunk one of her destroyer escorts, the *Hannan*. The *Yorktown* stayed afloat until the early hours of 7 June, when she suddenly rolled over and plunged to the bottom of the Pacific.

The Battle of Midway was the decisive battle in the Pacific war. America had had its revenge on the carriers whose planes had attacked Pearl Harbor. The Japanese Imperial Navy which, before Midway, matched the strength of the US Navy was now a shadow of its former self. Although Japanese pilots had beaten their American adversaries, who had lost eighty-five out of 195 aircraft, in the air, most of their elite fliers were dead. But, crucially, the Japanese shipyards could not hope to replace the carriers they had lost. The United States was already turning out new carriers in large numbers, and its aircraft factories were producing more powerful planes to put on them. With Midway, the Japanese expansion across the Pacific had reached its height. As the Japanese Imperial Navy turned for home, however, it left behind hundreds of small islands occupied by Japanese troops, which it would take a bloody campaign of island-hopping to clear.

The Allies would first win victory in Europe, but at a terrible price for both sides. In Berlin, few buildings were left undamaged.

V

VICTORY IN EUROPE

DATES OF LIBERATION
6 JUNE–24 JULY
25 JULY–14 SEPT.
15 SEPT.–15 DEC.

The liberation of Europe after D-Day, 6 June 1944.

SINCE THE SOVIET UNION had come into the war it had been urging Britain to begin a second front in western Europe. And when the United States entered the war, it wanted to make an attack on the Germans in France as soon as possible. The British were more circumspect. Having been in the war longer than their new allies, the British felt that it would be foolish to risk everything in one reckless operation. Many of the British commanders had experienced the carnage of World War I and were afraid of throwing men against enemy lines in a frontal assault – inevitable when making an amphibious assault against a fortified coastline. As First Lord of the Admiralty during World War I,

Churchill himself had been responsible for the disastrous amphibious assault at Gallipoli in the Dardanelles where 250,000 men, largely Australians and New Zealanders, were lost before the 83,000 survivors could be evacuated. Britain's worst fears were realized when 5,000 Canadians, 1,000 British and 50 US Rangers staged a disastrous raid on the Channel port of Dieppe in August 1942 – 2,600 men were lost. The US Army was still untested, so President Roosevelt was persuaded to join the war in North Africa.

When the war in the desert was brought to a successful conclusion, Churchill proposed an attack on the 'soft underbelly of Europe'. On 10 July 1943, an Anglo-American force landed on the island of Sicily. Italian resistance collapsed and, on 25 July, Mussolini fell from power and was arrested. The German forces, under Field Marshal Kesselring, were then evacuated from Sicily and prepared to defend the Italian mainland.

On 2 September, a small Allied force landed on the 'heel' of Italy and quickly captured the southern ports of Taranto and Brindisi. On 3 September, Montgomery's Eighth Army crossed the Strait of Messina and landed on the 'toe' of Italy, meeting little resistance. That day, the new Italian government agreed to change sides, and its capitulation was announced on 8 September. The following day, the combined US–British Fifth Army under General Mark Clark landed at Salerno on the 'shin'. This was where Kesselring had expected the attack to come. The situation was precarious for six days, but the Fifth Army eventually broke out, taking the city of Naples on 1 October.

On 13 October 1943, Italy declared war on Germany. This was not unexpected, and Kesselring had already consolidated his hold on central and northern Italy. And he held the Allies at the Gustav Line, a defensive line that ran right across the narrow peninsula of Italy some 100 km (60 miles) south of Rome. To get round this, the Allies landed 50,000 men north of the Gustav Line at Anzio, in Lazio. At first they met with little resistance, but, instead of driving directly on Rome, the landing force stopped to consolidate the beachhead. Kesselring quickly counterattacked, nearly pushing the Allies back into the sea.

The main Allied force was held up by the German defenders at Monte Cassino, a mountaintop monastery pivotal in the Gustav Line. The Eighth Army was then switched from the Adriatic side of the peninsula to the western flank. On the night of 11 May 1944, the Allies managed to breach the Gustav Line to the west of Monte Cassino, which was outflanked and fell to the Polish Corps of the Eighth Army on 18 May. On 26 May, the main Allied force joined up with the beachhead at Anzio and, on 5 June 1944, the Allies drove into Rome.

However, progress on such a narrow front up the Italian peninsula was bound to be slow. And it did little to divert German strength from the Russian front. By this time, the Red Army was making good progress against the Wehrmacht. By sheer weight of numbers, it would eventually overwhelm the German army and overrun Germany. Even if the Allies pushed Kesselring all the way to the Alps, it would have been impossible to cross the mountains before the Red Army had swept right across Germany and, perhaps, taken the rest of western Europe as many people feared. By the spring of 1944, a landing in France was politically vital.

The delay in staging an amphibious assault across the English Channel gave the Germans time to fortify the coastline. They built what they called the 'Atlantic Wall' down the west coast of Europe from the Arctic Circle to the Pyrenees. By the time of the invasion, 12,247 of the planned 15,000 fortifications had been completed, along with 943 along the Mediterranean coast. Half a million beach obstacles had been deployed, and 6.5 million mines had been laid.

The huge extent of the wall was partly due to a campaign of misinformation called Operation Fortitude, which the British used to feed the Germans the idea that a Western Allied landing might come anywhere at any

time. To defend his empire against possible attack from the west, Hitler would be forced to spread his forces thinly.

Operation Overlord

AT THE BEGINNING of the war, the British had arrested every German spy in Britain and turned many of them, so that they could be used to feed false information back to their spymasters in Hamburg and Berlin. False information was also conveyed by radio traffic that the Germans intercepted. The British had also broken the German Enigma code, so they could see whether their deception was working. On occasions, the British even fed the Germans information that the invasion would come in the South of France or Norway, through the Balkans or in the Black Sea. This meant that Hitler had to disperse his troops to the four corners of his empire.

The major thrust of Fortitude, however, was to convince him that the Western Allies would take the most direct route. They would take the shortest Channel crossing at the Straits of Dover to the Pas de Calais. It would be easy for them to support the landings with air and artillery cover from England there. And it would give them the shortest route to Paris and Germany itself. This deception was reinforced by the invention of the First US Army Group, or FUSAG. This was a nonexistent army, apparently mustered in Kent, ready for embarkation at Dover. Radio traffic poured out of Kent, and set-builders from theatres and film studios were employed to mock up tanks and landing craft that would look like the real thing in German aerial reconnaissance photographs. One badly wounded prisoner of war, a

The rubble generated by the bombing and shelling of Monte Cassino in March 1944 turned the Italian town into a mini-Stalingrad. Armour was next to useless, and the fighting was hand to hand.

The use of paratroopers had been perfected by the Germans during their attack on the Low Countries, but the losses of these crack troops in Crete were so high that Hitler decided not to use them again. The Allies used paratroopers to good effect. however, to support their amphibious landings.

Panzer officer who was being returned to Germany, actually saw FUSAG with his own eyes – although the tanks and trucks he saw were not in Kent at all, but in Hampshire, ready for embarkation at England's southern ports. He was also introduced to General Patton, who German intelligence had been led to believe was commanding officer of FUSAG. Hitler became so convinced that FUSAG existed and that this was where the attack would come that he kept his mighty Fifteenth Army in the Pas de Calais and his Panzers east of the Seine for seven weeks after the Allies had landed on the beaches in Normandy.

Slave Labour

THE ALVADOS COAST in Normandy was chosen as the site of the landings because it had a number of wide flat beaches so close together that the forces landing on them could quickly join up and form a single bridgehead. It was poorly defended. The fortifications there, and in other places, had been built by slave labourers who had weakened them with deliberate sabotage. Many of the defenders were Russians, Poles or other Eastern Europeans who had little motivation to fight against the Americans or the British.

What Germans there were among them were largely either too old to fight on the Russian front, too young or had been wounded there.

The other advantage of the Calvados coast was that it did not have a major port. The conventional wisdom was that, for an invasion to succeed, the landing force would have to seize a port to get men and materiel ashore quickly enough to defend against a counter-attack that would aim to push them back into the sea. This was another reason why Hitler and his High Command were so convinced that the attack would come in the Pas de Calais where there were three ports – Calais, Boulogne and Dunkirk. But the raid on Dieppe had taught the British that an attack on a heavily defended port was not a good idea. Even if a landing force managed to take it, the Germans placed demolition charges in the harbour facilities in all the ports they occupied. Once these had been set off, they could render the port useless and the invasion would inevitably fail. Instead, British planners came up with an ingenious solution – the Allies would bring their own port. Two prefabricated 'Mulberry' harbours would be built in sections which would then be towed across the English Channel and assembled at the landing beaches. The Americans laughed when they first heard the idea, but began to take it very seriously when they realized that landing in an area that had no existing port would give the invasion force the element of surprise.

The Allies' plans were well advanced when, in November 1943, Hitler sent his most trusted and most able commander, Field Marshal Erwin Rommel, to take charge of the Atlantic Wall. Rommel found it wanting, especially in Normandy, and began strengthening it – for example, supervising the laying of more than four million mines in little more than four months. Then, with just a week to go before the Allied landings, the battle-hardened 352nd Infantry Division, direct from the Russian Front, was posted to man the defences along what was to become Omaha Beach.

Massive German gun emplacements positioned atop the Atlantikwall (Atlantic Wall), Hitler's first line of defence along the French coast.

Huge Force

DURING THE LATE spring of 1944, southern England had become one huge parking lot for tanks, trucks and aeroplanes. There were weapons and ammunition dumps in country lanes, and village pubs were full of soldiers from every part of the English-speaking world, along with Poles, Czechs, Hungarians, Free French and Jews from Germany, Austria and all parts of Nazi-occupied Europe. In all, more than six million people were involved in the D-Day landings. Twenty US divisions, fourteen British, three Canadian, one French and one Polish division were billeted in southern England, along with hundreds of thousands of other men who belonged to special forces, headquarters' units, communication staff and corps personnel. Then, suddenly, as this huge force made its way to the embarkation ports, silently at night, these men simply disappeared.

In the ports and waiting out to sea were 138 battleships, cruisers and destroyers that would bombard the French coast. They were accompanied by 279 escorts, 287 minesweepers, 4 line-layers, 4 submarines, 495 motor boats, 310 landing ships and 3,817 landing craft and barges for the initial assault. Another 410 landing craft would join them as part of the ferry service to get more personnel and equipment ashore after the beachhead had been secured. A further 423 ships, including tugs, would be involved in the construction of the Mulberry harbours and the laying of the PLUTO (Petroleum Line under the Ocean) pipeline, which would pump petrol under the Channel, and the telephone cables that would connect the commanders on the ground to SHAEF (Supreme Headquarters, Allied Expeditionary Force) in London. Another 1,260 merchant ships would also be involved in supplying the landing force, making a total of more than 7,000 vessels.

Some 10,000 aircraft were also deployed in Operation Overlord. They would bomb key fortifications, drop paratroopers, tow gliders carrying airborne troops, attack enemy formations and protect the airspace above the beaches.

The head of the invasion force had to be an American for political reasons, and Churchill got along with General Eisenhower. who had demonstrated his competence as a commander in Operation Torch and during the landings on Sicily and Italy. Under him, however, actually running the landings, there would be four British officers – Eisenhower's deputy Air Marshal Sir Arthur Tedder; Admiral Sir Bertram Ramsay, commanding the operation at sea; Air Chief Marshal Sir Trafford Leigh-Mallory in the air; and on the ground General (later Field Marshal) Bernard Montgomery. This caused some resentment among American officers, who felt that they should have been represented at the high levels of command. However, one of the reasons Eisenhower had been picked as overall commander was the skill that he had already shown in handling the rivalries between the British and the Americans.

When Montgomery was appointed on New Year's Day 1944, the first thing he did was to throw away the invasion plans American planners had been working on since 1942. He considered that the front in the US plan was too narrow and that the assault force was not big enough to do the job. He upped the number of divisions landing on the beaches

Allied Supreme Commander of Operation Overlord General Eisenhower, accompanied by British officers, addresses men of the 101st Airborne Division, the 'Screaming Eagles', on the eve of D-Day. These paratroopers were to be the first Americans to set foot in Nazi-occupied France on 6 June 1944.

from three to five, and the number of airborne divisions from one to three. Montgomery presented his plan to the military commanders and senior politicians at St Paul's School in West Kensington, London, on 15 May 1944. It was accepted. A key part of the plan was that, on D-Day itself, equal numbers of British and US troops would be landed. But, as losses mounted, the battle-ravaged British would be unable to sustain this commitment, while the United States had an almost bottomless well of recruits. Eventually, the war in western Europe would become a predominantly American affair. To reflect this, Eisenhower himself would take over command of the land forces once the beachhead was well established.

Air Superiority

D-DAY WAS TO BE 5 June 1944. By that time, the Allies had exerted complete air superiority over France, and the bombing campaign had

A US soldier takes up position by the body of a dead German soldier in Normandy, July 1944. Behind him is a Waco glider, used to land reinforcements in the weeks following D-Day.

softened up the enemy. Much of the bombing was directed against the railways to prevent men, weapons and ammunition being brought to the front. Bombing and sabotage by the French Resistance had knocked out 1,500 of the 2,000 locomotives available. Eighteen of the twenty-four bridges over the Seine between Paris and the sea had been destroyed, along with most of those over the river Loire. Marshalling yards, crossings and other vital parts of the French railway system had been attacked, and bombs and rockets had knocked out nearly all the radar stations along the northern coast of France.

As 5 June approached, the fine, sunny days that had lasted throughout May came to an end. The defenders along the Atlantic Wall, who had been kept on constant alert by false alarms for months, began to believe that the Allies had missed their chance. Rommel himself took the opportunity to go back to Germany to see his wife on her birthday. On the following day, 6 June, he was to have a meeting with Hitler.

The Allied first-wave troops had already embarked on 4 June when the weather worsened and a storm blew up. Eisenhower had no option but to postpone the invasion.

That night, however, the meteorologists thought there might be a break in the weather the next day, and Eisenhower gave the order for the invasion fleet to sail. Navy minesweepers had swept broad lanes across the Channel and, as the invasion fleet headed out to sea, huge waves of RAF heavy bombers flew overhead to blast the coastal defences with 5,200 tonnes of bombs. As dawn broke on 6 June, the USAAF's medium bombers and fighters took over and continued the pounding of the emplacements behind the invasion beaches.

Under Montgomery's plan, the United States had two landing beaches: Utah at the base of the Cotentin peninsula and Omaha further to the east along the Calvados coast. The three British beaches – Gold, Juno and Sword – lay to the east of that. The two fronts were each about 30 km (20 miles) long. During the night, between midnight and 0300, one British and two American airborne divisions landed on what Hitler called *Festung Europa* – Fortress Europe – behind the Atlantic Wall. The British 6th Airborne Division landed east of Caen to seize vital bridges across the river Orne, to prevent the Panzers that were stationed to the east attacking the landing force's left flank, while the American 82nd and 101st Airborne dropped at the base of the Cotentin peninsula, to prevent troops stationed in Cherbourg from counterattacking. They were also to secure the causeways across the flooded areas behind the invasion beaches.

The paratroopers had been carried across the Channel on 1,100 planes from twenty different airfields. The British paratroopers were dropped too far east, but they caught the enemy by surprise, took the village of Ranville and secured the landing zones for the gliders

carrying more men and anti-tank guns that would arrive two hours later. These dropped close to the bridges and seized all but one of their objectives – the bridge at Troarn which carried the main road from Caen to Le Havre and Rouen. A team under Major Rosveare grabbed some explosives, commandeered a jeep, drove hell-for-leather for the bridge and blew it up. Meanwhile, 150 British paratroopers attacked the coastal battery at Merville, whose guns covered Sword beach. After hand-to-hand fighting which cost half their number, the paras took it and destroyed its guns.

British commandos advance into Normandy on D-Day, 6 June 1944.

First Town Liberated

THE AMERICAN AIRBORNE landings fared less well. Heavy flak and clouds caused the transports to disperse. The pilots flew too high and

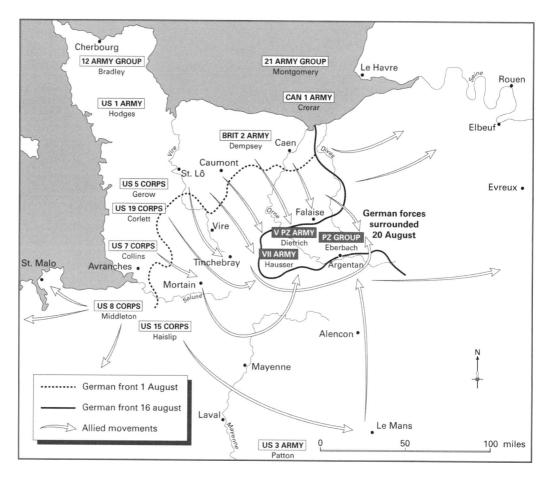

The destruction of the German troops in the Falaise Pocket, August 1944.

Cherbourg

12 ARMY GROUP
Bradley

21 ARMY GROUP
Montgomery

Le Havre

Seine

Rouen

US 1 ARMY
Hodges

CAN 1 ARMY
Crerar

Elbeuf

BRIT 2 ARMY
Dempsey

Caen

Dives

Vire

Caumont

St. Lô

Evreux

US 5 CORPS
Gerow

US 19 CORPS
Corlett

Orne

Falaise

**German forces
surrounded
20 August**

Vire

V PZ ARMY
Dietrich

PZ GROUP
Eberbach

US 7 CORPS
Collins

VII ARMY
Hausser

St. Malo

Avranches

Tinchebray

Argentan

Mortain

Seline

US 8 CORPS
Middleton

US 15 CORPS
Haislip

Alencon

N

Mayenne

German front 1 August

German front 16 august

Allied movements

Laval

Mayenne

Le Mans

0   50   100 miles

US 3 ARMY
Patton

too fast, scattering the paratroopers of the 101st Airborne over 970 sq km (375 square miles). Of 6,100 men dropped, only 1,000 made it to their rendezvous point. The 82nd had better luck and managed to capture St Mère Église on the road from Cherbourg. It was the first town in France to be liberated and, by dawn, the Stars and Stripes hung outside the town hall where the Nazi swastika had hung for four years. The American gliders also had a bad time. Only twenty-two of the fifty-two gliders landed in the drop zones, and most were badly damaged on

impact. This left the airborne troops short of transport, signals equipment and anti-tank guns, which made it impossible for them to capture the bridges across the river Merderet. The paratroops who were cut off west of the Merderet found they had been dropped into a region bristling with German strongpoints. They were so widely dispersed that all their efforts went into survival rather than securing their objectives. But although they did not take the bridges, they fully engaged the German 91st Division where it stood, and it made no move against the beaches.

Throughout the night, German headquarters received sporadic reports of paratroopers landing; however, the troops and the French Resistance set about cutting the telephone wires so that it was impossible for anyone in command to get a clear picture of what was going on. At 0245, General von Rundstedt's headquarters received a report saying, 'Engine noise audible from the sea on east coast of Cotentin.' This was dismissed, and the Germans became aware of the impending invasion only when the landing craft were 20 km (12 miles) off shore. Even then, it was thought to be a diversionary attack to draw the German defenders away from the Pas de Calais where the real invasion would come.

At first light, a combined Allied fleet of 200 warships began bombarding the Normandy coast. Then the landing craft started their run in. The seas were heavy and most of the men, who had been fed a hearty breakfast, were seasick. To add to their misery, they were soon soaked to the skin from the spray as waves broke over the front of the landing craft. A piper played a highland reel in the front of one of the British landing craft. In another Major C.K. 'Banger' King, of the East Yorkshire Regiment, read stirring extracts from Shakespeare's *Henry V* over the Tannoy. In front of the landing craft that carried the troops was a line of amphibious tanks. Behind, craft carrying the artillery and multiple rocket launchers opened up. The German fortifications had been built to withstand bombing and naval gunfire. Although the occupants were dazed from the bombardment, most of the emplacements were still intact and ready to mow down the infantry as they came rushing from their landing craft. But they did not expect artillery fire from the landing craft as they ran in, or to be confronted with amphibious DD (Duplex Drive) tanks trundling up the beaches ahead of the troops.

There were more surprises. Crabs, modified Sherman tanks with huge revolving drums of flailing chains mounted on the front, landed to clear minefields; AVREs (Assault Vehicle Royal Engineers) carried bridges or bundles of logs to breach walls or fill in ditches; perhaps most terrifying were the Crocodiles, Churchill tanks fitted with flame-throwers to clear out machine-gun nests. The whole idea of the Atlantic Wall was to destroy the invaders before they had a chance to get off the beaches. This would prove impossible.

Push Inland

MONTGOMERY'S PLAN WAS for the British to engage the German Panzers around Caen, hold them there and destroy them, while the Americans cleared the Cotentin peninsula. Once they had taken Cherbourg, the Allies could build up their strength and break out of the beachhead to the south. Key to this was for the British 1st Corps, which landed on Sword and Juno beaches, to join up with the 6th Airborne on the Orne. The British 3rd Division landing on Sword beach, near the mouth of the Orne, took less than an hour to secure the beach and push inland. They had travelled nearly 3.5 km (2 miles) from the shore when they were stopped by the infantry and the 88mm self-propelled guns of the 21st Panzers. This took the British troops by surprise. They had been trained extensively for fighting on the beaches, where many of them had expected to die. Once they had

US Landing Ship Tanks deliver troops and tanks to Omaha Beach, scene of the most ferocious fighting on D-Day. Barrage balloons protect the ships from enemy air strikes.

survived that, they were not quite sure what to do, and it took eight hours before they linked up with the 6th Airborne.

To the west of the British sector, the 50th Division – which had seen action in North Africa – and the 8th Armoured Brigade fought their way through the enemy defences within an hour. By 1200, the beachhead was 5 km (3 miles) wide and 4 km (2½ miles) deep. And by sunset, the British infantry and armour, supported by further naval barrages, had cleared the beaches around Arromanches, the site of one of the Mulberry harbours. With that, word was sent for the harbour's huge caissons to begin their journey across the Channel. And by the time it was dark, British patrols had reached the outskirts of the historic town of Bayeux, and the 50th Division's beachhead was 10 km (6 miles) wide and 10 km deep.

The Canadians who landed on Juno beach, which lay between Sword and Gold, had a harder time as their landing zone was obstructed by a reef which delayed their landing by half an hour. The amphibious tanks and obstacle-clearing tanks that should have gone ashore ahead of the infantry were held back. But when the tanks finally came ashore, it still took the Canadians several hours to overcome the enemy strongpoints at the mouth of the Seulles. Then they found that they did not have the specialized armour they needed to clear the beach exits, and men and vehicles backed up on the sands.

Probing

TO THE EAST of Juno, the lack of tanks meant the Canadians took heavy casualties in the 90-m (100-yard) dash to the shelter of the sea wall. But then a ship almost beached herself to blast the German defences, and the Canadians began to stream off the beach. By nightfall, they had taken the town of Bernières and had travelled 11 km (7 miles) inland – the furthest any of the Allied forces had reached

on the first day. They were probing the main Bayeaux–Caen road within 5 km (3 miles) of Caen and joined up with the British 50th Division, giving a joined Anglo-Canadian beachhead about 20 km (12 miles) long and almost 11 km (7 miles) deep.

On Utah Beach, to the west of the American section, thirty-two amphibious tanks went in under a huge bombardment by two battleships, two cruisers and twelve destroyers. Twenty-eight of the tanks made it the 3.5 km (2 miles) to shore. When the first wave of infantry hit the beaches, they found that, as they covered the 460 m (500 yards) to the foreshore, they were met by only occasional gunfire. This sector had been lightly defended because the area behind it was flooded and no attack had been expected there. The 4th Infantry Division had actually landed on the wrong beach. But within three hours it had cleared avenues through the beach obstacles and minefields, and its tanks rushed forward to seize the causeways over the flooded areas.

By contrast, the landings on Omaha Beach were little short of a disaster. The beach itself was far from ideal. The 275 m (300 yards) of sandy foreshore was backed by a steep bank of shingle. Behind that was a sea wall or sand dunes. Beyond was a 45-m (150-ft) plateau with defensive positions along the top. Four ravines cut the face of the plateau. These were the only beach exits, and they were well defended. And at either end of the plateau there were 30-m (100-ft) cliffs. Although the beach was unsuitable for an amphibious assault, it was chosen because the Allies had to take a beach between Gold and Utah if a single beachhead was to be established. To make matters worse, this was where the battle-hardened 352nd Infantry Division had been stationed. Allied High Command knew this, but the US troops, who were new to combat, were not told in case it sapped their morale.

Omaha was more exposed than Utah, and only four of the amphibious tanks made it the 6.5 km (4 miles) to shore without being swamped. Poor visibility meant that the initial bombardment had failed to neutralize the enemy's defences, and the rockets from the multiple rocket launchers that followed the infantry in landed harmlessly in the shallows.

When the landing craft hit the beaches and their ramps were dropped, the troops rushing out were met with a withering fire. Soon the sea was choked with blood and dead bodies. Those who survived did so by hiding behind beach obstacles that the engineers were supposed to blow up. The second wave of troops met a similar fate, apart from a small section who had managed to land on a part of the beach that was now wreathed in smoke. Nearly a whole infantry company, which had been blown to the east of its designated landing zone, managed to reach the sea wall and pick their way through the minefield behind. Strengthened by a formation of Rangers following behind, they made it up on to the plateau in time to prevent a counterattack on the beach. Even further to the east, two battalions had made it ashore under the cover of heavy smoke from undergrowth and a building set on fire by the naval bombardment. They made their way off the beach before German artillery got the range of those who followed them.

Pinned Down

THE MAIN FORCE found themselves pinned down behind the shingle bank, subjected to murderous machine-gun and artillery fire. Colonel G.A. Tayler rallied his regiment. 'Two kinds of people stay on this beach,' he told them, 'the dead and those who are going to die.' Some brave men then picked themselves up and attacked the German defences. Others scaled the cliffs to the left and moved off to join up with the British.

Even so, General Clarence R. Huebner, commanding officer of the 1st Infantry

Division, realized something drastic had to be done. He called in another naval bombardment on the German fortifications, despite the risk of hitting his own men. The destroyers sailed so close to the shore that they were hit by rifle fire, but they did their job so effectively that the Germans came out with their hands up. But it was not until 1900 that the paths through the minefields had been cleared and obstacles blown up or bulldozed aside so that the armour could leave the beaches. It advanced on the fortified villages behind.

By dusk, the Omaha beachhead was only 1,100 m (1,200) yards deep. Beyond it the enemy was massing for a counterattack. But instead of pushing the Americans back into the sea at Omaha, the Germans rushed all their armour towards what they considered a greater threat – the British and Canadians advancing on Caen. The mobile defence forces were sent against the British at Bayeux. One battalion of the 352nd Infantry Division was sent to deal with the American paratroops in Cotentin, while another was sent against the British, leaving only one battalion to check the Americans pouring off Omaha.

The following morning, the British from Gold turned eastwards to join up with the Canadians from Juno. Towards evening, they had cleared the remaining strongpoints between them, and the British beaches now formed one continuous beachhead. However, the move on Caen had stalled. The landscape of northern Normandy is known as *bocage* country. This is characterized by small fields separated by thick hedges on high banks and sunken roads. It is easy terrain to defend. Hundreds of German tanks and 88mm guns were dug in and camouflaged, and the Allied

forces had to fight their way hedgerow by hedgerow through this country. However, the Allies' bombers, fighters and accurate naval gunnery support – which were able to lob shells 26 km (16 miles) inshore – made it difficult for the Germans to line up into the formations necessary to stage a concerted counterattack. The best the defenders could do was slow the Allied advance, never halt it entirely or turn it back.

The 260 tanks of the Panzer Lehr Division, formed from various units of the German Army training and demonstration units – otherwise known as Lehr or teaching units, hence the name – which tank warfare expert Colonel General 'Fast Heinz' Guderian boasted would 'throw the Anglo-Americans into the sea', were beaten back by air assaults. On D+1 (i.e. the day after D-Day), an SS Division was sent to the front. But it simply

On 27 June 1944, Cherbourg finally fell to the Americans after days of fighting. Royal Navy frogmen were then called in to clear demolition charges from the harbour, while US flags were flown at the town hall to celebrate the Allies' victory.

disintegrated under air attacks using bombs and rockets, and its men ended up hiding in the woods until dark. The Allied planes did not even have to wait until the enemy reached the battlefield before engaging them. They would attack the remaining trains bringing them to the front up to 50 km (30 miles) away.

On D+1 the American airborne troops had begun to form themselves into a coherent fighting force. But the 16 km (10 miles) between Utah and Omaha beaches were still held by the enemy. However, with the help of RAF Typhoons and naval bombardment, Royal Marines from Gold beach had taken the small fishing port of Pont-en-Bessin halfway between Gold and Omaha's left flank, and the following day forces from the British and American beaches linked up.

Bloody Battles

MONTGOMERY KEPT UP the pressure on Caen, often in bloody battles designed to keep the enemy off balance. They were costly in British casualties, but forced the Germans to use their tanks as dug-in artillery and took the pressure off the Americans. The 160 British troops who took the key village of Breville suffered 141 casualties. Once it was taken, though, the eastern end of the beachhead was secure. After fierce fighting, US troops took Carentan on 12 June, and the Omaha and Utah beachheads were finally joined, giving the Allies one huge enclave along the Normandy coast 100 km (60 miles) long and 25 km (15 miles) deep. The German front in the west began to crumble. An American thrust across the Cotentin peninsula to Barneville on the Atlantic coast

cut off Cherbourg. Another push created a 32-km (20-mile) salient to the south.

By D+12, there were 50,000 men ashore. With twenty divisions now in Normandy, the Allies had managed to build up their forces faster than the Germans. The destruction of railways and bridges and constant air attacks – by then from planes flying from airstrips inside the beachhead – made it impossible for Rommel to bring battle-ready formations into the area. Divisions had to be broken up and travel at night, with the infantry often on foot or on bicycle. Tanks could not be massed for a large assault on the beachhead and were used piecemeal to plug the line. Two SS Panzer Divisions brought from the Eastern Front were devastated long before they reached the battlefield.

On 19 June, however, disaster almost overtook the Allies when the worst storm for nearly fifty years blew up in the Channel. Over three days and three nights, a dozen ships out to sea were sunk, and 800 vessels were driven ashore. The Mulberry harbour at Arromanches was badly damaged, but still usable. The one off Omaha beach was smashed to pieces. Suddenly, the Allies were short of supplies and ammunition, and robbed of their air cover. It was the perfect opportunity for Rommel to counterattack. But his forces were deployed for defence and were in no position to seize their last chance to push the Allies back into the sea.

Once the storm broke, the amphibious trucks used during the beach assaults were employed to ferry supplies ashore. By the end of the month, the daily tonnage landing was back to pre-storm levels. Bits of the Mulberry harbour at Omaha were salvaged and used to patch up the one at Arromanches. Within two

weeks, 700 out of the 800 ships beached were repaired and refloated, and, by 27 June, the port of Cherbourg was in American hands, although it had been so badly damaged and booby-trapped that it could not be used for several weeks.

The British had planned an attack on Caen on 19 June. This had been delayed and was finally launched on 26 June. With massive artillery support, the British managed to take the key highpoint Hill 112 to the south of Caen. The following day there was a massive armoured counterattack which employed both the remnants of the SS divisions brought in from Russia and a Panzer division that had been brought up from the south of France.

Despite heavy losses, Montgomery had to keep up the pressure on Caen to allow Patton and Bradley to break out of the other end of the beachhead.

A company of 'Le Régiment de Maisonneuve' march through Bons-Tassilly up to the Falaise front. They landed in Normandy with the 5th Brigade of the 2nd Canadian Division, 7 July 1944.

These formations came under withering air attack from the RAF's rocket-firing Typhoons. As the German tanks advanced through the *bocage* country, they were vulnerable to the British Piat anti-tank weapon that could be fired at close range from behind the hedgerows. Both sides threw everything they had into the fray. A five-day battle raged over Hill 112, and the fighting became so intense that the little river Odon was dammed with human bodies. The result was a stalemate, and the British did not completely overrun Hill 112 until 10 July.

It rained heavily throughout July. The fighting became – literally – bogged down, and both sides feared that the battle for Normandy

might turn into the kind of trench warfare and endless carnage seen in World War I. Public opinion in Britain and the United States became restive. Meanwhile, Hitler replaced his commander in the west Field Marshal Gerd von Rundstedt with Field Marshal Gunther von Kluge, fresh from the Russian Front.

At the cost of 11,000 casualties, US troops had crossed the fields and marshes of western Normandy to take the smouldering ruins of St-Lô. This stood at the head of a good road that ran south to the Loire Valley. A plan code-named Operation Cobra was hatched to make a break-out here with a fast-moving tank column under General Patton. To pull this off, Montgomery would need to keep the German tanks pinned down to the east. The Canadians attacked the airfield at Carpiquet, suffering grievous casualties. The British then launched a renewed onslaught on Caen, after the RAF had dropped 2,500 tonnes of bombs on it. After two days of fierce fighting, the British took the north-western part of the city, above the River Orne. A renewed attack from Hill 112 cost the British 3,500 casualties.

Montgomery planned to keep up the pressure with Operation Goodwood, a massive attack against prepared positions to the east and south of Caen. On the eve of the battle, Rommel was machine-gunned in his staff car by an RAF fighter. He took no further part in the fighting and committed suicide while convalescing after being implicated in the July plot to kill Hitler.

On the first day of Goodwood, the British lost 1,500 men and 200 tanks, and failed to make a breakthrough, although Montgomery kept up the pressure for three days before the offensive was halted by a thunderstorm.

Goodwood had one unexpected effect. It finally convinced Hitler that there was going to be no attack on the Pas de Calais – the Normandy landings were the real thing, and he ordered the 250,000 men of his Fifteenth Army into the battle. The devastation caused by Allied air attacks meant that it took them a month to reach Normandy. By that time, the Allies had 1,000,000 men ashore, and the Fifteenth Army proved to be too little too late.

Montgomery took a great deal of criticism for the failure of Operation Goodwood. But, as Field Marshal Brooke pointed out, not only had it drawn in most of the German armour as planned, but it had also destroyed it faster than it could be replaced. General Omar Bradley, now commanding the US forces in Normandy, also appreciated the strategy. It had allowed him to get his men in position for a break-out.

Patton had landed on Utah beach on 6 July without even getting his feet wet and, from a well-camouflaged bivouac on the Cotentin peninsula, he began to assemble his Third Army. With the Fifteenth Army on its way to the east of the front, Hitler felt that it was safe to move seven of his divisions, including two Panzer divisions, to the west, bringing the number there up to sixty-five. This strength-ened the German line against any US break-out; it also lured them into a death trap. On 25 July, 3,000 USAAF bombers dropped 4,000 tonnes of high-explosive, fragmentation and napalm bombs on an 8-km (5-mile) stretch of the German front to the west of St-Lô. The German commander General Bayerlein claimed that this raid turned the area into a *Mondlandshaft* – a moonscape. He estimated that 70 per cent of the German troops in that section were put out of action – either dead,

Opposite: Greeting the liberators – American GIs receive a warm welcome from Paris residents as they liberate the city, August 1944.

wounded or demented. Patton's troops slowly moved forward through the *bocage* country – what the GIs called the 'Gethsemane of the hedgerows'. By 27 July, Coutances was taken; by 30 July, Avranches. The German retreat had turned into a rout. Within twenty-four hours, Patton pushed three divisions through the 8-km (5-mile) gap that had opened at Avranches. His men were now out of the *bocage* country and on the open roads of Brittany.

Montgomery was still making slow progress in the east and turned his troops to the south with the Canadians advancing on Falaise. Bradley sent Patton and his Third Army on a long sweep south, then east, to encircle the Germans. Hitler saw the danger too late. He had ordered Kluge to switch four armoured divisions from the British front to attack the Americans, but Kluge could not disengage them until 7 August. Hitler planned a counterattack against the bottle-neck at Avranches, closing the gap there and cutting off Patton's supply lines. Hitler, however, was 1,300 km (800 miles) away in his headquarters, the Wolf's Lair, in East Prussia. His commanders on the ground in Normandy were against the attack. They knew that the battle of Normandy was lost, and that they should make an orderly retreat across the river Seine.

Hitler threw in four divisions of the Fifteenth Army, fresh from the Pas de Calais. Allied bombers cut off the German retreat by bombing the remaining bridges along the Seine. Meanwhile, Patton was making quick time across the open roads of northwest France, taking Le Mans on 8 August. To the north, on their way to Avranches, five Panzer and two infantry divisions ran into a single

American division at Mortain, which managed to hold them until other Allied units came to its aid. Powerful US formations struck back through Vire, while the British pushed from the north against Condé and Patton turned north closing the trap. The Germans were now caught in a small pocket between Mortain and Falaise, where the Allied air forces relentlessly bombed and strafed them. By 14 August, the only way out was through a 30-km (18-mile) gap between the Canadians at Falaise and Patton's Third Army. Patton wanted to drive on to Falaise and close the gap but, by then, his speeding army had lost its coherence and Bradley ordered him to stop. By this time, German units were being cut down by the French Resistance or surrendering wholesale to Allied forces. Kluge became lost in the confusion. Soon after he reappeared he was relieved of his command, and committed suicide. By 17 August, the Falaise gap was down to 18 km (11 miles) and the German forces were streaming eastwards through it. By 18 August, it was squeezed to 10 km (6 miles), and air attacks on it were so relentless that any attempt to get through it resulted in almost certain death. It was sealed on 20 August.

Eisenhower said later of the battle:

The battlefield at Falaise was unquestionably one of the greatest killing grounds of any of the war areas. Roads, highways and fields were so choked with destroyed equipment and with dead men and animals that passage through the area was extremely difficult. Forty-eight hours after the closing of the gap, I was conducted through on foot, to encounter a scene that could be described only by

Aux barricades!
The Paris uprising begins, 19 August 1944.

Dante. It was quite literally possible to walk for hundreds of yards at a time, stepping on nothing but dead and decaying flesh.

Some 10,000 Germans were killed in six days in the Falaise Pocket, and 50,000 prisoners were taken. Of the 20,000 to 50,000 who escaped, many more were killed before they reached the Seine. Thousands more who were cut off elsewhere gave themselves up. Two Panzer divisions and eight divisions of infantry were captured almost complete. In all, German casualties in Normandy amounted to 400,000 men, half of whom were captured. Allied casualties totalled 209,672 men, of whom 36,976 were killed.

The Germans also lost 1,300 tanks, 1,500 guns and 20,000 vehicles. What remained of the German army in western Europe ran headlong for the German border. On 25 August 1944, Paris was liberated.

Operation Market Garden

ON 1 SEPTEMBER 1944, Montgomery formally relinquished command of the Allied forces in France to Eisenhower. And while US forces dashed across France and Belgium towards the German border, Montgomery and his 21st Army Group headed north-eastwards to clear the V1 and V2 sites which were raining down flying bombs and ballistic missiles on London, liberate the port of Antwerp and drive into northern Germany.

Usually chided for his caution, Montgomery now planned a bold move. He wanted to use airborne troops to capture five bridges on the road from Eindhoven to Arnhem. He would then drive his Second Army down this corridor across the Netherlands through the German border defences and into the Ruhr, Germany's industrial heartland. The airborne part of the operation was code-named Market and the infantry and armoured part Garden. So the combined operation became known as Operation Market Garden.

The operation was to be mounted within a week. Although he gave the go-ahead, Eisenhower had misgivings. So did Lieutenant General Frederick Browning, deputy commander of the First Allied Airborne Army. In a planning meeting, he asked how long it would take for the Second Army to relieve the airborne troops holding the last bridge, the bridge at Arnhem. Montgomery said, 'Two days.' Browning studied the map and replied, 'Sir, I think we might be going a bridge too far.'

Five thousand aircraft were assembled for what would be the largest-ever airborne operation. Three divisions – the British 1st Airborne and the US 82nd and 101st Airborne, plus the 1st Polish Parachute Brigade – would be dropped over three days, as there were not enough planes to drop them in one go. The 101st Airborne would land around Eindhoven at the southern end of the corridor. The 82nd would take the central section around Nijmegen. The 'Red Devils' of the 1st Airborne and the Poles, under Major General Robert Urquhart, would take the final section at Arnhem. They would have the longest to hold out and, until the Second Army reached them, they would be on their own.

Aerial reconnaissance photographs and reports from the Dutch Resistance indicated that there were Panzers in the area of Arnhem, but the 1st Airborne were briefed to expect weak opposition from second-rate troops. The plan called for the 1st Airborne to take the defenders by surprise by being dropped near the bridge in close formation. But the pilots refused to fly slow, straight and level near the bridge, believing that it was defended by anti-aircraft batteries. Instead, the Red Devils would have to land on areas of open ground to the west, losing them the element of surprise.

Combat-hardened

THE HUGE FLEET of aeroplanes and gliders set off on the morning of 17 September. The landings in the early afternoon went well. However, the 1st Airborne soon found that the bunch of

old men and boys that they had been told they would be up against were actually two combat-hardened divisions of Panzers and a Panzergrenadier battalion armed with the new multi-barrelled, rocket-propelled mortars. But the 1st Airlanding Brigade fought off a German counterattack and held the landing zone, while the 1st Parachute Brigade set out for the bridge. Its progress was hampered by Dutch civilians, who treated them as liberators and wanted to ply the men with drinks and food, and the other spoils of victory. Later, they discovered that their radio sets were not working.

The 1st and 3rd battalions were stopped by heavy enemy fire on the main road, but the 2nd Battalion under Lieutenant Colonel John Frost advanced quickly along a secondary road alongside the river. The Germans had blown up a railway bridge before they could get to it, and a pontoon bridge upstream proved to be unusable. But the main road bridge, their objective, was still standing. As night fell, Frost and his men occupied houses overlooking the bridge's long northern approach ramp.

An attempt to take the bridge was repulsed by the Panzergrenadiers. However, Frost's men prevented the commander of Second SS Panzer Corps, under Lieutenant General Wilhelm Bittrich, sending one of his divisions across it to fight off the Allied attack at Nijemegen. Instead, Bittrich tried to get his tanks across the river using a ferry upstream – a slow business – and sent his remaining troops to take the bridge. A fierce gun battle broke out between the SS troops and the paratroopers, who managed to destroy a column of twenty-two half-tracks and scout cars that tried to cross the bridge from the south. The Germans brought down artillery fire on Frost's position at the north end of the bridge. Soon the houses there were on fire, and the cellars beneath were full of dead and wounded.

Unable to contact his men by radio, Major General Urquhart left his divisional headquarters in the drop zone. He grabbed a jeep and went to try to find out what was going on. Eventually he caught up with his deputy, Brigadier General Gerald Lathbury, commander of the 1st Parachute Brigade, who was advancing with the 3rd Battalion. It was then that fierce street fighting broke out. Lathbury was injured in the leg and was taken prisoner, while Urquhart had to hide in an attic overnight until he could make it back to British positions. He then discovered that divisional headquarters had been moved to the Hartenstein Hotel in Oosterbeek, 5 km (3 miles) west of Arnhem, and headed there. On the way his jeep was fired upon. When he arrived, he learned that, in his absence, he had been reported captured.

During the time he had been missing, the second wave of airborne troops had been delayed by bad weather, and the Germans had found a copy of the plan for Operation Market Garden in a crashed glider at Nijmegen. They organized a rough reception for the rest of the 1st Airborne when it arrived at 1600 on 18 September.

Urquhart's forces on the ground were scattered and had only rifles, grenades and Sten guns to hold off Tiger and Panther tanks, and self-propelled assault guns. However, the 2nd Battalion was still holding on north of the bridge, although it was taking severe losses. If Market Garden had been going to plan, the Second Army should have been nearing the bridge by them. But there was no sign of them.

Terrible Punishment

ON 19 SEPTEMBER, a renewed effort was made to join up with the 2nd Battalion, but this was halted a mile from the bridge by German reinforcements. The weather intervened again. Most of the 1st Polish Parachute Brigade was delayed. The glider force got through, though, but it landed in the middle of the battle zone and was caught in the crossfire. With the drop zones now in German hands, Urquhart radioed for supplies to be dropped near his headquarters at the Hartenstein Hotel. But the radio was still not working properly, and the message did not get through. Of the 390 tonnes of food, medical supplies and ammunition dropped by the RAF, only thirty-one tonnes arrived in Allied hands.

By nightfall on 19 September, the Second Army had broken through and British tanks were only 16 km (10 miles) away, down the road they were now calling 'Hell's Highway'. But the 1st Airborne was taking terrible punishment, and Urquhart took the reluctant decision to pull his scattered forces back into a box around the Hartenstein Hotel, leaving Frost's 2nd Battalion to fend for itself. Even in this defensive position his lines were only thinly defended, and the crossroads at Oosterbeek

The failure to take Arnhem left thousands of British and Canadians in German hands. More than 6,642 were listed as missing, captured or wounded, while 1,200 lay dead.

British, Polish and Canadian paratroopers descend from the sky during Operation Market Garden. Arnhem was the one huge failure of an airborne assault during World War II.

came under such intensive fire that the 1st Airborne called it the 'Cauldron'.

By the evening of the 20th, the Second Army had still not arrived. Colonel Frost was wounded. Ammunition was running low, and he realized that their three-day stand was coming to a close. That night, they were over-run. At dawn on 21 September, Bittrich's Panzers crossed the bridge and went to confront the Second Army. Later that day, the Polish paratroopers were dropped at Driel, south of the river, straight on top of the Germans. Those who escaped headed for a small ferry across the river. When they got there they found it was not working. Some 200 swam across the river to joint Urquhart, while the remainder dug in on the south bank.

Early on the morning of 22 September, a detachment of armoured cars from the Second Army reached Driel and made contact with the 1st Airborne across the river. Over the next two days, the British infantry came up, but the situation for Urquhart's men on the north bank was deteriorating. Their stores were running low, and attempts to resupply them had failed. The 4th Battalion of the Dorset Regiment tried to cross the river, but failed. Eventually, at 0600 on 25 September, Urquhart was ordered to withdraw. That night, with muffled boots, they slipped down to the Rhine, where a few boats waited to ferry them across.

No one had expected so many men to escape, and there was insufficient transport to carry them to the rear. So Urquhart's men, exhausted by eight days of fighting, had to march the 18 km (11 miles) to the Second Army's main position at Nijmegen. They left behind 1,200 dead, 6,642 wounded, captured or missing. The German casualties were 3,300, of whom a third were dead. The people of Arnhem also suffered. For greeting the British as liberators, the entire population of Arnhem was driven out of the town by the Germans. They were only able to return the following spring. When they did, they found that their homes had been reduced to rubble.

The Battle of the Bulge

THROUGHOUT THE SUMMER of 1944, the German army was on the retreat on all fronts. By then Germany was so weak that even Hitler realized that victory by force of arms was no longer within his grasp. But he thought that, if one decisive battle went in his favour, the situation might still be turned to Germany's advantage. A victory on the Eastern Front was out of the question as the Red

BATTLE OF THE BULGE: DECEMBER 1944–JANUARY 1945

.... Front line 16 December — — — Front line 20 December ——— Front line 25 December

Army was too strong. However, the failure of Operation Market Garden showed that the Western Allies with their overextended supply lines could still be halted, and he realized that they would be particularly vulnerable if he hit them between the advancing British and US armies. A decisive victory there might force the Allies to the negotiating table – and they

The Battle of the Bulge – Operation Herbstnebel – was Hitler's last-gasp assault on the Allies. It failed.

An abandoned Sherman tank ablaze in the Ardennes forest, during the Battle of the Bulge.

might even be persuaded to join their former enemy to take on Communist Russia together.

On 16 September, while listening to a situation report on the Western Front, Hitler suddenly announced, 'I shall go on the offensive … out of the Ardennes, with the objective, Antwerp.' An attack through the Ardennes had worked in 1940. As it fell between the British and American sectors, it was only lightly defended. A sweeping attack would sever the American's supply lines and cut off the British in Belgium and the Netherlands. The operation was called Wacht am Rhein – Watch on the Rhine – and it would put at risk twenty divisions. If it failed, there would be no stopping the Allies.

In the winter
of 1944, the
Germans' last-
ditch counter-
offensive in the
Ardennes cost
81,000 American
lives – along with
1,400 British and
10,000 German
lives. But the
counteroffensive
halted the Allied
advance by no
more than a
few weeks.

Caught: a captured Wehrmacht soldier identifies an SS prisoner as having taken part in the shooting of US prisoners in Malmedy, Belgium, during the Battle of the Bulge.

overwhelming number of men they could call on in 1940. It was the Americans who had the limitless numbers now. By the fourth day of the offensive, US reserves had doubled the number of men in the Ardennes to 180,000. But, running true to form, Hitler ignored what the professional soldiers told him and decided to go ahead. He was persuaded, however, to change the name of the operation from Wacht am Rhein to Herbstnebel (Autumn Fog) and delay the attack from 25 November to 10 December, then to 16 December to muster enough troops for the offensive.

Spearheading the break-out would be the Fifth Panzer Army under General Hasso von Manteuffel and the newly formed Sixth SS Panzer Army under Colonel General Joseph 'Sepp' Dietrich. They would be supported by the Seventh Army under General Erich Brandenberger. The Panzers would attack on a 145-km (90-mile) front from Echternach in the south to Monschau in the north. The Fifth Panzer Army would be on the left, the Sixth on the right, while the Seventh Army would protect the armour's southern flank.

To blunt any counteroffensive, Hitler sent a handpicked force of English-speaking troops behind the Allied lines carrying American weapons and wearing US uniforms. They would disrupt the Allied forces by misdirecting traffic and switching signposts. Their commander would be SS Colonel Otto Skorzeny, who had recently headed the daring raid to rescue Mussolini from his mountain prison, allowing Hitler to set the Italian dictator up in a new Fascist state in northern Italy.

Although Hitler was ill and exhausted, he switched his headquarters from the Wolf's Lair in East Prussia to the Eagle's Lair near Bad

Hitler and his closest aides planned the operation in secret. When Rundstedt, who had recently been reinstated as commander in the west, heard about it he was horrified. 'It was obvious to me that the available force was far too small for such an extremely ambitious plan,' he said after the war. 'It was a nonsensical operation, and the most stupid part of it was setting Antwerp as its goal. If we had reached the Meuse we should have got down on our knees and thanked God, let alone try to reach Antwerp.' Indeed, Rundstedt pleaded for a 'little solution' – an offensive that stopped at the Meuse.

Rundstedt had sent 2,500 tanks into France on the Blitzkrieg in 1940. Now, against far superior forces, Hitler planned to send just 1,420, which would have to supply their own fuel by capturing American gasoline on the way. The Germans had enjoyed air superiority in 1940. That was now lost. They had had 2,000 fighter-bombers back then. In 1944, they had just 1,000. And the Germans no longer had the

Neuheim in the Rhineland, where he would direct the battle personally. He had been there in Eagle's Lair in the 1940 when the German offensive had crushed the Allies in France. Those who accompanied him were increasingly of the opinion that he was rapidly losing touch with reality.

Sign of Hubris

IN NOVEMBER, while preparations were under way, the Allies had breached Germany's 'West Wall' frontier defences – the Siegfried Line – and had taken Aachen, the first German town of any size to fall to the Allies. However, the Allies were beginning to show signs of hubris. The front Hitler planned to hit was manned by just four divisions of the US 8th Corps, under Major General Troy Middleton. They were spread thinly. The 4th and 28th divisions had just been pulled out of the line to recuperate after heavy fighting, while the 9th Armoured and the 106th Division had never seen action before. On either side of the Ardennes front were the inexperienced and understrengthed First, Third and Ninth armies of General Omar Bradley's 12th US Army Group. This hardly seemed to matter, as Army Intelligence ruled out a German offensive in this area, despite the lesson of 1940.

No matter what they did, the Germans could not shift the US 101st Airborne Division from Bastogne, where they held out for six days. When asked to surrender, Brigadier General Anthony McAuliffe famously replied: 'Nuts!'

'1918? Never again,' the sign says. The Allies were afraid that the Germans would fight even harder once they were back on German soil. Instead, they fell apart, preferring to surrender to the British and Americans.

These men were about to be hit by three German armies, twenty-five divisions in all, eleven of them armoured.

Eisenhower was taken completely by surprise when, at 0535 on 16 December, 2,000 guns opened up in the Ardennes. The Germans attacked with a message from Rundstedt ringing in their ears. It read, 'Soldiers of the Westfront. Your great hour has arrived. Large attacking armies have started against the Anglo-Americans. I do not have to

tell you anything more than that. You feel it yourselves. We gamble everything. You carry the sacred obligation to give everything to achieve things beyond human possibilities for our Fatherland and our Führer.'

The offensive took place during a period of bad weather when the Allied air forces were grounded, and the Germans quickly developed a salient 80 km (50 miles) deep in the American lines. Churchill quickly dismissed this as the 'Battle of the Bulge', a title he had

divisions, reaching Celles, 10 km (6 miles) short of the river Meuse, where it was halted then the weather cleared and the Allied air forces took to the air again. Despite this initial success, the Fifth Panzers' supply route ran through the town of Bastogne, which was held by the 101st Airborne Division under Brigadier General Anthony McAuliffe. He found himself completely surrounded in what was called the 'hole in the doughnut'. When he was asked to surrender, he replied famously, 'Nuts!' The 101st held out for six days, supplied by air.

By 19 December, the offensive was stalled, but Hitler refused Rundstedt's suggestion that part of Dietrich's Fifth Panzers should be moved north to support Manteuffel's Sixth SS Panzers, who had done marginally better. Hitler wanted the SS to have all the glory. At a meeting at Verdun on the same day, Eisenhower told his generals, 'The present situation is to be regarded as one of opportunity for us and not disaster. There will be only cheerful faces at this conference table.' The outcome of the meeting was to shift Patton's Third Army 150 miles north to the left flank of the salient, while Montgomery, newly promoted to field marshal, would attack the northern side with some of Bradley's troops temporarily assigned to his command.

On 21 December, the Fifth Panzers took the town of St Vith, but Rundstedt felt the advance had run out of steam; on 22 December, he asked Hitler's permission to withdraw. It was refused. But on Christmas Day, Sixth Panzer Army suffered a crushing defeat, and the following day Bastogne was relieved, at the cost of 3,900 American dead and 12,000 Germans. The Americans lost 150 tanks in the action; the Germans 450.

first given to the 1940 Ardennes offensive. This time it stuck.

Skorzeny's troops in US uniforms went in first. They fooled no one, and most ended up facing a firing squad. Seventh Army was held up not far from their starting point, but the Panzers did better. The Sixth SS Panzers struck through what was called the 'Losheim Gap' and made significant gains, which they could not exploit due to lack of fuel. The Fifth Panzer Army swept through the 28th and 106th

German Atrocities

HITLER HAD NO CHOICE but to withdraw now as German atrocities had inspired the US troops to fight with renewed determination. In the advance guard of the German assault was Lieutenant General Jochen Peiper, commanding 140 tanks and a battalion of motorised infantry. At Honsfeld, his men shot nineteen GIs and robbed their dead bodies. At an airfield near Bullingen, Peiper forced captured Americans to refuel his tanks. Afterwards, he shot them. Eight more prisoners of war were killed at Lignueville. A hundred American prisoners were machine-gunned in Malmédy. Twenty Americans who miraculously escaped hid in a café. It was set on fire, and they were machine-gunned when they ran out. Hitler thought that news of these massacres would demoralize the American troops. In fact, it gave them a first-class incentive to fight back. By early January 1945, the front line was almost back where it had been before the Battle of the Bulge.

Hitler claimed that Herbstnebel had been worth it, but the autumn fog was dispersed by the crisp air of winter. The Germans had lost 10,000 men, the Americans 81,000 and the British, who played only a minor part in the action, 1,400. The Americans had also lost 733 tanks, while the Germans lost 600; an enormous number of guns and other equipment had been lost. The complete destruction of German cities by relentless bombing meant, however, that the Germans could not replace their equipment. The Allies could. All Hitler had bought with the loss of his final strategic reserve was six weeks to prepare the defences on the Rhine.

By the time the Allied forces reached the frontier of Germany, the total defeat of Hitler's Third Reich was only a matter of time. But, for the British and American forces, there was still one huge obstacle to overcome – the fast-flowing river Rhine that ran along much of Germany's western border.

The Crossing of the Rhine

IN THE EARLY weeks of March 1945, the US First and Ninth armies reached the Rhine, and a unit of the First Army, finding the railway bridge at Remagen only lightly defended, swept across on 7 March. On 22 March, Patton's Third Army established a bridgehead near Nierstein, ready for a drive across southern Germany. To the north, Montgomery's 21st Army Group had also reached the Rhine, and halted while the western bank was cleared. On the other side of the river were five divisions of Hitler's elite paratroopers, with one Panzer division and one Panzergrenadier division as a mobile reserve. They were a formidable force, and it was feared they would be highly motivated as they were now fighting for their home territory. And, after Arnhem, Montgomery had resumed his cautious demeanour. He was determined to cross the Rhine with the minimum loss of life for his men.

Montgomery planned an airborne assault called Operation Varsity, using the US 17th Airborne and the British 6th Airborne, and an amphibious assault called Operation Plunder, using the British Second Army and the US Ninth Army under his command. The airborne troops would seize the high ground on the other side of the river overlooking the crossing points to prevent the Germans

Opposite:
Triumphant American troops display a captured Nazi flag and a portrait of Hitler. Victory in Europe was now near.

deploying artillery there. To gain the element of surprise, he would reverse the usual order of things, with the airborne assault going in after the amphibious landings, rather than the other way around. First, bombers from the US 8th and 9th Air Forces would cut off the Ruhr on the other side of the river to prevent the Germans bringing up reinforcements, while 1,000 fighter-bombers of the 2nd Tactical Air Force would provide close air support.

At dawn on 24 March, the British Second Army crossed the Rhine. By that time, the British paratroopers had already left their bases in southern England. Meanwhile, the US troops, resting in Paris after the Battle of the Bulge, enplaned at seventeen bases around Rheims, Orléans, Evreux and Amiens. The two forces met up over Brussels. Between them they had 1,696 transport planes and 1,348 gliders carrying 21,700 men, 600 tonnes of ammunition and 800 guns and vehicles. And they were protected by a close escort of 889 fighters.

Airborne operations had been going on throughout the war, but there were still two schools of thought concerning tactics. The US forces liked to drop their airborne troops and release their gliders as low as possible to reduce the time they spent in the air, where they were particularly vulnerable. The British preferred to drop their airborne troops and release

The Americans and Soviets finally met up at Torgau on the Elbe. This effectively stopped the German armies defending Berlin.

Opposite: The US 17th Airborne Division descends near Wesel in the Duisburg area of Germany, during the Allied operations to secure the Rhine crossings.

Remagen Bridge over the Rhine, secured by units of the US First Army, 7 March 1945.

gliders high, to reduce the chances of the planes being hit by anti-aircraft fire. Both tactics worked in their fashion. The US suffered fewer casualties, but lost more planes. This was partly because they were using the Curtis C-46 Commando for the first time because it had two doors for the paratroopers to jump from, instead of the C-47 Dakota's one. But it also had a tendency to catch fire and was never used for paratroop drops again. However, flak suppression from the Allied artillery was so good that only forty-six transport planes and 3 per cent of the gliders were lost.

Both the British and American parachutists went in twenty minutes after the amphibious assault began. The British gliders followed three-quarters of an hour later; the American gliders forty-three minutes after that. The British 3rd Parachute Brigade landed on the

left, along the north of the village of Bergen. It came under heavy fire from anti-aircraft guns which were being used as ground support, but succeeded in taking the village of Schappenburg. The 5th Parachute Brigade suffered casualties during the drop. It landed near the woods on the Hammiklen–Rees road and rapidly moved on to take its objectives. The 6th Airlanding Brigade also sustained casualties in the air. It landed in open fields to the south of Hammiklen. Its objective was the village itself.

Although the US paratroopers were dropped lower, when they hit the ground they were more dispersed. Two battalions of the 507th landed in the drop zone between Diersfordterwald and the Rhine. The third battalion and the regimental headquarters, however, landed well to the north. They found themselves just short

of Diersfordt. A fierce firefight erupted, and the Germans put up stiff resistance for most of the day until, about 1500, they surrendered.

The 513th also landed north of its designated drop zone, and the men found themselves alongside the right-hand battalion of the 6th Airlanding Brigade and 13th Devons. Together they secured the British objective, Hammiklen village, before the 513th moved on to take its own objectives.

Crushed

DURING THE AIRBORNE operation, the British lost 347 killed and 731 wounded; the Americans 159 killed and 522 wounded.

A tank and German soldiers at Kursk. Once they were defeated, there was nothing the Germans could do to stop the Red Army pushing them all the way back to Berlin.

Russian T-34 tanks on the advance: General Heinz Guderian had warned Hitler before the war that Germany could never outstrip Soviet tank production.

Some 3,789 German prisoners were taken and the 84th Division practically annihilated. By dusk, the airborne troops had joined up with the Second Army's amphibious forces. German resistance, though initially stiff, was soon crushed, although the Allies took heavy casualties. Montgomery has been criticized for using such a great force to achieve so little. However, with the Allies now moving on to Germany's own soil, it was perhaps not unwise to think that the Germans might put up the fight of their lives.

By this time, though, most Germans wanted to see the Western Allies sweep through

Germany as quickly as possible, rather than let their country fall into Russian hands. Having suffered terribly at the hands of the Germans, the Soviets would doubtless be bent on revenge. And no one wanted to institute Hilter's scorched-earth policy in front of the advancing Allies.

On 25 March, the German Fifteenth Army containing the bridgehead at Remagen collapsed. The US First Army then broke through. The Third Army crossed the river Main at Aschaffenburg and Hanau. Then the First and Third armies used the autobahn system, which Hitler had built to move his troops, to race across southern Germany.

On 15 April 1945, near where the Rhine crossing had been made at Bergen, horrified British troops found a concentration camp: Bergen-Belsen. Between the villages of Bergen and Belsen, it had been designed for 10,000, but it then held 41,000 people. Although this was not an extermination camp – there were no gas chambers there – some 37,000 prisoners died as a result of starvation, over-work and disease, and their corpses were bull-dozed into mass graves. Anne Frank, whose wartime diary would later become world famous, died of typhus at Bergen-Belsen in March 1945, while the Allied armies were massing a matter of miles away.

The Battle of Berlin

FOLLOWING THE BATTLE of Stalingrad, Germany was on the run in Russia. However, the German Field Marshal von Manstein, who had nearly managed the relief of Paulus's trapped Sixth Army at Stalingrad, had managed to get his Army Group Don, named after the Russian river Don, back to the river Donetz. Then, in February 1943, he retook Kharkov in the Ukraine, leaving the Soviet troops around the city of Kursk in a salient. This stretched 240 km (150 miles) from north to south, and protruded 160 km (100 miles) into the German lines. In an attempt to regain the initiative on the Eastern Front, the Germans planned a surprise attack on the salient in a pincer movement from both north and south. They hoped to cut off, surround and destroy the Red Army in the bulge.

For the attack, the Germans massed almost fifty divisions containing 900,000 troops, including seventeen motorized or armoured divisions with 2,700 tanks and self-propelled assault guns. However, the Soviets had anticipated the German attack and had withdrawn their main forces. They had built eight concentric circles of defences and had massed forces that were numerically superior to the Germans in both men and tanks. When the Germans launched their attack on 5 July, they soon found themselves embroiled in deep anti-tank defences and minefields, and only advanced into the salient 50 km (30 miles) in the south and 16 km (10 miles) in the north, losing many of their tanks along the way. On 12 July, the Soviets counterattacked. They successfully developed a broad front and recovered the nearby city of Orel on 5 August and Kharkov on 23 August.

The Battle of Kursk was the largest tank battle in history and involved some 6,000 tanks, 2,000,000 troops, and 4,000 aircraft. It was the last German offensive on the Eastern Front and, from that point on, the German armies in the east were always on the retreat.

Vigorous Protest

IN EARLY 1945, the race to Berlin was on. Although the Soviets had three army groups poised on the Oder-Neisse Line, the present-day Polish border, Montgomery's 21st Army Group was moving at such a pace that it was thought that it might reach the German capital first. Montgomery proposed a single thrust in overwhelming strength from the Ruhr to take Berlin and finish the war. However, Eisenhower vetoed his plan. He had favoured Montgomery over his own generals throughout the invasion; now he switched his resources to General Omar Bradley's 12th Army Group in southern Germany which, he thought, could make a quick dash to join up with the Red Army in the area around Dresden. This would cut Germany in two. Eisenhower feared that Hitler might abandon Berlin and prolong the war, fighting in the mountainous region to the south. On 28 March, he sent an outline of his plans to Stalin and asked about the Soviet plans. When Churchill found out, he protested vigorously. He wrote to the ailing Roosevelt, pointing out the political necessity of taking Berlin as the 'supreme symbol of defeat'. But Churchill had another agenda. He was a fervent anti-communist and had been one of the architects of the 1919 Allied intervention into Russia, which attempted to strangle the Bolshevik state at birth. He now feared that the Russians might roll on across western Europe and had even made plans to rearm the German army, once Hitler was dead, to fight Stalin.

'If the Russians take Berlin, will not their impression be that they have been the overwhelming contributor to the common victory be unduly imprinted on their minds, and may this not lead them into a mood which will raise grave and formidable difficulties in the future?' he wrote. It was of utmost necessity that Berlin be taken by an Anglo-American force.

Leaving the politics aside, however, Eisenhower was right militarily, and his staff

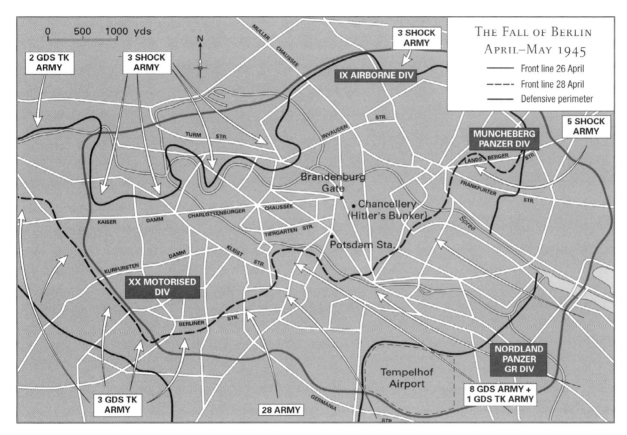

The Fall of Berlin
April–May 1945
—— Front line 26 April
- - - - Front line 28 April
—— Defensive perimeter

3 SHOCK ARMY
IX AIRBORNE DIV
2 GDS TK ARMY
3 SHOCK ARMY
5 SHOCK ARMY
MUNCHEBERG PANZER DIV
Brandenburg Gate
Chancellery (Hitler's Bunker)
Potsdam Sta.
XX MOTORISED DIV
NORDLAND PANZER GR DIV
Tempelhof Airport
3 GDS TK ARMY
28 ARMY
8 GDS ARMY + 1 GDS TK ARMY

The Battle of Berlin: the final reckoning between the Red Army and the Third Reich.

backed him. Stalin replied on 2 April, agreeing that the plan for their two armies to meet up near Dresden was strategically sound. As a result, he said, he would send only a second-rate force against Berlin which had 'lost its former strategic importance'. Nothing could have been further from the truth. Stalin was a politician, not a general. He knew the political importance of taking Berlin and suspected that Eisenhower was playing a trick on him. Before he replied he spoke to his two senior field marshals, Ivan Koniev and Georgii Zhukov. They were great rivals and both begged for the chance to take Berlin. He gave them each forty-eight hours to come up with a plan.

Although Stalin told Eisenhower that he intended to attack Berlin in May, Koniev and Zhukov were clear that he wanted to do it before that, even though their armies were exhausted after weeks of heavy fighting. Koniev's 1st Ukranian Front – or Army Group – was on the eastern bank of the river Neisse, some 120 km (75 miles) south-east of Berlin. He proposed starting his offensive with a two-and-a-half-hour artillery bombardment with 7,500 guns. At dawn, he would lay a smoke-screen, and force a river crossing with two tank armies and five field armies, more than 500,000 men in all. He would keep his tanks on his right flank. They would smash through the

German defences, then swing north-westwards and make a dash for Berlin. Unfortunately, his plan relied on two extra armies that, although promised, could not be relied on to arrive in time.

Zhukov's 1st Belorussian Front was on the river Oder, 80 km (50 miles) east of Berlin, with a bridgehead on the western side of the river at Küstrin. He proposed pre-dawn bombardment with 10,000 guns. He would then turn 140 anti-aircraft searchlights on the German defenders, blinding them while he attacked. Two tank armies and four field armies would stream out of the Küstrin bridgehead, with two more armies on each flank. With complete air superiority and 750,000 men at his disposal, Zhukov was confident of a quick victory.

Stalin gave Zhukov the green light as he was closer to Berlin and better prepared. But, still encouraging the rivalry between the two field marshals, he also let Koniev know that he was free to make a dash on Berlin if he thought he could beat Zhukov to it. The starting date set for the offensive was 16 April. The two field marshals had just thirteen days to prepare.

On 15 April, the Americans entered the race when Lieutenant General William Simpson's Ninth Army crossed the Elbe. Between him and Berlin stood the remnants of the German 12th Army under General Walther Wenck. There would be little that it could do to prevent Simpson making a dash for the capital. But Eisenhower ordered Simpson to halt on the Elbe until the link-up with the Red Army had been made at Dresden. The following morning at 0400, three red flares lit up the skies over the Küstrin bridgehead. It was followed by the biggest artillery barrage ever mounted on the Eastern Front. Mortars, tanks,

self-propelled guns, light and heavy artillery – along with 400 Katyushas – all pounded the German positions. Entire villages were blasted into rubble. Trees, steel girders and blocks of concrete were hurled into the air. Forests caught fire. Men were deafened by the guns and shook uncontrollably. They were blinded by the searchlights. Then, after thirty-five minutes of pounding, the Soviets attacked.

Little Flags

IN HIS FORTIFIED BUNKER under the Reichskanzlei (the Reich Chancellery) Hitler still believed that he could win. He predicted that the Russians would suffer their greatest defeat at the gates of Berlin. His maps told him so. They were still covered in little flags representing SS and army units. Unfortunately, most of these little flags were just … little flags. The units they represented had long since ceased to exist or were so chronically understrength that they were next to useless. Anyone who pointed this out was dismissed. Even 'Fast Heinz' Guderian was relieved of his position as Chief of the General Staff on 28 March for suggesting that it was time to negotiate.

Hitler also sacked Reichsführer-SS Heinrich Himmler, the chicken farmer who had become Hitler's secret policeman and the architect of the Holocaust, from his position as Commander of Army Group Vistula. Although named Vistula, after the river that runs through Warsaw, this army group had not in fact seen the Vistula for some time. Himmler was replaced by a veteran military man, Colonel General Gotthard Heinrici. At his disposal was the Third Panzer Army under

Final hours: the last photograph of German dictator Adolf Hitler, hours before his death in his Berlin bunker.

General Hasso von Manteuffel, which occupied the northern part of the front. The centre was held by General Theodor Busse's Ninth Army, while the south was held by the depleted army group of Field Marshal Ferdinand Schörner. And there were 30 other divisions in the vicinity of Berlin he could call on.

Heinrici was an expert in defensive warfare. On the eve of the Soviet attack, he had pulled his frontline troops back so that Zhukov's massive bombardment fell on empty positions. The Ninth Army had dug in on the Seelow heights, blocking the main Küstrin–Berlin road. Zhukov's men attacking down the road suffered terrible casualties. They eventually overwhelmed the Seelow line with sheer weight of numbers, but then they came up against more German defences, reinforced by General Karl Weidling's 56th Panzer Division, and were halted. Stalin was furious. He ordered Koniev, who was making good progress to the south, to turn his forces on Berlin. And, on 20 April, Marshal Konstantin Rokossovsky's 2nd Belorussian Front made a separate attack on Manteuffel.

Busse's Ninth Army began to disintegrate, and Zhukov got close enough to Berlin to start bombarding the city with long-range artillery. Koniev's forces were also approaching from the south, and the German capital was caught in a pincer movement. To ensure that the Americans would not come and snatch their prize at the last moment, both Zhukov and Koniev sent forces on ahead to meet up with

Simpson on the Elbe. They made contact at Torgau on 25 April, to find Simpson sitting on the Elbe facing no one. Two days earlier, Wenck had been ordered back for the defence of Berlin. By 28 April, he had reached the suburb of Potsdam. There he met fierce Soviet resistance, but managed to extricate his force and tried to link up with remnants of the Ninth Army. He then headed westwards in the hope of surrendering to the Americans. Hitler cursed his treachery.

Soldiers of the Red Army during the street fighting in Berlin, April 1945.

Fortress Berlin

WHAT PROPAGANDA MINISTER Joseph Goebbels now called 'Fortress Berlin' was defended by 90,000 ill-equipped boys from the Hitler Youth and elderly men from the Volkssturm, the Home Guard. The two million Berliners still trying to go about their business in the ruined city joked, 'It will take the Russians exactly two hours and fifteen minutes to capture Berlin – two hours laughing their heads off, and fifteen minutes to break down the barricades.'

Himmler, Goebbels and other top Nazis left the city. Hitler refused to go, pretending, for a while, that the situation could be reversed. He issued a barrage of orders to his nonexistent armies. Then, as the Soviets drew the noose tighter and 15,000 Russian guns began to pound the city, Hitler dropped all pretence of running things and announced that he would commit suicide before the Russians arrived.

As Soviet troops entered the city, Hitler sacked his designated successor, Göring, for trying to take over while he was still alive, and Himmler, for trying to put out peace feelers to the British and Americans. Grand Admiral

Karl Dönitz was named as his new successor. Then news came that Mussolini was dead. Captured while trying to escape into Austria in a German uniform, he was executed with his mistress, Claretta Petacci, on 28 April, and their bodies were hung upside down in the Piazza Loreto in Milan. On 29 April, Hitler married his mistress Eva Braun. The following day, he dictated his will and his final political testament. That afternoon, in their private quarters, Hitler and his wife of one day committed suicide. Their bodies were burned in a shallow trench in the Chancellery Gardens.

Both Zhukov's and Koniev's troops were now in the city. But Koniev was ordered to halt so that Zhukov's men would have the honour of raising the Red Flag on the Reichstag. Zhukov's resulting popularity was seen as a threat by Stalin, who banished him to obscurity in 1946.

There were still pockets of resistance, and those remaining in Hitler's bunker tried to negotiate surrender terms. The Soviets would accept nothing but unconditional surrender – which General Weidling conceded on 2 May. The surrender of the German forces in north-western Europe was signed at Montgomery's headquarters on Lüneburg Heath on 4 May. Another surrender document, covering all the German forces, was signed with more ceremony at Eisenhower's headquarters at Reims.

And by midnight on 8 May 1945, the war in Europe was officially over.

It is not known how many people perished in the Battle of Berlin. Estimates put the number of German dead as high as 200,000 and the Russian at 150,000. The Soviet troops then went on an orgy of drinking, looting and raping. It is thought that as many as 100,000 women were raped – often publicly – during that period in Berlin; an estimated two million in the whole of eastern Germany. The Russians often shot their victims afterwards. Other women committed suicide. In one district of Berlin alone, 215 female suicides were recorded in three weeks.

It had been agreed at the Yalta conference in the Crimea in February 1945 that Berlin would be divided between the four powers – Britain, France, the United States and the Soviet Union. By the time the Four Power Control Commission arrived to take control the orgy was over. Almost immediately, the Cold War started. The part of the city in the hands of the western powers became West Berlin, an enclave of democracy and free-market capitalism deep inside the region dominated by the Soviet Union that extended, by common consent, 160 km (100 miles) to the west of the capital. This would become a bone of contention for the next fifty-five years, until the reunification of Germany in 1990.

The Reichstag, the German parliament building practically unused after Hitler's accession to power in 1933, still stands amidst the rubble of Berlin in this poignant photograph.

Victory would also come in the Pacific, leaving some of the most idyllic scenery in the world littered with wreckage. This Japanese wreck was beached in Iron Bottom Sound off Guadalcanal in the Solomons.

VI

VICTORY
IN THE
PACIFIC

*The Pacific
Theatre, 1941–45.*

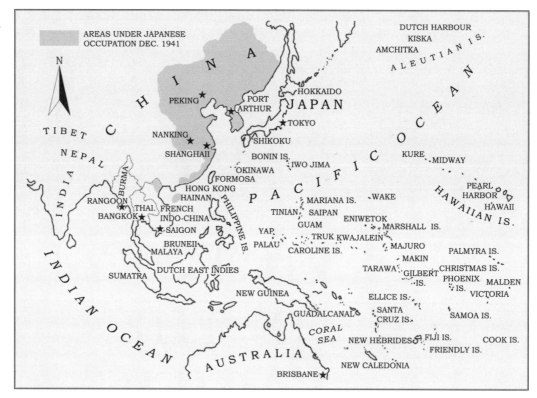

D URING THE EXPANSION of their 'Co-Prosperity Sphere', the Japanese had occupied much of Southeast Asia and numerous Pacific islands. While the British fought their way back across Southeast Asia, the Americans turned their attention to the Pacific islands.

Island Hopping

THE AMERICAN STRATEGY was to hop island by island across the Pacific, until they were within striking distance of Japan itself. As they were pushed back closer and closer to their homeland, however, the Japanese put up an increasingly fanatical defence of their island conquests.

The defeat of the Japanese at the Battle of Midway called for an immediate American initiative. The plan was to start from the south, where their own men could be supplied easily from Australia and New Zealand. There would be two thrusts: one up through Port Moresby to clear northern New Guinea, while the other would come though the Solomon Islands. Both would have as their objective the capture of Rabaul on the northern tip of New Britain, which was, by then, the principal Japanese naval base in the south-western Pacific.

The Japanese had landed on New Guinea at Salamaua, 320 km (200 miles) due north

194

from Port Moresby on the other side of the island. They were kept at bay by a successful guerrilla campaign in the mountains. The main invasion force heading for Port Moresby itself was turned back in the Battle of the Coral Sea. This allowed the Allies to reinforce the island with the Australian 6th and 7th divisions who had returned from Europe. By June 1942, the Allies had 369,000 Australian and 38,000 US troops on the island, under overall command of General Douglas MacArthur.

There were two areas considered crucial by both sides. One was Buna, which lay on the north side of the island at the head of the Kokoda trail, a track just wide enough for men to travel single file across the mountains to Port Moresby. The other was Milne Bay, which lay at the extreme eastern end of the island. Two Australian brigades, under Brigadier Porter, were on their way down the Kokoda trail when, on the night of 21 July, 1,800 Japanese landed at Sanananda, just north of Buna. They met at Wairope on 23 July, where the Australians held them for four days, before falling back on Kokoda. The Japanese were soon reinforced in overwhelming numbers and forced the Australians back. But the Australians conducted a valiant rearguard action, inflicting heavy casualties on the Japanese forces that now numbered 13,000. The Japanese had other problems. They were constantly harassed from the air; their supply lines were overextended; and they could not handle the steamy jungle climate. But still they kept coming.

On 29 August, the Japanese received orders not to advance past Ioribaiwa, 50 km (30 miles) from Port Moresby, which they reached on 17 September, while resources were concentrated on Guadalcanal. On 28 September, the Allies,

under General Blamey, began a counter-offensive. By now, the Australian troops were experienced in jungle fighting. The Japanese put up no more than token resistance and, by 2 November, the Allies had retaken Kokoda. The Japanese continued retreating throughout November, but found themselves in difficulties at Wairope, where the bridge had been destroyed. The Japanese commander General Horii was drowned while trying to ford the river and was replaced by General Adachi. The Australians took Gona, which was strongly fortified, after two attempts, then made straight for the Japanese base at Sanananda, while US troops came under some criticism for their feeble attacks until their commander was replaced by Lieutenant General Eichelberger. Buna fell on 2 January and Sanananda on 22 January 1943. By this point in the campaign, the Japanese had lost 12,000 men; the Australians and the Americans 2,800 – although they experienced three times as many casualties from disease as from fighting.

Once Gona, Buna and Sanananda were in Allied hands, 5,400 Japanese fled westwards towards Salamaua, Lae and the Markham Valley. They hacked their way through the jungle and, on 30 January, attacked the airfield at Wau. This was held by the local Kanga force, and the Japanese were repulsed with 1,200 casualties. Troops were sent from Rabaul to reinforce them, but, on 3 March, 3,000 were drowned when their convoy was sunk in the Battle of the Bismark Sea.

The Japanese retreated towards Mubo and dug in. To break the deadlock, on the night of 20 June, 1,400 US troops made an amphibious landing at Nassau Bay and threatened Salamaua. General Adachi considered

Opposite: US Marines in the jungle at Hell's Corner on Guadalcanal, as a naval scout plane flies overhead, 20 October 1942.

Salamaua so important to the defence of his position at Lae that he sent all but 2,000 of his 11,000 troops to defend it. This allowed the Australians to take Mubo on 17 July, then advance around the ridges behind Salamaua. Rather than be encircled, the Japanese withdrew, and US troops entered Salamaua on 11 September. During this operation, the Japanese lost 2,722 killed and 7,578 wounded; the Australians 500 killed and 1,300 wounded; and the United States 81 killed and 396 wounded.

The Allied forces then split in two. The Australian 7th Division pushed down the Markham Valley towards Madang on the coast, cutting off the Huon Peninsula. They reached Dumpu, some 80 km (50 miles) from Madang in early October. Meanwhile, the Australian 9th Division and the US forces hopped along the coast of the Huon Peninsula in a series of amphibious landings, although they were held up by fierce fighting along the Bumi River and a counterattack outside Sattelberg, which they eventually took on 25 November.

General MacArthur then halted the advance to allow the Allies to build up supplies. This pause further weakened the Japanese, who now had no air or naval support in the area. Six understrength Japanese divisions had been left to fight 15 Allied divisions. On 2 January 1944, the US 32nd Infantry landed at Saidor, 160 km (100 miles) ahead of the Australians advancing from Sattelberg. This cut off 12,000 Japanese on the Huon Peninsula. The Australian 7th Division forced its way over the mountains west of Saidor and took Bogadjim, Madang and Alexishafen on 24–26 August, forcing General Adachi's Eighteenth Army and his remaining 30,000 men back towards Wewak. The Allies left Adachi's men, along with 20,000 civilians, there without supplies while they made a series of further amphibious landings up the coast, taking their objectives with no significant opposition. Meanwhile, Adachi tried to break out, but the US II Corps was ready for him. Some 8,800 Japanese died, while US troops suffered 450 killed and 2,500 wounded.

MacArthur decided that the tactic of leaving enclaves of Japanese troops in position without any supplies worked well and made a further series of amphibious assaults isolating enemy troop concentrations. However, someone would eventually have to take the enclaves on. The Australians advanced through the Toricelli mountains under terrible conditions; they took Wewak on 11 May at the cost of 442 killed and 1,141 wounded. Another 16,203 were hospitalized. The Japanese lost 9,000. But Adachi and his remaining 13,500 men surrendered only at the end of the war, which had long passed them by.

Guadalcanal

AT THE SAME TIME as the offensive in New Guinea, the United States made an advance in the Solomons, landing on a small, volcanic island that would give its name to one of the most famous engagements in Marine Corps history – Guadalcanal. The largest island of the Solomon Islands – some 5,300 sq km (2,047 square miles) in area – it was named by the Spaniard Álvaro de Mendaña de Neira when he visited it in 1568, but in 1942 it was a British protectorate. Its mountainous spine, the Kavo Range, rises to 2.447 m (8,028 ft) at Mount Makarakomburu. Many short, rapid streams, including the Mataniko, Lunga and Tenaru, tumble from the jungle-clad

mountains to the coast, which is dotted with mangrove swamps.

On 3 May, Admiral Takagi had landed a small force unopposed at Tugali, immediately to the north of Guadalcanal across the Iron-bottom Sound. On 1 July, a radio message from Martin Clemens, a young British district officer on Guadalcanal, reported that 1,000 Japanese troops had landed at Lunga, on the north of the island. By 5 July, they were clearing an area just inshore from their beachhead to build an airstrip. This made an attack on Guadalcanal a priority. It was to be under the strategic command of Vice Admiral Robert Ghormley and the tactical commander would be Rear Admiral Fletcher.

Operation Watchtower – or Operation 'Shoestring' as the invasion of Guadalcanal and Tugali became known among the men – was prepared hastily. Its commanders fell out, and the troop morale was low. The under-strength 1st Marine Division commanded by Major General Archer Vandergrift, a gritty Virginian of thirty-three years' service, was assigned the task. With just a few weeks to go before the attack, half of Vandergrift's men were in Samoa or still at sea. They were green – few of them had been in uniform before the beginning of the year. However, time was of the essence. Once the airfield was up and running, and the Japanese moved their Zeros and attack-bombers in, any amphibious invasion would be suicidal.

All Vandergrift knew about the island came from a handful of old photographs taken by missionaries, an ancient maritime chart and a short story by Jack London. He was getting good reports from Clemens, however, whose local scouts now said that there were between 2,000 and 10,000 Japanese troops on the island, with a smaller force on Tulagi and the twin islands to the north, Tanambugo and Gavutu.

As D-Day for Guadalcanal approached, some Australians were found who had lived on the Solomons. They were flown in to advise Vandergrift and helped him to draw up sketch maps of the landing area. These would be out of range of the guns that now domi-nated the beaches at Lunga, east of the Ilu River. Unfortunately, the Australians mis-iden-tified the Tenaru River as the Ilu. Usually this stream was dry in August, but a sudden deluge had turned it into a raging torrent.

Things did not augur well. Unseasonable rains also soaked the men who were loading the transports. These were inadequate, only carrying enough ammunition for ten days' fighting and enough food and fuel for sixty days. The 19,000 men of the 1st Marines were to be put ashore by a huge invasion fleet of eighty-nine ships. Vandergrift had hoped that the US Navy would give his Marines artillery and air support throughout the operation. But Admiral Fletcher was convinced that the invasion was going to be a failure. He did not want to risk his three precious aircraft carriers in the restricted waters of the Solomons and planned to pull out after two days.

Fortunately, the enemy were no better prepared. The Japanese Army commander Lieutenant General Haruyoshi Hyakutake in Rabaul had not been told about the Imperial Navy's defeat at Midway. He believed the propaganda claims that numerous American ships had been sunk and their planes annihi-lated, so he dismissed the possibility of an American counterattack. The navy had not even told him about the airstrip they were

building on Guadalcanal. So he concentrated all his forces on the invasion of New Guinea, imagining the seas around him were patrolled by the all-powerful Imperial fleet.

At 0613 hours on 7 August, the Japanese were still asleep on Tulagi and Guadalcanal when the bombardment began. Clemens had picked out key targets, which were taken out by Dauntless dive-bombers and Avengers. On Tulagi, the Marines, supported by a battalion of Raiders and paratroopers, overran most of the island with hardly a shot being fired. Then they encountered fierce resistance. In the end, it took 6,000 Marines two days to defeat 1,500 Japanese soldiers. On 9 August, Admiral Gunichi Mikawa, commander of the Japanese naval task force 965 km (600 miles) to the north-west, received a despairing message. It read, 'The enemy force is overwhelming. We will defend our positions to the death, praying for everlasting victory.'

However, Gavutu and nearby Florida Island fell easily. But the Marines who stormed Tanambugo met withering fire. The island had to be bombarded by dive-bombers and destroyers before it fell the next day.

By comparison, Guadalcanal was a walkover – at first. At 0900, the Marines came swarming ashore on the palm-fringed beaches practically unopposed. The 2,200 Japanese on the island were largely construction workers who had fled when the first bomb fell. By nightfall, 17,000 Marines were ashore. The 10,000 men of main force had then moved on to Landing Beach Red in the middle of Guadalcanal's northern coast. Again they stormed 1,800 m (2,000 yards) of sandy beach unopposed. The 5th Marine Regiment moved westwards towards the fishing village of Kukum, while the 1st Marine Regiment who followed them ashore advanced south-west towards the high ground that overlooked the airstrip. The heat and humidity were overpowering, and they made slow progress through the jungle and over the switchback terrain. The rain came down in torrents, and they had to wade chest-deep through unexpectedly swollen rivers. But 6.5 km (4 miles) inland they reached the grassy knoll above the airstrip. There they dug in for the night, alert for the enemy. But all they heard were the grunting of wild pigs, eerie bird calls, the scuttling of land crabs and the whine of ubiquitous mosquitoes. It was all too easy.

Into the Jungle

ADMIRAL MIKAWA HAD also picked up a message from Guadalcanal. It said, 'American landing forces encountered, we are retreating into the jungle.' He passed this on to Admiral Nagumo, who ordered the fleet to make the recapture of Guadalcanal its immediate objective. And Mikawa was given permission to launch a night attack on the US fleet in the New Georgia Sound, the narrow body of water that runs the 480 km (300 miles) north-west from Guadalcanal to Bougainville Island. Soon twenty-four Mitsubishi G4M 'Betty' torpedo bombers, escorted by twenty-seven Zeros, were on their way. They were spotted by the fleet when they were still an hour's flight away, and six Wildcats went up after them. They waited at 6,100 m (20,000 ft), shot several of the Betties down and harassed the rest enough to make their bombing ineffective. A number of Zeros were downed, too, and, of the fifty-one planes the Japanese sent, thirty were shot down.

After an uncomfortable night on the knoll, 1st Marines seized the airfield with hardly a shot being fired. They found it was much more than an airstrip. Some 17,000 Japanese naval pioneers had already built a road to the shore and dug deep bunkers housing a radio station, warehousing facilities and power and oxygen plants. This was quickly named Henderson Field, after Major Loften Henderson, a Marine flying ace who had been killed at Midway.

9 August, the Marines had set up a perimeter along the high ground and rivers surrounding Henderson Field and Kukum. With the airfield not yet operational, they were still being supplied across the beaches. Dozens of small craft shuttled back and forth bringing food, fuel, water, arms and ammunition quicker than it could be moved from the dumping grounds on the shore up to the airfield. These small craft were sitting ducks – or so the Japanese thought. Escorted by Zeros, another forty-five Betties attacked. But in the withering fire put up by the US Navy, only one limped away, having caused little damage.

Despite these two easy victories, Fletcher felt that the risk to his three carriers was too great and withdrew them, along with their escort of sixteen destroyers, six cruisers and one battleship. But Admiral Mikawa was not discouraged by the failure of his fliers. He steamed southwards towards the New Georgia Sound, aiming to attack the transport fleet bringing in the Marines' supplies. Luck was on his side. US daylight reconnaissance planes did not spot him and, when he was sighted at last, the report took eight hours to reach Admiral Richmond Turner at his headquarters in Australia. He was furious when he discovered that Fletcher had withdrawn, leaving the Marines undefended, and ordered Rear Admiral Sir Victor Crutchley, commanding the Australian naval squadron, to block the western approaches of the Sound, while another naval force under Rear Admiral Scott would block the eastern approaches.

However, the Japanese spotted Crutchley's squadron of six heavy cruisers and four destroyers in the narrow straits between Guadalcanal and Savo Island, and attacked. Within half an hour the American cruisers

On Guadalcanal, the US Marines quickly adapted to jungle fighting. Although it cost the Americans 1,592 lives, the Japanese lost 50,000 – some 9,000 of those to disease.

The 5th Marine Division took Kukum unopposed and found that the Japanese defenders had fled in panic. They had abandoned their rifles, uniforms, mosquito nets and large amounts of mouldering rice. By

Astoria and *Quincy*, along with the Australian cruiser HMAS *Canberra*, were blazing hulks, bound for the bottom of Ironbottom Sound. The USS *Vincennes* hit the Japanese cruiser *Kinugasa*, but followed the others to the bottom. Another cruiser was badly damaged, 1,270 men were killed, drowned or devoured by sharks, and more than 700 wounded were rescued. In memory of this action, the next US Navy heavy cruiser to be commissioned was named *Canberra*, the only American warship ever to be named after a foreign city.

Turner had to withdraw the undefended transports and supply vessels to New Caledonia. Next morning, when the Marines from Henderson Field arrived at the beach, all they could see was blue sea, the supply ships and warships gone. They were now on their own.

They gathered up what supplies remained on the beach, then set about completing the airstrip in the hope that they might get some fighter support. To hold the airfield, which would become their lifeline, they had to maintain a perimeter that was 3,200 m (3,500 yards) deep at its widest and 6,860 m (7,500 yards) long. It ran inland from the beach between Kukum and the village of Tenaru to a tortuous ridge of hills along the southern flank. The Matanikau River and Kukum hills formed the western flank, the Tenaru River the eastern. Defences were dug and positions manned, while Vandergrift massed his artillery and tanks in the middle of the enclave so that he could bring down concentrated fire on any point around it. The airfield was defended by 90mm ack-ack guns dug in to the north-west of the airstrip and 75mm guns on half-tracks which were dug into the north. Positions were also prepared for the half-tracks on the beaches, so

that they could defend against any seaborne landing. This was where Vandergrift expected the Japanese to attack, so extensive trenchworks were dug along the top of the beaches, with other further defensive lines inland.

The first air attack came on 9 August. Antipersonnel bombs that burst into a thousand flying steel slivers were dropped, along with 500-pound bombs. Next came a naval bombardment from Admiral Mikawa's cruisers and destroyers sailing up and down the coast in what the Marines came to call the 'Tokyo Express'. Three days later came the gruesome curtain-raiser to the land battle, when a Japanese force landed at night near Matanikau. On 12 August, they ambushed a 26-man patrol, cutting the Marines down with hidden machine guns. The three survivors who made it back told their fellow Marines that the wounded had been hacked to death with sabres. From then on, the Marines decided that they would be every bit as brutal.

On 13 August, General Hyakutake received orders from Imperial General Headquarters in Tokyo to retake Guadalcanal without delay. He sent Colonel Kiyono Ichiki with 2,000 crack troops who had been trained for the invasion of Midway. On 16 August, Colonel Ichiki and the 915 men in his preliminary force set sail on six destroyers. The rest would follow later in slower craft. The main advance force landed at Taivu Point, 35 km (22 miles) east of the Tenaru River, with a diversionary force going ashore to the west. Vandergrift had every reason to know about the landings. At night, in the South Seas, the wash of boats becomes luminous. This had been spotted by a sharp-eyed sentry. Clemens and ten of his scouts had put themselves at Vandergrift's

service and told him of the arrival of the Japanese. US Naval Intelligence confirmed the reports. On top of that, a message bound for the original Japanese force hiding to the west of Kukum fell within the perimeter. It read, 'Help is on the way. Banzai.'

The Imperial High Command believed that the battle for Guadalcanal would force the United States to return the remains of its Pacific fleet to the area. Eager for revenge for Midway, Yamamoto mustered three aircraft carriers, three battleships, five cruisers, eight destroyers and a seaplane carrier, and sent them to the Solomons. Admiral Mikawa already had four cruisers and five destroyers there, supported by 100 warplanes flying from Rabaul.

Yamamoto was right in his assessment of the situation. When the Allies saw where his

The Leathernecks advance in the Solomon Islands. Nowhere was safe from the Japanese, who continued to fight tenaciously even when they had no chance of victory.

fleet was heading, Ghormley ordered Fletcher to guard the approaches to the Solomons and sent the carrier *Hornet* and its escort of destroyers and cruisers as reinforcements.

Unsure of the enemy's deployment, Vandergrift sent three companies of Marines to attack the Japanese defences along the Matanikau. At the same time, he sent a patrol in force to the east. The Matanikau attack was successful, and the Marines mounted an amphibious assault further to the west at Kukumba. This came under fire from the Tokyo Express and a Japanese submarine. But the Marines made it ashore and managed to drive the Japanese defenders into the jungle.

A patrol from Colonel Ichiki's force to the east was surprised by the Marine patrol, and a map was taken from them showing that Ichiki knew the weakest point along the Tenaru defence line. Vandergrift strengthened it immediately. Shortly after 0010 on 21 August, 500 of Ichiki's men rushed the Americans guarding the sand spit at the mouth of the Tenaru River. Mortars rained down on the defenders. The attackers yelled 'Banzai!' and sprayed the Marines' positions with automatic and machine-gun fire. But the Marines kept their cool and held their fire – then opened up with everything they had. It was a blood-bath. At 0500, Ichiki sent a second wave of 400 men. This time they were cut down before they even reached the American wire. Ichiki's elite force was wiped out without even making so much as a dent in the American line. In shame at his utter failure, Ichiki burnt the regimental colours and shot himself. But some of his men fought on. Wounded Japanese soldiers tried to kill the American medics who were going to help them. Vandergrift sent in light tanks to make sure that there was no further resistance.

But Yamamoto was not to be thwarted. Operation Ka to recapture the airfield on Guadalcanal would continue. The remaining 1,500 men of Ichiki's main force were still on their way. Yamamoto reinforced them with another 1,000 men sent on fast transports. Meanwhile, he was determined to get the better of Fletcher. On 22 August, he sent twelve submarines to set up a screen south-east of Guadalcanal, while his main force was concentrated 320 km (200 miles) north of the southernmost of the Solomons. The light carrier *Ryujo* was then sent out as bait. Yamamoto's plan was to destroy the American carriers while their planes were attacking the *Ryujo*. Then his massive battleships could sail though Ironbottom Sound and annihilate the Marines, while his troops retook the airfield.

Fletcher took the bait, and torpedo planes and dive-bombers from the *Enterprise* and the *Saratoga* obliterated the *Ryujo* completely. Yamamoto had counted on Fletcher keeping his three carriers together for the attack, but Fletcher had already sent the *Wasp* to refuel. He was also ready for Yamamoto's counter-attack. The *Enterprise* had kept back fifty-three Wildcats, which were circling in the clouds as the carrier waited for its attack planes to return from the *Ryujo*.

Then thirty Val dive-bombers came screaming from the sky. The battleship *North Carolina* fired a canopy over the *Enterprise*, but still three dive-bombers found their mark. The *Enterprise* sped on at 27 knots, ablaze. An hour later she was able to swing into the wind to pick up the returning planes, but after that she was out of action for two months. In the

Battle of the Eastern Solomons, however, the Japanese lost daytime control of the sea, along with one more carrier and numerous planes, although some of the surviving Japanese pilots claimed that two US aircraft carriers had been sunk. In Rabaul, Admiral Mikawa gave the okay for the invasion convoy to continue on to Guadalcanal.

In preparation for the invasion, Admiral Tanaka, commander of the invasion fleet, sent five destroyers into New Georgia Sound to bombard Henderson Field. This left the convoy undefended. On the night of 24 August, with the transport slightly more than 160 km (100 miles) from Guadalcanal, a formation of Dauntlesses caught up with them. The Japanese were so confident that the US carrier force had been dealt a serious blow in the Battle of the Eastern Solomons that they did not even have their guns loaded. The American dive-bombers hit Tanaka's flagship, the cruiser *Jintsu*, and a large troopship laden with men. They then called up Flying Fortresses, which finished off the burning transport and a destroyer that was trying to rescue the men. The other ships turned northwards and fled out of range.

Yamamoto then decided to change tactics. Instead of landing a large invasion force, he would build up slowly, landing men on the island by stealth at night. Next ashore was to be the crack Kawaguchi Brigade. But its advance units were so eager to get into the fray that they left Borneo on destroyers at night, guaranteeing that they would be in New Georgia Sound in broad daylight. Marine dive-bomber pilots spotted them, and soon two of the four destroyers had been torn apart with explosions, while a third was on fire.

General Kawaguchi and his main force were on shore in the Shortland Islands south of Bougainville with Yamamoto. A row broke out. Kawaguchi refused to have his men transported by destroyers, insisting that they be landed by barge. A compromise was reached. Eight destroyers would carry the bulk of the force. The rest would follow in the limited number of barges available. Some 3,500 men were landed from destroyers at Taivu Point on Guadalcanal on the night of 31 August. Several nights later, the remaining 1,000 men turned up in their barges, but a heavy swell prevented them from landing. At first light, they were caught out to sea by the Marine aircraft now flying from Henderson Field, and decimated.

The Imperial General Headquarters was now getting impatient with the loss of life the recapture of Guadalcanal was costing. It sacked Admiral Tanaka, although he had frequently warned against the use of barges, and made the taking of Henderson Field its top priority. The already overstretched General Hyakutake was ordered to go on the defensive in New Guinea and concentrate his forces against Guadalcanal. This halted the Japanese forces within 50 km (30 miles) of Port Moresby and allowed the Allies to regroup for their counteroffensive, which eventually pushed the Japanese back across the island. The entire resources of the Southeast Area Air Force would also be put at Hyakutake's disposal, and he would be supported by the powerful 8th Fleet.

Henderson Field was being bombed daily, and the Japanese were now deploying fifty-eight more planes against it. However, Henderson now had its Cactus Air Force – as they called themselves – who quickly shattered the myth of the invincibility of the Zero with their new Wildcats. With its superior firepower, the formation flying of the US pilots outweighed the greater speed and manoeuvrability of the Zeros. Spotters along the coast gave Henderson an early warning of the approach of enemy aircraft. This meant that the stubby radial-engined Wildcats could get airborne and attack the incoming bandits out of the sun. Enemy planes were being shot down at a rate of between six and eight for every Wildcat lost. They could do nothing, however, to counter the nightly Tokyo Express and the US Navy still did not dare to enter the New Georgia Sound.

Dysentery and Malaria

THE SITUATION AT Henderson Field grew dire. The Japanese forces around the Marines were building up. The Tokyo Express meant that the men got little sleep at night and were subjected to surprise attacks during the day. They were also suffering from dysentry, jungle rot, malaria and the effects of eating little but stodgy rice. But things picked up when the World War I fighter ace Brigadier General Roy Geiger flew in to take command of the Cactus Air Force, and a battalion of Navy Seabees, expert in airfield construction, arrived to make improvements to Henderson Field.

Vandergrift was short of reinforcements and called in the Raiders and paratroopers from Tulagi. They were ferried across the Ironbottom Sound at night by the light destroyers *Gregory* and *Little*. But after they had delivered their precious cargo, the ships were mistakenly illuminated by an American flare and shot to pieces by the Japanese navy.

With the airfield now extended, Skytrain air transports brought in machine guns and took out the wounded. This became a regular service and did much to boost the Marines' morale. Then two transports got through with reinforcements, bringing the garrison up to a total of 23,000 men.

On 12 September, the Japanese began a massive air and sea bombardment to cover the advance of Kawaguchi's 6,200 men in a three-pronged attack. However, he had overestimated how quickly his men could move through the slimy swamps and tangled jungle that characterized the terrain. Soon they were strung out and disorganized.

Forewarned, Vandergrift reinforced the steep ridges the Japanese were aiming for and brought his headquarters up. But the bombardment left Henderson Field with only 11 Wildcats airworthy. Despite protests, Admiral Nimitz ordered Fletcher to sent twenty-four of his fighters from the *Saratoga* to reinforce Henderson. This was done reluctantly, as Vice Admiral Robert L. Ghormley, at the time Commander of the South Pacific Area and South Pacific Force, now considered the position of the Marines on Guadalcanal untenable. As there was no way that the US Navy could risk taking on the Japanese Imperial Navy in the confined waters of the Solomons, he ordered the fleet to stay away.

On the night of 12 September, the American defenders on the ridge above the Tenaru River saw a rocket. Next, they heard the crackling of automatic fire and the cry of 'Banzai' as the Japanese came charging up the hill. In some places, they forced the Marines back. In others, they broke through. But Kawaguchi had misjudged the jungle. He had sent his

first wave in, while the second wave was still clawing its way through the undergrowth. Vandergrift then concentrated artillery fire on the places the Japanese had broken through, causing any who had survived the bombardment to flee back into the forest. A counter-attack by the Marines at dawn retook what they were now calling 'Bloody Ridge'. As it seemed certain that the Japanese would attack there again, they rolled out barbed wire and cleared the slopes so that, next time, the Japanese would have to charge across a hundred yards of open ground raked by machine-gun fire.

Back at Henderson Field, three air raids had depleted the complement of Wildcats again, but sixty more planes, including six Avenger torpedo bombers, arrived from the *Wasp* and the *Hornet*. At the same time, 140 new planes arrived at the Japanese bases on Bougainville and at Rabaul.

Henderson was given a day's rest, while General Hyakutake waited for the news that Kawaguchi had taken the ridge. His planes would, instead, be sent to bomb Tasimboko, to Kawaguchi's rear, where there had been an erroneous report of an American landing. Mistaking them for Americans, the Japanese planes made a devastating raid on Kawaguchi's rear echelon troops.

Killing Grounds

IN THE JUNGLE below Bloody Ridge, Kawaguchi tried to muster his remaining 2,500 troops into an organized assault. That night, while Henderson Field was under bombardment from seven destroyers, he sent 2,000 men in six waves up the slope against just 400 Raiders under 'Red Mike' Edson. Some made it across the newly prepared killing grounds and threw themselves into hand-to-hand fighting. The US artillery decimated the oncoming Japanese. Others were knifed to death as they jumped into American foxholes. The Japanese also called their naval gunfire from the Tokyo Express, although soldiers from both sides were in the close combat. The American line bent, but held. The surviving Japanese were put to flight by P-400s swooping in low with cannon firing, and chased away by five Marine tanks. The Raiders had suffered 224 casualties, the paratroopers 212, and the Marines who had been sent in as reinforcements 263. The Japanese dead were uncountable, and Kawaguchi's men carried away 400 wounded on litters through the jungle towards Matanikau. Meanwhile, six more transports got through carrying 4,000 more Marines. They had been escorted by a substantial force, including the *North Carolina*, the *Hornet* and the *Wasp*. These big ships were quickly withdrawn under cover of darkness on the night of 14 September. The following day, the *Wasp* was fatally hit by torpedoes, and a battleship and destroyer were damaged, but Yamamoto could not follow up and finish off the US fleet because his ships had been recalled for refuelling, only for the carriers to be ordered back to home waters. Instead, he continued his tactic of building up the ground forces on the island, sending in the battle-hardened Nagoya Division and the crack Sendai Division.

On 18 September, in a lightly defended convoy, Admiral Kelly Turner landed more Marines inside the perimeter at Guadalcanal. He also brought 155mm 'Long Toms' and

Although Japanese troops often fought to the death rather than surrender, on Guadalcanal, as elsewhere, they were let down badly by a command structure that was indifferent to their fate.

5-inch naval guns. Also on their way were USAAF Lightnings, diverted from the Anglo-American landings in North Africa, which had the necessary range to attack the Tokyo Express when the ships stayed away from the island during the day.

Although the conditions at Henderson Field were by no means luxurious, the Japanese out in the jungle were in a pitiful state – disease-ridden and starving, with no prospect of evacuation. Vandergrift decided to increase their woes. On 27 September, he sent a three-pronged attack against their strongpoint at Matanikau. The Marines would rush across the sand spit at the mouth of the river, while the Raiders were to cross the river about

1.5 km (1 mile) inland, wheel around to the Japanese rear and meet up with another Marine battalion that was to land behind them. But the Marines charging across the spit were driven back, the Raiders were pinned down and the landing force found that they had walked into a trap. Vandergrift cancelled the offensive.

The monsoon was on its way, and Admiral Nimitz landed amid heavy rain to reassure the defenders that he would support them with the 'maximum of our resources'. The embattled defenders were in need of reassurance. The ground troops arrayed against them seemed to increase every day. The Marines were, however, winning the war in the air. The next two air raids on Henderson Field cost the Japanese six fighters and twenty-nine bombers, without destroying a single American plane. By the end of September, the Cactus Air Force had lost thirty-two planes, while the Japanese had lost more than 200.

Determined to make sure that the Japanese forces did not fail again, Hyakutake left Rabaul for Guadalcanal on 9 October to direct operations personally. He estimated Vandergrift's strength at just 10,000 – it was more than 19,000 – and believed that his Sendai Division alone could vanquish them. Nevertheless, Hyakutake did take the precaution of bringing the 38th Division in from Borneo, and established his Seventeenth Army headquarters on Guadalcanal. The plan was to attack in force from Matanikau on 17 October.

The Sendai commander Lieutenant General Masoa Maruyama issued an order of the day setting the tone for the engagement. It said: 'The occupying of Guadalcanal island is under the observation of the whole world.

Do not expect to return, not even one man, if the occupation is not successful.'

At the same time, Vandergrift decided to launch another attack, this time in more force, against Matanikau. On 7 October, the Marines and the Japanese met head-on in the jungle. Furious fighting ensued. By nightfall, both sides were pinned down as the monsoon started. The following day, the Marines caught a battalion of Sendai resting in a ravine and called artillery fire down on them, killing them all. Around 1,000 Japanese died at the cost of sixty-five Americans, and the unbeatable Sendai were then forced to retreat.

As the Marines had held their position on Guadalcanal for two months now, their prospects were now viewed with more optimism. Even the US Army chipped in. The 164th Infantry Regiment sent 3,000 men on two transports from New Caledonia and the USAAF sent twenty Wildcats. And Ghormley sent all the warships available to challenge the Japanese's dominance in the New Georgia Sound. The landing on Guadalcanal had started out as a small-scale engagement. Now it was a major battle.

The Japanese were reinforcing, too. Hyakutake brought in 1,000 more men from the Sendai Division on six destroyers, and another battalion on seaplane carriers. The convoy was guarded by a huge force including three cruisers, two destroyers and numerous aircraft. Artillery, stockpiles of medical supplies and ammunition, and sixteen tanks were landed. The ships, under Admiral Aritomo Goto, were then to bombard Henderson Field, putting it out of action. That night, 11 October, they were to run straight into Rear Admiral Norman Scott's convoy coming in from New Caledonia, which had four cruisers and five destroyers protecting the troopships. Goto felt safe, believing that the Americans would not attack after nightfall. But Scott's convoy had radar, so he could see where the Japanese ships were, and his crews had been extensively trained in night fighting.

Scott's fleet almost gave its position away when a spotter plane caught fire on take-off, but Japanese look-outs mistook the conflagration for a signal fire on the landing beaches. At 4,570 m (5,000 yards), the US ships opened fire. The first salvos hit the cruiser *Aoba*, Goto's flagship, setting it on fire and fatally wounding the Admiral. To take stock in the midst of the confusion, Scott ordered a ceasefire. Not all the gun crews heard the order, and before the guns fell silent the cruiser *Surutake* was also on fire. Searchlights also revealed that the destroyer *Fuvuki* had been blown to pieces. On the US side, the destroyer *Duncan* had been caught in the crossfire and sank, and the cruiser *Boise* was badly damaged. The Battle of the Cape of Esperance, as the engagement became known, ended Japanese domination of the waters around Guadalcanal for the time being. This point was rubbed home when the Japanese destroyers that landed the Sendai reinforcements were attacked by dive-bombers from Henderson Field and annihilated.

Progress was being made by the US forces, but painfully slowly. As the 3,000 American infantry men Scott had brought set foot on Guadalcanal, there was a massive Japanese air raid. Japanese ground troops had attacked and killed the coastal spotters, so Henderson Field had no warning. The Wildcats could not climb fast enough to intercept the attackers. Planes on the ground were badly damaged

and fuel stores set ablaze. The Japanese had now brought in artillery that could outrange the American guns and an artillery barrage hit the runways, putting the airfield out of action for the first time.

Another 10,000 Japanese troops were to be landed on the night of 14 October, ready for an all-out offensive on the 20 October. They were supported by Yamamoto's massive fleet, which comprised five aircraft carriers, five battleships, fourteen cruisers and forty-four destroyers. The battleships bombarded Henderson Field for an hour and a half, leaving the men there speechless and barely sane. Forty-one had been killed, many of them pilots. All thirty-four Dauntlesses had been badly damaged, along with nearly all the Avengers and sixteen out of the forty Wildcats. Both runways were pitted with huge craters.

The Seabees got to work on the runways and, using fuel siphoned from two wrecked Flying Fortresses and a slash captured from the Japanese, the remaining twenty-four Wildcats got airborne to fend off further air raids. Ten Zeros and nine bombers were shot down at the cost of one US Army pilot and two Marines. Then, working around the clock, the mechanics managed to patch up the P-400s, Aerocobras, Dauntlesses and more Wildcats, which went out to strafe and bomb the incoming troopships. Fuel was flown in and, towards the end of the day, a formation of Flying Fortresses from the New Hebrides joined in the attack. Four motor torpedo boats began harassing the convoy by night, while the Cactus Air Force threw everything it had at them by day. Two of the transports were wrecked. Another three turned back. In all, Hyakutake only got 4,500 of the reinforcements for his big offensive.

Screaming from the Sky

YAMAMOTO'S FLEET CONTINUED pounding Henderson. On the night of 15 October, hundreds of 8-in shells finished off the fuel stocks and smashed the planes until there were only twenty-seven left. The converted destroyer *McFarland* arrived with 40,000 gallons (152,380 litres) of aviation fluid. It was unloading as fourteen Japanese dive-bombers came screaming from the sky. At that moment, a squadron of Wildcats sent in from the New Hebrides, at the limit of the range, arrived. With his fuel tanks almost empty, the squadron's leader, Lieutenant Colonel Harold Bauer, shot down four Vals in one swoop, and the *McFarland* was able to finish unloading.

Hyakutake now prepared his attack with 22,000 men. General Maruyama was to take 7,000 men on the same route as Kawaguchi's ill-fated assault. But, this time, a road would be hacked through the jungle. He would then break through the perimeter and take the airfield. Meanwhile, the remaining 15,000 men would stage diversionary attacks to prevent the Americans reinforcing Bloody Ridge. And the defenders would be harassed constantly by land-based planes flying from the airfields at Rabaul, on the nearby island of Buka, and from the Buin airfield on Bougainville. They would be joined by planes from Yamamoto's carriers and the fleet would be on hand if any further bombardment were needed. The Japanese strength was so over-whelming, Hyakutake believed that the whole thing would be over in two days.

However, the jungle came to the defenders' rescue again. On 22 October, after five days' marching, General Maruyama's Sendai had only covered 47 km (29 miles) of the 56 km (35 miles) to their starting point. Nevertheless, Maruyama reported that he would be ready to start the battle on 23 October. That day, the Japanese sent in a formation of bombers. The Wildcats took off to greet them and take on their escorts. In the attack, twenty Zeros were downed for the loss of not a single Wildcat. None of the bombers got through.

On the ground, things were going even more badly for the Japanese. Maruyama was in position, but Kawaguchi, who was supposed to attack on his right, was not yet in place. Kawaguchi was relieved of his command, and the attack was rescheduled for the 24 October. News of the delay did not, however, get through to Major General Sumoyoshi. At dusk, he attacked across the mouth of the Matanikau River. His men and his tanks were blown to pieces by the American artillery.

Vandergrift was away at the time, seeing the new commander in the South Pacific Admiral William Halsey. Intelligence reported that an all-out attack was expected on the night of 24 October. Halsey sent in the *Enterprise* and *Hornet* to take on Yamamoto's fleet while the battle raged on land. In Vandergrift's absence, Geiger was in command. Sumoyoshi's premature assault on the Matanikau River convinced Geiger that the attack would come from the west, and he switched a battalion from the southern defence line to reinforce his right flank.

Maruyama's attack was due to begin at 1700. But at that moment the monsoon came. The jungle tracks turned into seas of mud. His units lost touch with each other, and communications broke down. Maruyama postponed the attack for two hours. At 1900, the rain had stopped, but Kawaguchi's successor, Colonel Shoji, had still not managed to get his men up to the start line to the right. Nevertheless, Maruyama sent his left wing in. The jungle was so dense that it was impossible to advance with any degree of stealth. An American outpost warned their comrades on the ridge that the attack was coming. The Marines held their fire until the Japanese reached the wire. The first wave was cut down to a man. The second wave of men tried to scramble over the corpses of their fallen comrades, but even the Sendai could not take this kind of slaughter, and a few survivors fled back into the forest. At one point, however, the Japanese did make it through. Led by Colonel Furumiya, with his sword held high, they rushed the American machine guns, killing a number of Marines. The line simply closed behind them and, when the Japanese were all dead, the positions were remanned.

At 2130, the Sendai tried again. This time Shoji had his men in place on the right wing, and they were determined to cleanse the dishonour of being late for the battle with their ferocity. At a number of places they managed to penetrate the Marines' line. Thinking that his men had got through, Maruyama radioed that he had taken the airfield, and Hyakutake sent a message to Admiral Mikawa asking him to land the remaining men he had on three destroyers at Koli Point to the east of Tenaru to finish off the Americans once and for all.

All this was very premature. The Marines' line had been penetrated, but not broken. Soldiers were sent up to fill the gaps, and the Japanese troops who had got through were hunted down and killed. At 2330, a fourth wave of Sendai warriors was sent in. Instead of finding the line broken, the Sendai were met with intense fire. When the slaughter abated, a few survivors slunk away into the dark depths of the jungle. At dawn, the Americans saw the terrible carnage around their positions. At one place, an anti-tank gun had hit an entire Japanese column point-blank, blasting them to pieces. Shamefacedly, Maruyama radioed Hyakutake, 'Am having trouble capturing the airfield.'

But it was too late to stop the landings. As the destroyers carrying the troops approached Koli Point, they met 5-in shells from the Marines' guns and were forced to turn away. Once the morning sun had dried out the airfield, a wing of Dauntlesses took off to attack the convoy. They set one Japanese cruiser on fire, sent four destroyers fleeing for the open seas and forced another on to shore. Twenty-six Japanese planes were shot down over Henderson Field, and Admiral Nagumo, fearing another Midway, turned tail, taking with him the carrier *Junyo*, whose planes were to have landed at Henderson, once it was safely in Japanese hands.

Full Retreat

THAT NIGHT MARUYAMA tried to redeem his honour with one more assault. This time he got all his men in place and in communication. Then they came screaming out of the jungle. Hundreds were slaughtered, but as the battle developed the attack swung towards Hill 67 and the sea. The Sendai charged headlong at the machine-gun nests. Those who got through hacked at the

Marines with knives and swords. Such was the ferocity of the attack that some of the machine-gun positions were overrun. But the Marines counterattacked, forcing the Sendai back, leaving some 2,500 of their dead on the ground. Maruyama ordered a full retreat. The land battle had been won. There now followed a battle at sea.

While the Sendai were being decimated in the jungle and the United States was winning its first land battle of the war, the *Enterprise* and the *Hornet* were steaming with their escort ships towards Guadalcanal from the Santa Cruz Islands in the south-east, under the command of Admiral Thomas Kincaid. The huge Japanese fleet, with its four carriers,

American Marines display a Japanese flag captured during the taking of Guadalcanal.

turned south looking for them. On 26 October, a reconnaissance plane from the *Shokaku* found the US ships 320 km (200 miles) to the east. Admiral Nagumo sent bombers from all three of his carriers, while the *Junyo*, a 160 km (100 miles) to his rear, launched a separate attack. At about the same time, an American spotter plane found Nagumo's fleet.

Shortly before 0700, a patrol of Dauntlesses came hurtling down through the canopy of Zeros onto Nagumo's carriers. They quickly made smoke and zigzagged, but two bombs hit the *Zuiho*, putting her out of action.

The Japanese pilots could not find the *Enterprise*, which was hidden under cloud. But the *Hornet* was caught out in the open by fifteen dive-bombers and twelve torpedo planes. A Japanese pilot smashed his plane through the flight deck in a kamikaze attack, starting a huge fire. Two torpedoes then struck home, followed by three bombs. Although the whole ship threatened to blow up, the fires were soon brought under control.

Meanwhile, the *Hornet*'s dive-bombers had located the *Shokaku*. Diving through heavy flak, they put 1,000-lb bombs through her deck, setting the whole ship on fire. Unfortunately, the Avenger torpedo bombers did not find her to finish her off. Instead, they disabled the Japanese cruiser *Chikuma*. The *Shokaku* also headed out of the battle, but in nine months she was at sea again.

While she was turning to avoid torpedoes from a Japanese submarine, the *Enterprise* was hit on the flight deck by two bombs. She evaded more torpedoes dropped by Kates and survived in good enough shape to take on her returning aircraft. The battleship *South Dakota* downed twenty-six of the Japanese dive-bombers that attacked her, taking scarcely a scratch herself. The *Hornet*, which was being towed by the cruiser *Northampton*, was hit again by Japanese bombers, and Admiral Kincaid ordered that she be scuttled. American destroyers tried to torpedo her but, of the eight Mark 15 torpedoes launched by the USS *Mustin*, only three ran straight. And they failed to do the job. So, while American floatplanes illuminated the target with flares, the destroyer hit the *Hornet* with 430 5-in shells. Still, she would not go down and had to be abandoned. Eventually, the Japanese sunk her with four 'Long Lance' torpedoes.

As Kincaid sped away from the advancing Japanese fleet, the Japanese announced that they had won the Battle of the Santa Cruz Islands. But Nagumo was replaced. He had won victory at too high a price. The *Shokaku* and the *Zuiho* had been put out of action, and more than 100 planes, along with their highly trained crews, had been lost. On top of that, the *Hiyo* had damaged its engines during the engagement. But at least the defenders on Guadalcanal did not have to worry about being attacked by carrier-borne planes for some time.

Since late October, things on the island had turned into a stalemate. But soon both sides began to reinforce again. It had come to the attention of President Roosevelt how crucial the battle for Guadalcanal was becoming. Cactus Air Force was now down to 29 planes, and he ordered all available aircraft, ships and weapons to be rushed there. Meanwhile, Japanese Imperial Headquarters planned yet another all-out offensive from Matanikau, accompanied, once again, by a massive naval bombardment.

On 1 November, Vandergrift did his best to upset these plans by sending 5,000 Marines to stop the Japanese consolidating their position to the west of Matanikau and to silence their long-range artillery there. Fierce fighting between the two sides ensued; however, the Japanese were eventually pushed back. Then two battalions of 155mm 'Long Tom' guns were delivered to the defenders, giving the US artillery the ascendancy again.

On 3 November, Nagumo's successor, Admiral Tameichi Hari, transported more troops to reinforce the Sendai survivors who were quietly starving at Koli Point, and renewed the Tokyo Express with three cruisers and eight destroyers. By 10 November, the Japanese had built up their forces on the island to 30,000, against Vandergrift's 20,000 Marines and 3,000 soldiers. Another 6,000 were on their way. Before they were to attack again, however, the Japanese wanted overwhelming superiority.

They planned to land 28,000 more troops on the night of 12 November, and add two aircraft carriers, four battleships, eleven cruisers and forty-nine destroyers to the Tokyo Express. These were spotted by Australian coastal watchers on occupied Bougainville and Halsey decided that he would have another crack at the Imperial fleet.

In Nouméa harbour on New Caledonia, hundreds of engineers were working day and night on the *Enterprise*. The Imperial Fleet was expected to arrive at Guadalcanal on 12 November. On 11 October, the *Enterprise* sailed from Nouméa with repair teams still working on board. She was escorted by the battleship *Washington* and the damaged *South Dakota*, two cruisers and eight destroyers.

Under cover of a rainstorm, the Japanese fleet slipped into New Georgia Sound. US reinforcements were landing when eight Zeros and twenty-four Betties flying from the fleet attacked. But the guns of the American naval escort downed three Zeros and twenty-three Betties in just a couple of minutes.

In the forthcoming battle, the planes on Henderson Field were a vital asset, so Admiral Turner sent two heavy cruisers, the *Portland* and the *San Francisco*; three light cruisers, the *Atlanta*, the *Helena* and the *Junea*; and eight destroyers to attack the Japanese fleet in an attempt to stop it bombarding Henderson Field. Admiral Hari had not anticipated this. When his fleet arrived off Savo Island, its decks were stacked with high-explosive shells to bombard Henderson. When the look-outs spotted the American ships, there was consternation. One shell hitting the ammunition would blow the ship out of the war. Quickly the high-explosive shells were taken below, the gunners reloading with armour-piercing shells to take on the American ships.

The American ships, under Rear Admiral Callaghan, advanced in a single line because his ships had not trained together as a squadron. Even this simple manoeuvre required more co-operation between the ships than they could manage, and the situation was not helped by the fact that Callaghan's flagship *San Francisco* did not have radar. At 0140, in the darkness, the destroyer *Cushing* almost ran into the two Japanese destroyers, *Murasame* and *Yudachi*. Only five minutes later did Callaghan give the order to open fire. Almost immediately, the *Cushing* was blown to bits by the battleship *Hiei*. A point-blank blast from the *Laffey* set the *Hiei* on fire, but the

counterblast blew the *Laffey* out of the water. The *Portland* and the *San Francisco* hit the *Hiei* and damaged two Japanese destroyers, the *Yudachi* and the *Akatsuki*. But when Callaghan found that the *San Francisco*'s guns had also crippled the *Atlanta*, he gave the order to cease fire. This allowed the 14-in guns of the battleship *Kirishima* to fire a massive broadside into the *San Francisco*, killing Callaghan and his staff. The crippled *Atlanta* was also caught in the Japanese searchlights and blasted, killing Admiral Scott. In the maelstrom, the Americans lost five destroyers and two light cruisers, and the *San Francisco* was badly damaged. Only one of the Japanese ships, the *Akatsuki*, sank, although the *Yudachi* had to be abandoned. Nevertheless, the Japanese abandoned their plans to bombard Henderson and withdrew, leaving the damaged *Hiei*. The next day, it was bombed and sunk.

Too Far Away

BUT HENDERSON WAS not to be spared for long. The next night, Admiral Mikawa's flagship, the *Chokai*; three heavy cruisers, the *Kinugasa*, the *Maya* and the *Suzuya*; and six destroyers arrived off Savo Island at midnight. The *Enterprise* was still too far away to be of any help. Kincaid sent the greater part of his escort – the battleships *South Dakota* and *Washington*, and four destroyers – but they would not arrive before dawn. Mikawa's ships bombarded Henderson at will on the night of the 13 November, destroying eighteen planes. But next morning the Cactus Air Force would have its revenge. Its planes torpedoed the *Kinugasa* and the destroyer *Izuso*. Then planes from the

Henderson Field on Guadalcanal was named after Major Loften Henderson, a Marine pilot lost at Midway, and was home to the Cactus Air Force. Despite being bombed every day, the Cactus pilots soon showed that their Grumman Wildcats were superior to the Japanese Zero.

Enterprise turned up to finish off the *Kinugasa*. Soon after noon, eleven Japanese troop transports were spotted by US planes some 240 km (150 miles) from Guadalcanal. By nightfall, there were only four left.

On the night of 14 November, the Japanese attempted to bombard Henderson Field again. A squadron under Vice Admiral Kondo – the heavy cruisers *Atago*, *Kirishima* and *Takao*, the light cruiser *Nagara* and three destroyers – sailed into Ironbottom Sound. The US submarine *Trout* spotted them as they passed Savo Island and warned Rear Admiral Willis Lee. The *Washington* and the *South Dakota*, supported by four destroyers, went to attack them. But the Japanese had split their force into four groups. The cruiser *Sendai* was sent to shadow the American ships. When Lee realized this, he opened fire. While the *Sendai* returned fire from the rear, the *Ayanami* and the *Uranami* attacked them in front. In the gun battle that followed, the US destroyers *Preston* and *Walke* were sunk.

The destroyer *Gwin* was also out of action, and a shot from the *Kirishima* knocked out the *South Dakota*'s electrics so that it could not move its guns. At this point, only the *Ayanami* was damaged, so Kondo and his squadron closed in. They fired three torpedoes at the *South Dakota*. All three missed. The *Washington* retaliated. Soon the *Kirishima* was crippled, and sank. Kondo broke off at 0030, his destroyers also having been badly mauled. However, the Japanese did manage to drive their transports aground at Tassafaronga, and the reinforcements disembarked under fire. Only 2,000 got ashore, along with 250 cases of ammunition and 1,500 bags of rice. On 30 November, eight Japanese destroyers attempted to land more troops and were beaten off in the Battle of Tassafaronga, losing one destroyer sunk and one crippled – the cost to the Allies was one cruiser sunk and three damaged.

Even though the Japanese forces on Guadalcanal outnumbered their American counterparts, the Japanese had lost the battle for the sea: the forces on Guadalcanal could not be resupplied. During the naval battle, they had lost two battleships, one cruiser and three destroyers to the Americans' two cruisers and five destroyers. It would become increasingly difficult to resupply their men while the Americans still held Henderson Field. The Japanese mounted a fifth and final offensive on Guadalcanal, but it never really got off the ground. And the Japanese troops on the island were soon reduced to eating grass and roots.

On 4 January 1943, after bitter disputes between the army and the navy, Imperial General Headquarters decided to evacuate its forces from Guadalcanal. Between 1 and 7 February, the Japanese withdrew the 13,000 survivors so stealthily that the Marines, now 50,000 strong but still fearful of a new attack, did not even know about it. Nevertheless, Guadalcanal was the first land victory in the South Seas and the beginning of the end for the Japanese Empire. During the six-month campaign on the island, the Japanese lost 50,000 men, 25,000 of those on land and 9,000 to disease. But the greater loss, militarily, was 600 planes and their crews – all for what the Imperial High Command called, at the time of the first US landing, an 'insignificant island in the South Seas'.

Guadalcanal had cost the Marines 1,592 lives. And for the United States the island was

not so insignificant. It kept open the route to Australia, which was fast becoming a forward base in the war against Japan. The battle for Guadalcanal had also been well covered in the press and newsreels, and victory there gave the Allies' morale a much-needed boost.

Rabaul

ON 21 FEBRUARY 1943, the US infantry landed on the Russell Islands to support advances on Rabaul. In the summer of 1942, British forces had begun an invasion of Vichy French–held Madagascar. Hostilities ceased on 5 November, and the Free French took over on 8 January 1943. In the North Pacific, the United States had decided to expel the Japanese from the Aleutians. Landing forces on Adak in August 1942, they began air attacks against Kiska and Attu in September, while a naval blockade prevented the Japanese from reinforcing their garrisons. Bypassing Kiska, American forces invaded Attu on 11 May 1943 and killed most of the island's 2,300 defenders in the following three weeks, and the Japanese evacuated Kiska. With bases in the Aleutians, the United States could bomb the Kuril Islands at the north of the Japanese archipelago.

In mid-1943, the Allies drew up new plans for the invasion of Japan proper. It was decided that the main offensive should come from the south and the south-east, through the Philippines and through Micronesia, rather than from the Aleutians or from the Asian mainland, where the Chinese – with Allied backing – were still involved in fighting the Japanese, while the British were taking on the Japanese in Burma.

The key to the invasion plan was the Philippines, which the Japanese had taken in 1941. Retaking them would disrupt Japanese communications with the East Indian islands and Malaya. And the conquest of Micronesia, through the Gilbert Islands, the Marshalls, the Carolines and the Marianas, offered the prospect of drawing the Japanese into a naval showdown and winning land bases for massive air raids on the Japanese mainland in the run-up to any invasion.

To reach the Philippines, it would be necessary to encircle Rabaul – the strategy was to isolate it rather than attack it directly. The encirclement of Rabaul began with the capture of the Treasury Islands in the Solomons by New Zealand troops in October and November 1943. And on 1 November, US troops landed at Empress Augusta Bay on the west of Bougainville. US reinforcements subsequently held off Japanese counterattacks in December 1943, when the Japanese sank two American destroyers, and in March 1944, when they killed some 6,000 men. But by then what remained of the Japanese garrison on Bougainville no longer had the strength to fight, although it did not surrender until the end of the war.

On 15 December 1943, US troops landed at Arawe on the south-west coast of New Britain. This drew the Japanese away from Cape Gloucester on the north-west coast, where there was a major landing on 26 December. By 16 January 1944, the airfield at Cape Gloucester had been secured. Talasea, on the road to Rabaul, was captured in March 1944. With western New Britain now in American hands, the Allies controlled the vital straits between New Britain and New Guinea.

On 15 February, New Zealand troops took the Green Islands south-east of New Guinea. American forces invaded Los Negros in the Admiralty Islands on 29 February and captured Manus on 9 March. With the fall of the Emirau Islands on 20 March, the Allies' stranglehold on Rabaul was virtually complete, and the 100,000 Japanese troops there could be ignored for all practical purposes. Then when the Allies subdued the Japanese in western New Guinea in 1944 and built air bases there, they were all set to push on towards the Philippines.

Tarawa

ALTHOUGH THERE WAS no plan to make a major offensive westwards across the Pacific until mid-1944, the US Joint Chiefs of Staff decided to launch a limited offensive in the central Pacific in 1943, hoping to draw the Japanese away from other areas and to speed the pace of the war. In November 1943, Admiral Nimitz's central Pacific forces invaded the Gilbert Islands. Makin fell easily, but the amphibious landings on the Tarawa atoll became another bloodbath.

Tarawa is an atoll to the north of the centre of the Gilbert Islands, comprising fifteen islets, with a total land area of 31 sq km (12 square miles). They are laid out in the shape of a right-angled triangle – the hypotenuse being the north-eastern side. This is made up of a string of islands. The southern side is the same, but the western leg is largely a reef which shelters the central lagoon. The only entrance to the lagoon is through a break in the reef on the western side, just north of Betio Island in the south-western corner. Before the

war, Betio had been the British administrative headquarters and, on the north side, in the lagoon, there was a pier where a small boat could land at high tide. The island was just 3 km (2 miles) long and only a few hundred yards wide. But it was flat, rising no more than 3 m (10 ft) above sea level. The Japanese had built an airstrip there for medium bombers. It was the main air facility in the region. Consequently, the island was well fortified.

Despite the island having been British territory before the war, detailed information about it was scant. The only charts of the area were more than a hundred years old and carried no information about currents and tides. However, aerial reconnaissance had located an estimated 90 per cent of the Japanese defensive positions. It was also estimated that the Japanese had 200 artillery pieces on Betio, ranging from 8-in guns to 20mm cannon. As the island was so small, almost all the beaches were within range of almost all the guns. Although the island had palm trees and a little undergrowth, there were absolutely no natural features to provide cover. Any invasion was going to be bloody.

With little information to go on, the 2nd Marine Division, which was to make the assault, decided to use amphibious tractors – Amtracs – to get its men ashore, although these had only been used to land supplies on beaches before. The Marines acquired seventy-five of them and began fixing machine guns to them and welding armour plating in position, while Marine drivers were taught how to manoeuvre them over coral. Fifty more Amtracs, of a newer type designed for beach assaults, were shipped out from San Diego in California the day before the invasion. But even that was not enough. The divisional

commander Major General Julian C. Smith's plan called for 100 tractors to carry the first three waves of the assault, with twenty-five tractors being held in reserve. That meant that the fourth and fifth waves would have to be brought in on landing craft. These would need at least 1.2 m (4 ft) of water over the reef which ran between 730 and 1,100 m (800 and 1,200 yards) out to sea all around the island.

No one knew much about the local tides but, for strategic and logistical reasons, the assault would have be made during a neap tide. If they waited seven days for a spring tide, the high tides came at night, which was no good for a beach assault. Delaying for over a month until spring high tides came during the day would have been too late. So D-Day was set for 20 November 1943, and H-Hour was 0830.

US Marines storm a peak on the island of Tarawa, November 1943.

At Tarawa, the US Marines found themselves pinned down on the beaches. After two days, however, the Japanese defenders made a suicidal assault allowing the Americans to expand their toehold.

The Japanese were expecting an invasion. At the top of the beach all around the island they had built a wall of palm logs 1–1.5 m (3–5 ft) high, reinforced with wire. Behind it were dug machine-gun emplacements and rifle pits. Behind those there were more well-fortified machine-gun posts made of logs, coral and reinforced concrete, and covered with sand. They were hard to see and even more difficult to silence. Further back were another twenty-five pillboxes and concrete emplacements with 75mm field guns and 37mm anti-tank guns trained on the shore. At each corner of the island and dotted in between the other emplacements were fourteen coastal defence guns ranging in calibre from 80mm to 203mm. Their magazines and crews were protected by bombproof shelters. The guns were trained on the sea approaches and the beaches themselves, and concrete beach obstacles had been laid to concentrate any invasion force into their field of fire. The Japanese also had seven Type 95 light tanks, each armed with two machine guns and a 37mm, acting as a mobile reserve.

The defenders were commanded by Rear Admiral Keiji Shibasaki. Under his command, there were 1,497 sailors from the 7th Special Naval Landing Force and 1,122 sailors from the 3rd Special Base Force. Also ashore were 2,170 Korean construction workers.

Careful study of aerial photographs showed that the south and west of the island were most heavily defended. The Japanese plainly expected the attack to come from the open sea. But the beaches there lay in a series of concave bays where it would be easy for the defenders to concentrate their fire. The northern beaches, however, were convex, so it was decided to attack the island from the lagoon side. A scouting platoon would be sent in to clear the jetty there, which could be used for resupply and the evacuation of the wounded. Three reinforced battalions would then land on the beaches Red 1 and Red 2 to the right of the pier, and Red 3 to the left. A separate landing would take place on Green Beach at the western end of the island. The 2nd Marine Regiment, under Colonel David M. Shoup, was to lead the assault on Betio, reinforced with a battalion of the 8th Marines.

The 2nd Marines had some experience of jungle fighting on Guadalcanal, but their intensive training with the tractors gave them the impression that they were going to be involved in a landing rather than an assault. They thought it was going to be a walkover.

On 18 November, the 2nd Marines were joined by the 27th Army Division, under Major General Ralph C. Smith. Along with the 2nd Marines divisional commander Major General Julian C. Smith, there was yet another Major General Smith involved in the operation, the Marine Corps commander Major General Holland M. Smith – known to his men as H.M. 'Howling Mad' Smith – who supervised the 27th Division's amphibious training on Hawaii.

On the night of 19 November, the assault force closed on Tarawa. Long before they reached the beaches things began to go wrong. Unbeknownst to the planners, the area where the Marines were supposed to transfer from their ships into the Amtracs and landing craft was subject to strong currents. The ships began to drift, and in the darkness what was supposed to be an orderly transfer turned into chaos.

Air raids over the previous few nights were supposed to have knocked out the shore batteries. At first light, it was discovered that they had not. However, the Japanese aim was bad – perhaps because the fire control system had been damaged. No ships were hit, but shells landing all around them in the water did little for the men's morale. The US Navy then opened up in an attempt to silence the Japanese guns, but the vibration knocked out the communications equipment on board the command ship USS *Maryland*. This meant that the invasion force had no communication with the carrier-borne air attack that was to come in and soften up the beach defences. This had been scheduled for 0545, so the US Navy stopped its bombardment at that time to avoid hitting its own planes. When no planes appeared, they started it again. When the bombers eventually turned up at 0615, the naval bombardment had kicked up so much dust that they could not see their targets.

Smokescreens

AT THE SAME TIME, two minesweepers moved into the lagoon, followed by two destroyers which laid smokescreens and bombarded the beaches from close range. The gunfire was supposed to slacken after an hour, as it was assumed that the Marines would be nearing the beaches, but a strong offshore wind had

The Japanese believed that they were bullets made from flesh, that their Bushido code was bound to bring victory. But at Tarawa, once again, they found that all their sacrifice was in vain.

slowed their progress and they were still nowhere near their start line. This line was supposed to be marked by the minesweepers, but one of them had drifted out of position, adding to the confusion. Rear Admiral Harry Hill worked out that it would take the Amtracs forty minutes to travel from the start line to the beaches, so he stopped his bombardment at 0855 to avoid hitting his own men as they landed. However, the Amtracs were a lot slower in the water than he had calculated. So, when the bombardment stopped, the tractors were still a long way from the beaches.

The carrier-borne planes were then supposed to strafe the beaches but, due to the breakdown in communication, few turned up, and those that did left a full ten minutes before the first Marine arrived. Meanwhile, the carrier pilots were telling their debriefers that the island's defences had been completely destroyed. Along with their bombing and strafing, 3,000 tons of shells had hit Betio, and the Marines, it was said, would walk ashore.

Shortly before 0910, Lieutenant William D. Hawkins and his scout patrol arrived on the pier and cleared it of Japanese snipers. A few minutes later, the three assault battalions reached the beaches and landed with little opposition. They ran up the beaches to the log wall, where they stopped. By this time, the Japanese began to recover their senses after the bombardment. A few men got over the log wall, but the majority were pinned down behind it.

The men coming in behind them were in even more trouble. There was only 1 m (3 ft) of water over the reef, so the landing craft had

to drop them at the edge and let them wade ashore, presenting irresistible targets to the Japanese gunners. Amphibious assaults from landing craft were at this time still relatively new. By the time the Allies stormed the Normandy beaches, they had learned to put the officers and NCOs at the back. At Tarawa, they were at the front and were shot down, leaving those men that did get ashore leaderless. Only one of the battalion commanders from the landing craft reached the beach alive. The men from the landing craft were in danger not just from enemy fire, but also from the reef itself, which had deep holes in it. Fully laden Marines disappeared into them and drowned.

At noon, the next wave arrived with the tanks. These drove in across the reef. On Red 3, one platoon of four medium tanks helped the 2nd Battalion of the 8th Marines under Major Henry P. Crowe consolidate its position, but it made little progress inland. By the end of the day, three of the tanks had been destroyed – two of them hit by American bombs. A battalion from the reserves, under Major Robert H. Ruud, was sent in to help Crowe. Again, it took heavy casualties crossing the reef, especially among the officers and NCOs, although Ruud himself made it ashore; by the time the men reached the beach, their number was fewer than that of the battalion they had come to support. There was no prospect of making an attack on the Japanese and, by nightfall, the Americans controlled a stretch of beach only 275 m (300 yards) long and had penetrated no further than 230 m (250 yards) inland.

On Red 2, the situation was worse. Intense fire during its landing had dispersed the landing force, and its commander had been landed so far to the right that the men effectively had no leader. But a liaison and observing officer from Corps Headquarters, Lieutenant Colonel Walter I. Jordan, was with them. He took charge but, as he pointed out later, Marines are not inclined to take orders from people they do not know. Nevertheless, under his command, the Marines moved inland some 70 m (75 yards) before being pinned down by sniper and machine-gun fire.

Seeing that the centre of the beach was in trouble, Colonel Shoup committed his 3rd Battalion. Enough of the Amtracs had made it back through the intensive shelling to the start line to carry two of its three companies back to the beaches. The other company would have to wait until the Amtracs dropped off those men and made the hazardous return journey.

The first two companies approached the beaches at about 1130. On their way, they passed the mouth of a small valley which was bristling with Japanese guns. They took 200 casualties before the tractors even hit shore. Some landed on the wrong beach, and those who had arrived on the right one had lost most of their equipment.

Shoup followed them ashore, followed by four 75mm howitzers. He set up a command post and established contact with Crowe to his left. But no communication was possible with Red 1, as the Japanese were dug in between them. He had no communication with his divisional commander J.C. Smith either, as most of the radio sets had become wet during the landings and were not working.

Neither Smith nor Shoup had any idea what was happening on Green Beach. The 3rd Battalion under Major Michael P. Ryan landing there found it was facing a considerable

Japanese force. But with stragglers who had drifted there from other beaches he managed to consolidate a position on the north-west tip of the island. At midday, two tanks drove in across the reef to support them. Engineers then blew a hole in the log wall and, following the tanks, Ryan's men advanced 460 m (500 yards) before the tanks were knocked out. They were unable to hold this forward position, however, as they had bypassed several Japanese positions, lacking the heavy weapons to take them out. So, at nightfall, Ryan fell back to a defensive perimeter.

That evening, one of Ryan's radios dried out sufficiently to work. He reported to J.C. Smith that, without heavy weapons, he could not advance. Smith got the impression that the situation was far worse than it was and, although reinforcements could have been landed safely, he sent none. Instead, he called up the Corps reserve and prepared to send the 1st Battalion of the 8th Marines to make a fresh landing east of Crowe, fearing that the Japanese had a force there set to counterattack. Due to a mix-up, this landing never took place – which was fortunate as it would surely have resulted in a massacre. Before Smith had issued his orders, a Marine spotter plane saw Shoup's howitzers going ashore on Red 2 and assumed it was the 1st Battalion. Smith was told that the 1st Battalion had already been committed and binned his plan. As it was, the men of 1st Battalion suffered an uncomfortable night in the landing craft. The following morning, they were sent to Red 2. A message from Shoup saying that there was a deep-water channel running all the way up to the jetty did not get through, and the 1st Battalion sustained heavy casualties as the men waded ashore across the reef. The survivors were sent

to defend Shoup's right. He then pushed forward and, by the end of the day, Marines from Red 2 had made it across the island to the opposite shore, cutting the Japanese in two.

Although Ryan had been denied troop reinforcements, he received two more medium tanks and some flame-throwers during the night. Air strikes were called in on the Japanese artillery, and at 1000 hours he moved out against little opposition. Soon Ryan had cleared the western beach and arrived at the southern coast opposite the pier.

That evening, two battalions of the 6th Regimental Combat Team under Colonel Maurice Holmes were to land on Green Beach. In the morning they were to advance on the airstrip, while the rest of the Marines were to attempt to break out of their beachheads. The Japanese had been seen moving off Betio onto the next island in the southern chain, Bairiki. As J.C. Smith's orders were to clear the entire atoll, he sent a battalion of 75mm howitzers and a battalion of the 6th Marines to Bairiki to prevent the enemy making a stand there. On Bairiki, the Marines met two machine-gun posts manned by fifteen Japanese. But Bairiki was also used as a fuel dump. A preliminary air strike strafed the island and hit the dump with .50 incendiary bullets. The resulting explosion burnt out the machine-gun posts, and the Marines landed unopposed. Once the howitzers were in position, they could cut off the retreat of the Japanese, leaving the infantry free to return to the battle on Betio.

Late that afternoon, the 1st Battalion of the 6th Marines under Major William K. Jones landed on Green Beach. It was the first unit to reach the island in an organized condition.

During the night, the men moved forward to reinforce Ryan's position. The following morning, they pushed along the southern coast until they met up with the Marines who had crossed the island from Red 2 the day before. With the aid of flame-throwers, naval gunfire, the one remaining medium tank and seven light tanks, they pushed forward 2.5 km (1½ miles) by midday. The rate of progress slowed that afternoon, partly because the light tanks were found to be ineffective. Their 37mm guns made little impression on even the defensive positions made out of coral and logs, and they did not have enough weight to crush them. However, the M4 medium tank worked wonderfully and, by the end of the day, they had joined up with Crowe, Ruud and the 8th Marines at the end of the Japanese air base's runway. With the exception of small pockets, the Japanese forces were now corralled in the eastern end of the island. There they were pounded by naval gunfire and the howitzers on Bairiki.

On the morning of 23 November, Shoup began clearing the remaining Japanese resistance in the valley that ran inland from Red 2. By midday, he had driven through to the southern tip. Meanwhile, the 3rd Battalion of the 6th Marines passed through the American lines and advanced on the Japanese positions. At 1312 hours, J.C. Smith announced that Beito was clear. The rest of the atoll was cleared by 28 November. The defenders lost 4,690 killed, and 146 were taken prisoner. Only seventeen of them were Japanese. The rest were the remnants of the benighted Korean construction workers.

Tarawa had cost the Marines more than 1,000 killed and 2,100 wounded. The casualty list would have been longer if the Japanese commander had not depended on stopping the invasion on the beaches and prepared a more effective defence inland – admittedly, as Admiral Shibasaki was killed by a shell in the preliminary bombardment, he was in no position to organize this as the battle developed. But as it was, the Battle of Tarawa shocked the American public because of the huge number of casualties sustained in so short a time. However, it had taught the military some important lessons. Programmes were developed to improve the accuracy of naval gunfire and aerial bombing and strafing, and changes were made to the organization of amphibious assaults that would pay dividends on other islands and on the beaches of Normandy.

The Marianas

HAVING LOST THE Gilbert Islands, the Japanese defended the Marshalls in an effort to tie up Allied forces and put a strain on their extended lines of supply. Nimitz made his first attack on the Kwajalein Atoll, which he subjected to so heavy a preliminary bombardment that the Allied infantry had no problems landing on 30 January 1944. Enewetak fell on 17 February.

To support their landings on the rest of the Marshall Islands, the US fleet began day and night attacks on the Japanese base at Truk in the Carolines on 17 February, destroying 200,000 tonnes of merchant shipping and around 300 aircraft. That put the base out of action, and the Allies could safely bypass it. The Allies then mustered over 125,000 troops and 500 ships to attack the Mariana Islands, which lay 5,600 km (3,500 miles) from Pearl

Harbor and 1,600 km (1,000 miles) from the westernmost limit of their advance, Enewetak.

Knowing the attack was coming, the Japanese planned to counterattack using their remaining 1,055 land-based aircraft in the Marianas, the Carolines, and western New Guinea, along with the 450 aircraft on their nine aircraft carriers. But in the spring of 1944 the Allies were winning the war in the skies. Yamamoto had died when his plane had been shot down over Bougainville in April 1943, and his successor, Admiral Koga Mineichi, who had come up with the plan, was killed along with his staff in a plane crash.

A dead Japanese soldier and a burnt-out tank bear witness to the successful US recapture of Saipan in the Mariana Islands, July 1944.

In the Battle of the Philippine Sea, the Japanese Imperial Navy once again found itself under attack because Allied cryptographers had broken the Japanese codes and were thus able to anticipate the enemy's every move.

counterattack, the biggest of its kind in the war. Some 8,000 civilians also committed suicide en masse by jumping off the cliffs at Marpi Point. Only 1,000 out of the garrison of 32,000 survived. In all, 22,000 civilians also perished. American casualties were also high – 3,426 were killed and 10,595 wounded.

The loss of Saipan was such a setback for the Japanese that prime minister Hideki Tojo and his entire Cabinet resigned. Even some in the Imperial High Command realized that the loss of the Mariana Islands meant the war was lost, but dared not say so. Even so, Tojo was succeeded by General Koiso Kuniaki, who pledged to carry on the nation's historic fight with a renewed vigour. The loss of Saipan meant that the United States could build bases there for its new B-29 Superfortresses, which had been developed for the sole purpose of bombing Japan. Now the Japanese would have to suffer air raids like their German allies. The first flight of 100 B-29s took off from Saipan on 12 November 1944. It bombed Tokyo, the first air raid on the city since 1942.

While the Japanese were still resisting on Saipan, Admiral Jisaburo Ozawa put Admiral Mineichi's plan into action. The Japanese Combined Fleet was steaming from its anchorages in the East Indies and the Philippines to take on the US 5th Fleet, under Admiral Raymond Spruance. Ozawa had nine aircraft carriers against Spruance's fifteen, but he could count on help from land-based planes from Guam, Rota and Yap. They met west of the Marianas in the greatest carrier battle of the war, known as the Battle of the Philippine Sea. It is also known as the 'Great Marianas Turkey Shoot'. Battle was joined on 19 June, but Ozawa had already lost. He did not know that

On 15 June, two divisions of US Marines went ashore on Saipan Island in the Marianas. But the 30,000 Japanese defending it put up a fierce fight. The Japanese fortified themselves in underground caves and bunkers that protected them from American artillery and naval bombardment. The same defensive tactics were used on other small islands. The only way to deal with the defenders was to clear out the bunkers and caves one at a time. This was time-consuming and caused such a high rate of casualties that an entire US Army division had to be brought in as reinforcements. Gradually, the Japanese defenders were pushed into smaller and smaller pockets. The Japanese position was hopeless. To encourage their men to fight to the last, Admiral Nagumo, now the Commander in Chief on Saipan, and Lieutenant Gaito, head of the garrison, committed suicide. Organized resistance ended on 7 July with a suicidal

raids on the Japanese airfields had put his land-based aircraft out of action. At 0830 Ozawa sent 430 planes in four waves against Spruance's ships. As the second wave left, the carrier *Taiho*, Ozawa's flagship, was hit by a torpedo from a submarine. US planes intercepted the Japanese aircraft, and only twenty planes from the second wave got through to inflict minor damage on the *Wasp* and *Bunker Hill*. At 1220, the *Shokaku* was recovering the thirty of its planes that had made it back when it was hit by a torpedo from the US submarine *Cavalla*. The *Shokaku* blazed for three hours before it sank. Shortly after, at 1532, the *Taiho* exploded. Even then Ozawa did not realize what a disaster the battle had been, believing that his missing planes had landed on Guam. In fact, more than 300 planes had been shot down. Hoping that they might return Ozawa held on until late in the afternoon of 20 June. US aircraft counterattacked, sinking the *Hiyo*, damaging the *Zuikaku*, putting a hole in the flight deck of the *Chiyoda* and destroying nearly 100 more planes. As the Japanese fleet retreated northwards towards Okinawa, the American pilots tried to make it back to their ships in the growing dark. That night only 43 of the 216 aircraft launched in the air strike found their carriers. Many ditched in the sea and most of the crews were picked up. The United States lost only 16 pilots and 33 aircrew.

Despite the American aircraft losses, the Battle of the Philippine Sea was ultimately of more strategic importance than the fall of Saipan. After it, Nimitz's forces could occupy other major islands in the Mariana Islands. Of particular satisfaction was the retaking of Guam, which had been an American possession since the Spanish-American war in 1901.

Garrisoned by 365 Marines, it was the first US possession to fall into Japanese hands when it was invaded on 9 December 1941.

The island of Guam was about 16 km (10 miles) long and 50 km (30 miles) wide. There were mountains to the south, and the centre was a flat limestone plateau. It had a fine anchorage in Apta Harbour, and the Japanese had built an air base on Orote peninsula, next to the old Marine Corps barracks. The invasion was delayed because the Marines were held up by the prolonged fighting on Saipan, so the Army's 77th Infantry Division was brought in from Hawaii to reinforce the assault force. After eleven days of bombing and shelling, the 3rd Marine Division was put ashore at 0829 on 21 July at Asan. By mid-afternoon they held a beachhead just 1,830 m (2,000 yards) wide and 1,100 m (1,200 yards) deep, with the Japanese pouring fire down on them from the surrounding hills. Mortars were fired from the caves on the front of the hills and artillery from the reverse, causing huge casualties among the Marines. But accurate naval gunfire helped them fight their way up the slope and, on 24 July, they held the ridge. The following night seven battalions of Japanese soldiers with bayonets fixed charged, shouting, 'Banzai' and 'Wake up Yankee and die.' In heavy fighting, some of the enemy got so far through the American line that the wounded in the field hospital had to pick up rifles and defend themselves from their beds. But the ferocious Japanese counterattack failed to push the Marines back into the sea. It petered out, leaving massive Japanese casualties.

A second landing on 21 July by the 1st Provisional Marine Brigade (Shepherd) to the south on Agat beach came under heavy Japanese artillery fire the moment it hit the

The first wave of Marines go ashore in Saipan. Of the 30,000 defenders, only 1,000 survived, and thousands of civilians killed themselves by jumping off cliffs. Once Saipan had fallen, the Japanese home islands were in bombing range.

beaches. Some 350 Marines died, and 24 Amtracs were destroyed. But once ashore the Marines made rapid progress, soon penetrating to a depth of 1,830 m (2,000 yards). On the first day, they also managed to land 3,000 tonnes of supplies and a platoon of Sherman tanks which helped them hold off Japanese counterattacks on the following few nights. When reinforcement arrived from the 77th Infantry, the Marines fought their way out of the beachhead and joined up with the Marines at Asan to the north. Together they fought north until they had cut off the Orote peninsula. This was defended by an infantry battalion, whose commander told his men to drink whatever alcohol they could lay their hands on. Intoxicated on beer, saki and synthetic whiskey, the Japanese staged a night attack. They charged, giggling hysterically, reeling about and firing their weapons indiscriminately. But just because they were drunk did not mean that they were not dangerous. They were shelled and machine-gunned. In the morning, the Marines counted more than 400 Japanese corpses.

The 1st Provisional Marine Brigade then fought its way yard by yard up the Orote peninsula against fierce resistance. But fire support from naval artillery helped force the enemy back. Resistance cracked on 27 July. By 29 July, the peninsula had been cleared and the airfield was in action again – this time for American planes – on 31 July. But there were still Japanese units who put up a tremendous fight on the island. Gradually the 1st Marines and 77th Infantry drove them up into the northern tip of Guam. Resistance ceased on 10 August. Of the 54,891 US troops landed, 1,440 were killed, 145 were missing and 5,648

were wounded. Of the Japanese garrison 10,693 were killed and ninety-eight taken prisoners. The rest disappeared into the jungle to fight on. A lieutenant colonel and his 113 men surrendered on 4 September 1945, but the last known survivor, Colonel Yokoi Shoichi, emerged in January 1972.

The last important island in the Mariana Islands, Tinian, fell on 24 July, when two Marine Divisions from Saipan landed on the beach, taking the Japanese commander Admiral Kakuda and his 9,000-man garrison by surprise. By the evening, the Marines had established a large beachhead, and 1,200 Japanese died when they tried to force them back into the sea. The 4th Marines cleared the southern part of the island, while the 2nd took the north. Within a week, the island was in American hands. The Marines had lost 327 killed and 1,771 wounded. The Japanese had lost their garrison almost to a man. In all, the Marianas cost the Japanese 46,000 killed or captured; the Americans, 4,750 killed.

The Philippines and Borneo

ON 28 JULY 1944, President Roosevelt had approved General MacArthur's plan to take the Philippines Archipelago. This was of special interest to MacArthur as he had been commander of the US forces on the Philippines when the Japanese attacked in 1941. With 180,000 men under arms, he thought he could hold the islands, but by 27 December he was forced to abandon the capital Manila and withdraw to the peninsula of Bataan. The men fought a delaying action there, but found themselves short of supplies. MacArthur left on 11 March 1942 with the

words, 'I will return.' The men in Bataan fought on until 8 April. Six days later, they were subjected to a march into captivity, the infamous Bataan Death March. Some 16,000 died. A small US force fought on, on the island of Corregidor until 6 May.

In preparation for the invasion, MacArthur's forces from New Guinea seized Morotai, the most north-easterly island of the Moluccas, in mid-September 1944. This was on the direct route to Mindanao, the southernmost landmass of the Philippines. Meanwhile, Nimitz's fleet from the east landed troops in the Palau Islands.

US intelligence had discovered that the Japanese forces were unexpectedly small both on Mindanao and on Leyte, a smaller island north of the Surigao Strait. It was decided that they should bypass Mindanao and begin the invasion of the Philippines on Leyte. On 17 and 18 October 1944, US forces seized offshore isles in Leyte Gulf. And, on 20 October, they landed four divisions on the east coast of Leyte itself. The threat to Leyte was the cue for the Japanese to put into action their latest plan *Sho-Go* – 'Operation Victory'.

Under Sho-Go, the next Allied invasion would be met with concerted air attacks. The problem was that the Japanese army and navy air forces had only 212 planes in the immediate area. However, Admiral Ozawa would send four carriers with 106 planes south from Japanese waters. It was also hoped that this carrier force would lure the US aircraft carriers into a new engagement. By this point in the war, the Japanese were training 'kamikaze' pilots who would fly planes loaded with fuel and explosives into the Allied shipping. They hoped to knock out the US carrier fleet in a desperate effort to protect their homeland.

At the same time, a Japanese naval force from Singapore would split itself into two groups and converge on Leyte Gulf from the north and from the south-west. The weaker of the two groups, with two battleships, one heavy cruiser and four destroyers under Vice Admiral Nishimura Teiji, would pass through the Surigao Strait. The stronger group, consisting of five battleships, twelve cruisers and fifteen destroyers under Vice Admiral Kurita Takeo, would enter the Pacific through the San Bernardino Strait, which lies between the Philippine islands of Samar and Luzon. On the way, two of Takeo's heavy cruisers were torpedoed by US submarines on 23 October, and one of the mightiest of Japan's battleships, the *Musashi*, was sunk in an air attack the next day. However, three groups of US escort carriers Takeo met on the way also suffered heavy damage.

Tanks of the US 77th Division fight their way through a jungle clearing in the northwest of Leyte Island in the Philippines.

As the commander of the US 3rd Fleet, Admiral Halsey had diverted his main strength towards Ozawa's fleet farther to the north, Takeo made his way unopposed through the San Bernardino Strait on 25 October. But Teiji's fleet had been spotted going through the Surigao Strait and, when it arrived in Leyte Gulf in the early hours of 25 October, it had been practically annihilated by the US 7th Fleet under Admiral Kincaid. Finding himself all alone in Leyte Gulf, Takeo turned back. Meanwhile, Halsey had destroyed all of four Ozawa's carriers, together with a light cruiser and two destroyers. 'Operation Victory' had been a terrible defeat. Japanese losses amounted to one large aircraft carrier, three light carriers, three battleships, six heavy cruisers, four light cruisers and eleven destroyers. The US had lost only one light carrier, two escort carriers and three destroyers. This was the first time, however, that the American fleet faced the kamikaze in force, and their deliberately suicidal attacks meant that the war was going to be hard-won.

After the Battle of Leyte Gulf, the Japanese navy was no longer a threat, and the way was clear for the invasion of the Philippines. But that did not mean the Japanese were going to give them up easily. Even after their naval defeat in the Leyte Gulf, they landed reinforcements on the west coast of Leyte. Japanese resistance was so stubborn that the Americans had to be reinforced before the main city of Ormoc fell on 10 December 1944. Only on Christmas Day could the United States claim control of the whole of Leyte – even then, there was still some mopping up to be done. The defence of Leyte cost the Japanese some 75,000 killed or taken prisoner.

On leaving the Philippines in March 1942, the commander of US forces there, General Douglas MacArthur, vowed famously: 'I will return.' On 21 October 1944, he fulfilled his promise when he landed on the central island of Leyte.

The US Marines
would meet further
fanatical resistance
when they landed
on Iwo Jima. There
were huge losses on
both sides.

From Leyte the Americans took Mindoro, the largest of the islands immediately south of Luzon, on 15 December. Again the kamikaze made the victory costly. Suicidal attack continued after the US forces surprised the Japanese by landing at Lingayen Gulf on the west coast of Luzon itself, the most important island of the Philippines, on 9 January 1945. There was no hope of reinforcement and, in the long run, there was no prospect of victory, so the Japanese commander Lieutenant General Yamashita Tomoyuki tried to tie down the American forces as long as possible in the mountains. Manila itself was strongly defended. One American corps approached it from Lingayen over the Central Plains. Another was landed at Subic Bay, at the northern end of the Bataan Peninsula, on 29 January. The two corps met up at Dinalupihan a week later. More troops landed at Nasugbu, south of Manila Bay, on 31 January, surrounding Manila. It fell on 3 March, but Japanese resistance continued in the mountains until mid-June 1945. Meanwhile, an American division landed on Mindanao at Zamboanga, on the south-west peninsula, on 10 March, and a corps began the occupation of the core of the island on 17 April.

While US forces consolidated their positions in the Philippines, the Australians started the reconquest of Borneo by bombarding Tarakan Island, off the north-east coast, on 12 April. On 30 April, they landed on nearby Sadau Island in the Baragan Straits, from where they could shell the beach fortifications. They landed on Tarakan on 1 May. After four days of fighting, the town of Tarakan fell at a cost of 225 Australians killed and 669 wounded; 1,540 Japanese were dead. On 10 June, 2,900 Australians went ashore in Brunei on the north-west coast, where they met little opposition. And Balikpapan, on the east coast far to the south of Tarakan, was attacked on 1 July, and the Japanese defences collapsed, depriving Japan of oil supplies for southern Borneo. The British then began preparing an advance base for the retaking of Singapore there. But by the time the air base in Borneo was built, Japan had surrendered.

Iwo Jima and Okinawa

WHILE THE CAMPAIGNS on the Philippines and on Borneo were still under way, plans were being laid for invasion of Japan. This would begin, the planners decided, with landings on Kyushu, the most southerly of the major Japanese islands. In preparation, B-29 Superfortresses under General Curtis E. LeMay stationed on the Mariana Islands began a campaign of bombing in the closing months of 1944. But it was a round trip of 4,830 km (3,000 miles) from Saipan to mainland Japan, a long flight even for the Superfortresses. However, if US forces took the little volcanic island of Iwo Jima in the Bonin Islands, which lay some 1,220 km (760 miles) south-east of Japan, they would halve the distance to Tokyo and, with fighters stationed there, the USAAF would be able to defend its bombers over their targets. Iwo Jima was a doubly important target because Japan considered the island its 'unsinkable aircraft carrier'. It was a radar and fighter base whose aircraft intercepted the Superfortresses on their bombing missions over Japan.

Irregularly shaped, Iwo Jima is about 8 km (5 miles) long and anything from 730 m (800 yards) to 4 km (2½ miles) wide. The Japanese were determined to hold on to it. They garrisoned the island with 21,000 troops under Lieutenant General Kuribayashi Tadamichi, and it had the strongest defences of all the Japanese possessions in the Pacific. It had been under constant bombardment since the fall of the Marianas, but the prolonged fighting in the Philippines had delayed the attack, giving the Japanese a few months to build up the island's already formidable fortifications. As on other Pacific islands, they had created underground defences, making the best possible use of natural caves and the rocky terrain.

For days before the landings, Iwo Jima was subjected to massive bombardment by naval guns, rockets, and air strikes using bombs carrying the recently developed napalm. But the Japanese were so well dug in that no amount of shelling or bombing could knock them out.

On 19 February, the 5th Amphibious Corps under General Harry Schmidt went ashore on the south of the island, with Schmidt confidently predicting that he would take the island in four days. Of the 30,000 men landing on the beaches on the first day, 2,400 were hit by the Japanese. The Marines soon had a

US Marines storm the beaches of Iwo Jima, dragging heavy assault cannons behind them.

3,660-m (4,000-yard) long beachhead, but were slowed inland by the island's ashy volcanic soil. The 5th Marines then divided their forces. Half struck inland and took the first of the two Japanese airfields – a third was under construction. The other half turned south to take Mount Suribachi, an extinct volcano soon nicknamed 'Meatgrinder Hill' for the casualties taken there. The Marines eventually took Mount Suribachi on 23 February. The raising of the American flag on its summit was photographed by Joe Rosenthal of the Associated Press. It became one of the best-known images of the Pacific war, and statues, paintings and American postage stamp designs have been based on it. However, the photo-

graph actually depicts a second flag being raised over Mount Suribachi. The first flag was raised some hours earlier, but it was too small to be seen by the other troops on the island.

While the 5th Marine Division moved up the west coast, 4th Marines fought their way up the east, but the fighting was so fierce that 3rd Marines, a floating reserve, had to be landed. They moved up the centre, and by 9 March they had reached the north-east coast. On 26 March, the Japanese staged their last suicidal attack, with 350 men, near Kitano Point on the northern tip of the island. After that, resistance collapsed. Some 20,000 Japanese were killed and the remaining 1,000 captured. The Marine and US Army losses were 6,812 killed

Flying the Flag: the Stars and Stripes is hoisted over Iwo Jima, 23 February 1945. That there were still Japanese troops who had not surrendered is obvious from the watchful pose of the soldier in the foreground.

The USS Missouri *under attack from a kamikaze pilot. Japanese troops still fighting in the Philippines were told that these suicide attacks had been a great victory and that the Americans had been pushed back into the sea.*

and 19,189 wounded. The Battle of Iwo Jima was a costly but decisive victory. Now the all-out assault on the Japanese mainland could begin and, in the next five months, more than 2,000 Superfortresses flew bombing missions from the airfields of Iwo Jima.

While the fighting on Iwo Jima had been going on, the war in the air took a new turn. The USAAF abandoned high-altitude strikes during daylight, as they seemed to be making little impact on Japan's industrial output. Instead, they began low-level strikes at night, using napalm. These were a startling success.

As Japan was in an earthquake zone, buildings were traditionally made out of lightweight wood and paper. They burnt easily. In the first fire-bomb raid on the night of 9 March 1945, about 25 per cent of Tokyo's buildings were destroyed, killing more than 80,000 people and leaving 1,000,000 homeless. Strategic planners then came to believe that Japan could be defeated without an invasion by ground troops and the massive casualties that would entail. Similar fire-bombing raids were launched against other major cities – Nagoya, Osaka, Kobe, Yokohama and Toyama. However, the

invasion plans were not discarded immediately, and there would be one more island hop before the end of the war. It would be the largest amphibious operation of the Pacific war. Its objective was Okinawa, an island some 110 km (70 miles) long and 11 km (7 miles) wide just 560 km (350 miles) south of Kyushu. Okinawa was considered the last stepping stone before the invasion of Japan itself.

American reconnaissance planes put the strength of Okinawa's garrison at 65,000. In fact, the Thirty-Second Army under General Mitsuru Ushijima was almost 120,000 strong. Some 10,000 aircraft defended the island, and the Imperial Navy sent a task force headed by the *Yamato*, the biggest battleship ever built.

For the invasion of Okinawa, code-named Operation Iceberg, the commander of the US ground forces Lieutenant General Simon Bolivar Buckner assembled the largest array of battle-hardened troops yet deployed in the Pacific. There were three Marine Divisions and four Army Divisions: more than 155,000 men in all. But by the time the fighting was finished, more than 300,000 Americans had been committed to battle. Admiral Spruance assembled more than 1,300 vessels of all sizes for the landing, including a large British carrier force under Vice Admiral Sir Bernard Rawlings.

Air raids on Okinawa began as early as October 1944 and culminated in March 1945 in an attack that destroyed hundreds of Japanese planes. The invasion was scheduled for 1 April, and preliminary naval bombardment began on 18 March. US forces then began taking some of the outlying islands, including the Kerama Islands, which would be used as a forward base. On the Keramas, 77th Infantry captured 200 suicide boats, packed with explosives that would have posed a major threat to the 5th Fleet, which was already being harassed by kamikazes. In all, twenty-seven suicide pilots penetrated the wall of fire the escorts put up to reach their target. Four carriers were damaged in the run-up to the landings. The USS *Franklin* and the *Wasp* were knocked out; kamikaze also hit a battleship, a cruiser, four destroyers and six other ships.

On 1 April, the island was bombarded with 44,825 rounds of 5-in and larger shells, 32,000 rockets and 22,500 mortar rounds. The troops clambered into landing craft at 0400 for the four-and-a-half hour run into Hagushi beach, newly cleared of mines, on the west coast of the island. They hit the beaches at 0830 and found, to their surprise, no opposition. By nightfall, 60,000 men were ashore, holding a beachhead 13 km (8 miles) wide by 5 km (3 miles) deep.

The next day, US troops drove across the island to the east coast, occupied the entire central zone of the island and captured two airfields. Buckner then sent three Marine divisions south, while 6th Marines went north, where they met some resistance on the Motubu Peninsula. By 21 April, they had cleared the north of the island, killing 2,500 Japanese defenders at a cost of 218 Americans killed and 902 wounded.

On 4 April, the 24th Corps under Major General John Hodge reached the Japanese southern defences at Shuri, where Ushijima was determined to fight a war of attrition that he could not win. Meanwhile, on 6 April, the 77th Infantry Division took the small island of Ise Shima off the north coast of Okinawa. It was held by 2,000 Japanese, who put up a fierce fight for five days.

That same day the kamikaze resumed with new vigour. Some 700 suicide planes attacked the 5th Fleet, damaging or sinking thirteen destroyers. The *Yamato* and its escort of the cruiser *Yahagi* and eight destroyers were also sent on a suicide mission. With their tanks filled with nearly all Japan's remaining stocks of oil, they did not have enough fuel to sail back to port. So the flotilla had been ordered to beach itself on Okinawa and to use their guns to defend the troops there. But the mighty *Yamato* was spotted by a submarine just off the southernmost tip of Kyushu. She had no air cover and was a sitting duck when carrier planes caught up with her the next day. In two hours, she was hit by seven bombs and twelve torpedoes, blew up and sank. In what proved to be the last naval action of the war, the *Yahagi* and four destroyers were also sunk.

Meanwhile, despite reinforcements, 24th Corps could not make much of a dent in Ushijima's defences and was suffering high casualties. Even though his men were suffering ten times the casualty rate of the US force, on 12 April, Ushijima went on the offensive. For two days, he sent wave after wave of men in suicidal attacks on the American positions. All of them were repulsed. Then 32nd Army went back on the defensive again.

That same day a new Japanese suicide weapon – christened the *baka* by the Allies from the Japanese word for 'fool' – claimed its first victim, the US destroyer *Abele*. The baka was a rocket-powered glider that was towed into range by a bomber. When released, its solitary pilot flew at the target. There was no parachute and no way to get out. Dropped usually from an altitude of more than 7,600 m (25,000 ft) and over 80 km (50 miles) out, the baka would

US amphibious tanks and landing craft approaching a beach during Operation Iceberg to secure Okinawa, April 1945.

glide to about 5 km (3 miles) from the target before the pilot ignited its three rocket engines, accelerating the craft to more than 960 km/h (600 mph) in its final dive. The explosive charge in the nose weighed more than a tonne. Plane, pilot and – in thirty-four cases – ship were destroyed in one massive explosion.

Frustrated with the slow progress on land, Buckner ordered a more intensive bombardment. But the Japanese fortifications were well prepared and costly to overrun, and the Marines could make no breakthrough. On 2 May Ushijima went on the offensive again, but was driven back, losing 5,000 men. On 11 May, Buckner ordered a new offensive to push back the Japanese flanks. Fearing that he was about to be encircled, Ushijima pulled back on 21 May to make a final stand on the southern tip of the island. A rearguard continued a ferocious fight against the 24th Corps, while the rest of Ushijima's men made an orderly retreat to a new line. On 31 May, the city of Shuri finally fell, after its defences and been reduced to rubble by bombardment.

The US Tenth Army made a last push, aided by 6th Marines, who made an amphibious landing on Oroku Peninsula on the south-west corner of the island to take out a strongpoint and an airfield there. Buckner's main force moved forward painfully slowly, using flame-throwers and high explosives to clear enemy positions. The Japanese fought on fanatically, but the front gradually began to crumble.

On 18 June, General Buckner was wounded and, later, died. He was replaced by General Geiger for the final stages of the battle. Three days later Ushijima was also dead, by his own hand. Scorning an American offer of surrender to prevent any further unnecessary loss of life, on 21 June he and his Chief of Staff knelt outside their headquarters and committed hara-kiri. His final order was that his men should revert to guerrilla warfare. They continued fighting until the end of the month when some 7,400 gave themselves up, the first time the Japanese had surrendered in large numbers. At least 110,000 Japanese soldiers were dead, and there had been a large number of civilian casualties. For the Allies, it was the costliest operation in the Pacific, with some half a million men involved in the fighting. US ground forces had lost 7,203 killed and 31,807 wounded. The navy had lost some 5,000 killed and a similar number wounded.

Japan had lost its entire navy and, during the Battle of Okinawa, 7,800 Japanese aircraft had been destroyed for the loss of 763 Allied planes. The Japanese mainland now lay wide open. It had no defence against the continual bombing raids the USAAF flew against it, and the British and American fleets that surrounded the islands could shell it at will.

General Joseph 'Vinegar Joe' Stilwell was brought in to command the Tenth Army, and plans were laid to bring over the First Army, which had recently been victorious in Europe. They were to form a new army group under General Douglas MacArthur, ready for the invasion of Kyushu, which was scheduled to begin on 1 November. But they were upstaged by history.

President Roosevelt had died on 12 April, and President Harry S. Truman was now in the White House. Military assessments of the situation given to Truman estimated that it would take well into 1946 to defeat Japan, at a cost of perhaps a million casualties. But on 16 July 1945, the atomic bomb was tested

successfully in a desert area at Alamogordo, New Mexico. It had an explosive power equivalent to that of more than 15,000 tonnes of TNT, vastly more devastating than any previous weapon. Truman realized that it might be used to bomb Japan into surrender rather than waste more American lives in the invasion of the Japanese homeland.

When the victorious Allies met in the Berlin suburb of Potsdam in July 1945, they put out peace feelers to Japan, but received no reply. So, on 6 August 1945, an atomic bomb was loaded onto a specially equipped B-29 Superfortress *Enola Gay* on Tinian Island in the Marianas. At 0815 local time, *Enola Gay* dropped the bomb on Hiroshima, at the

The road to Naha: the 6th Marine Division, equipped with flame-throwing tanks, mops up Japanese resistance on Okinawa, April 1945.

It's over: signing the Japanese surrender, which brought World War II to a close, aboard the USS Missouri, *2 September 1945.*

southern end of Honshu Island. The combined heat and blast obliterated everything in the immediate vicinity. Fires burned across 10 sq km (4 square miles) of the city. Between 70,000 and 80,000 people were dead or dying, and more than 70,000 others were injured – though as many, if not more, were killed by conventional bombing and shelling that day. When this did not achieve the Japanese surrender, a second bomb was dropped on Nagasaki on 9 August. This killed between 35,000 and 40,000 people.

On 8 August, the Soviet Union declared war on Japan, threatening the huge Japanese

army now cut off on the mainland of Asia. On 10 August, the Japanese government agreed to surrender on the terms offered at Potsdam on the understanding that Japan could retain the Emperor. The Allies agreed.

On 14 August, Emperor Hirohito spoke on the radio for the first time and urged the Japanese people to accept the unacceptable. On 2 September, General MacArthur formally accepted the Japanese surrender, signed by Japan's foreign minister Shigemitsu and General Umezu, on the deck of Nimitz's flagship, the USS *Missouri*, in Tokyo Bay. World War II was over.

Bibliography

Beevor, Anthony, *Berlin: the Downfall 1945*, Viking, London, 2002.

Beevor, Anthony, *Stalingrad*, Viking, London, 1998.

Carver, Michael, *Dilemmas of the Desert War: A New Look at the Libyan Campaign 1940–42*, Batsford/Imperial War Museum, 1986.

Cawthorne, Nigel, *Fighting Them on the Beaches*, Arcturus, London, 2002.

Churchill, Winston S., *The Second World War*, Penguin, London, 1985.

Deighton, Len and Hastings, Max, *Battle of Britain*, Wordsworth, Ware, 1999.

Evans, Martin Marix, *The Fall of France*, Osprey, Oxford, 2000.

Forty, George, *Road to Berlin: The Allied Drive from Normandy*, Cassell, London, 1999.

Gawne, Jonathan, *The War in the Pacific: From Pearl Harbor to Okinawa*, Greenhill Books, London, 1996.

Hamilton, Nigel, *Montgomery of Alamein, 1887–1942*, Allen Lane, London, 2001.

Hastings, Max, *Overlord*, Michael Joseph, London, 1984.

Healy, Mark, *The Battle of Midway*, Osprey, Oxford, 2000.

Kershaw, Robert J., *The Battle of Kursk*, Ian Allen, Shepperton, 1999.

Kershaw, Robert J., *War Without Garlands: Operation Barbarossa 1941–42*, Ian Allen, Shepperton, 2000.

Kiriakopoulous, G.C., *Ten Days to Destiny: The Battle for Crete 1941*, Franklin Watts, New York, 1985.

Latimer, John, *Tobruk 1941*, Osprey, Oxford, 2001.

Mueller, Joseph N., *Guadalcanal 1942: The Marines Strike Back*, Osprey, London, 1992.

Perrett, Bryan, *Allied Tanks in North Africa*, Arms and Armour, London, 1986.

Prange, Gordon W., *At Dawn We Slept: The Untold Story of Pearl Harbor*, Penguin, London, 2001.

Ryan, Cornelius, *A Bridge Too Far*, Wordsworth, Ware, 1999.

Whiting, Charles, *The Battle of the Bulge*, Sutton, Stroud, 1999.

Wright, Derrick, *The Battle for Iwo Jima 1945*, Sutton, Stroud, 1999.

Index

Picture Credits

Mirco de Cet : 2-3 (title page), 6, 7, 8, 21, 22, 24-5, 27, 28-9, 34, 36-7, 44, 48, 50-1, 53, 54, 59, 62, 64, 65, 70-1, 72-3, 78-9, 90-1, 94-5, 100, 103, 110, 113, 114, 118, 123, 124, 126-7, 128, 129, 134-5, 139, 144-5, 146, 157, 159, 160, 167, 168, 171, 173, 174-5, 176, 179, 181, 182-3, 200-1, 203, 208, 216-7, 222, 224-5, 230, 232-3, 236-7, 238, 242

Getty Images: 14, 15, 16, 18, 19, 20, 23, 26, 32, 33, 39, 40, 49, 56-7, 67, 74, 82, 87, 88, 92, 93, 98-9, 105, 108, 115, 116, 117, 132, 138, 140, 147, 149, 150, 151, 154-5, 163, 164, 170, 172, 178, 180, 187, 188, 191, 192, 197, 213, 221, 229, 235, 240, 241, 244-5, 247, 248-9